D1368589

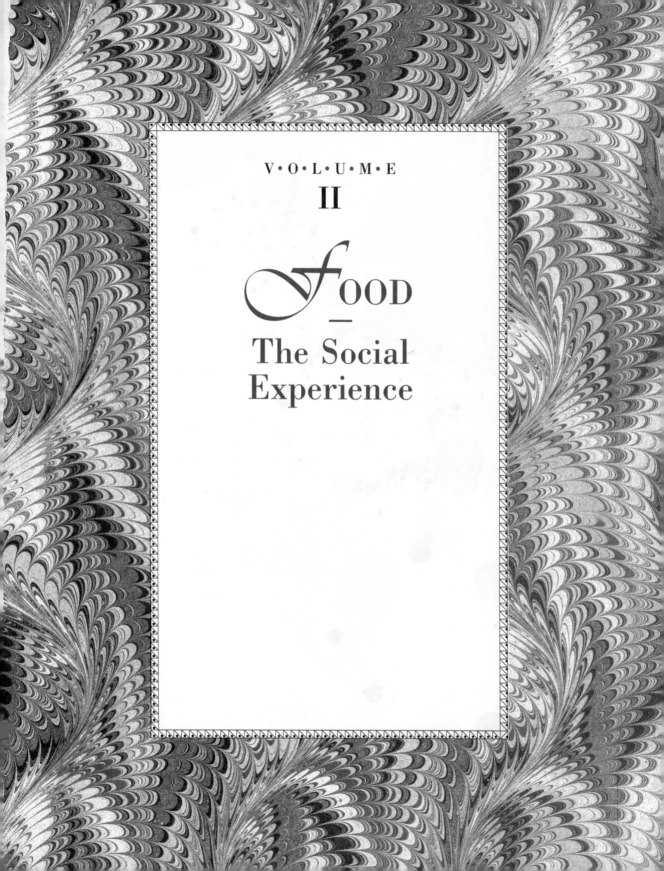

V·O·L·U·M·E

II

*F*OOD

The Social
Experience

V·O·L·U·M·E

II

$\mathscr{F}$OOD

The Social Experience

Educational Task Force

Johnson & Wales University
College of Culinary Arts

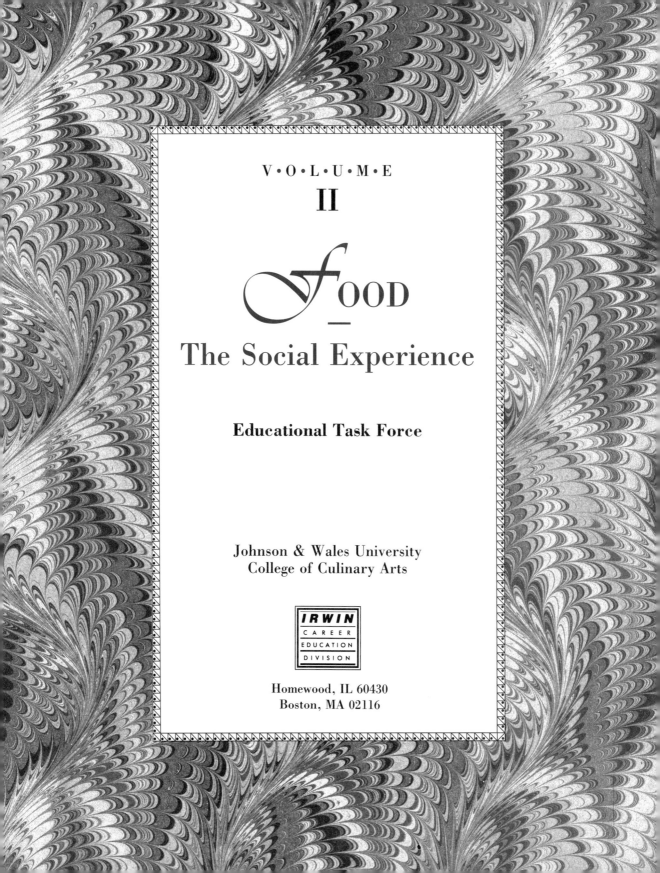

IRWIN
CAREER
EDUCATION
DIVISION

Homewood, IL 60430
Boston, MA 02116

Executive editor: Carol A. Long
Developmental editor: Anna Drake
Marketing manager: Lynn Kalanik
Project editor: Jean Roberts
Production manager: Bob Lange
Cover designer: Mercedes Santos
Interior designer: Maureen McCutcheon
Artist: Roger Gustafson
Compositor: The Clarinda Company
Typeface: 10/12 Sabon
Printer: R. R. Donnelley & Sons Company

**Library of Congress Cataloging-in-Publication Data
(Revised for vol. 2)**

    Food.
      Contents: v. 1. The fundamentals—v. 2. The
    social experience. v. 3. The recipe.
      1. Cookery.   2. Food.   I. Long, Carol A.
    II. Johnson & Wales University. College of Culinary
    Arts. Educational Task Force.
    TX663.F66   1992   641.5   92–7208
    ISBN 0-256-11741-1 (v. 1)
    ISBN 0-256-11742-X (v. 2)
    ISBN 0-256-11743-8 (v. 3)

Printed in the United States of America
1 2 3 4 5 6 7 8 9 0 DOC 9 8 7 6 5 4 3 2

Messages

At the end of the year, one takes account and tries to look into the future. Please allow me to say thank you to Johnson & Wales University, who undertook the job of promoting a new generation of foodservice professionals. Every time I visit the United States I am astonished by their expertise and dedication.

Johnson & Wales successfully took their task beyond the borders of the United States. Nevertheless, we shouldn't deceive ourselves that the future will be less difficult for all of us, Europeans and Americans alike. Isn't it a challenge to our profession to look ahead to a joint future with no national borders for our youth in the field of gastronomy?

Therefore, let us master whatever new problems challenge us, whether technical or nutritional, and go hand in hand in human friendship.

Dr. H. C. Siegfried Schaber
President V.K.D. Verbandes der Köche Von Deutschland
Vice President W.A.C.S. World Association Cooks Society

As you prepare for your culinary careers here at Johnson & Wales University, it is very important for you to realize the responsibility and pride you constantly must exercise to uphold the professional ethics, human values, and culinary fundamentals set forth by this great institution.

As the future bearer of the white toque, I encourage you to continuously try perfecting yourself, take great pride in what you do, exercise patience, and allow yourself to grow within your limits, share your knowledge and wisdom, respect your peers, and perform every day to the best of your ability.

The culinary profession is an exciting profession where you set the groundwork of your own limits.

Hans J. Schadler, C.E.C., A.A.C.
Executive Chef, Director of Food and Beverage
Williamsburg Inn

When deciding what you want to do as your life's work, think of those things you would do even if you didn't get paid for them. Those things you love doing, that don't get boring, that always have something new to teach you. Become a chef only if you love cooking and are fascinated by the infinite variety of foods and how they work. A cook is basically a chemist, mixing and blending ingredients to find the perfect combination.

When serving others, remember that the customer should always come first. We are there to please them, not the other way around. I always put this note on my menus:

> The "no substitution" rule is not fair and no fun! We reject it since it denies your inalienable right to choose what you want to eat. We believe you should be free to enhance your meal according to your own taste. In other words, be our guest! Make yourself at home! And try to enjoy yourself as much as we enjoy serving you!

It works. Try it.

Raymond G. Marshall
Former Owner & CEO
Acapulco y Los Arcos Mexican Restaurants

For the past decade, the world of gastronomy has looked to the United States as a leader for prime quality food products, great advances in the production of fine wines, and top-quality education for young culinarians in schools of culinary arts. The demand for cooks and chefs trained in the United States is greater now than ever. When I started in the kitchen as a young man over 50 years ago, there were no schools teaching culinary arts and opportunities were few.

At Johnson & Wales University, you are attending a world-class culinary school—perhaps the best in the country. You have the finest instructors to teach you not only the basics but also the advanced techniques needed in today's foodservice industry. Learn well, set your goals, and be all that you can be. Don't be discouraged by disappointments or setbacks, but use them as opportunities to do better.

John L. Bandera, C.E.C., A.A.C
Grand Commander
Honorable Order of the Golden Toque

Johnson & Wales University has continued to be a dynamic force in educating students in culinary arts. Through the creative talents of program founders to the present staff, all have endeavored to be the best they can be. My personal involvement with Johnson & Wales through the Distinguished Visiting Chef program and other activities has been a gratifying experience to me. Working with students has always been enjoyable because I now have the opportunity to give something back in return for all the help given to me as a young culinarian.

I tip my toque to the entire staff of Johnson & Wales for their great contribution to the future of the culinary arts.

Michael L. Minor
U.P. Professional Services
L. J. Minor Corp.

It is the good fortune of a present-day student of the culinary arts to become engaged in a calling that has been recognized by our federal government as a fully acknowledged profession, on a par with law, education, medicine, and the arts. This recognition is a weighty matter. It carries with it the obligation of complete commitment and personal dedication to the entire spectrum of academic preparation for the field of culinary arts. The student must never forget that the obligation is never ending. The health and safety of our nation is technically in your hands and, like all perfect professionals, your complete preparation is the only acceptable foundation for true dedication, technical expertise, and personal success.

Joseph P. Delaney
Retired Educator

FOREWORD

Though critics of the beverage alcohol business may be blind to our trade's long record of good works—purposely, at times, I'm convinced—there are few industries in this country with a more sensitive social conscience. Medicine, scientific research, higher education, and all sorts of philanthropies that assist the poor and underprivileged have benefited from profits generated by wine, beer, and spirits sales almost since the repeal of the 18th Amendment.

With its growing success, Banfi Vintners has assumed an increasingly broader societal role. Like other firms, year after year, we donate to worthy causes, both national and local. Yet some time ago, we began experiencing twinges of the corporate conscience because we hadn't made any serious contribution to the trade—and the people of the trade—most responsible for our company's success. We asked ourselves: How can we assist the future development of the hospitality trade; further, how can we assist the people who will lead and administer that trade in decades to come?

The answer was obvious. Through the Banfi Foundation, we now endow schools that specialize in hospitality education; for example, providing them with basic facilities such as the dining room at Johnson & Wales, where food and wine service can be taught under ideal conditions. Equally important, through scholarships and fellowships we help worthy students interested in pursuing a hospitality career. About 15 schools and dozens of students are currently benefiting from Banfi's decision.

The corporate conscience is not at ease, but are our motives entirely altruistic? Admittedly, no. We're convinced that a better and more widely informed hospitality staff will stimulate greater business for hotels and restaurants, including the wines they serve. Experience has proved that, for us anyway, the "trickle down" theory really can work. Well and good. Profits from wine sales fund the Banfi Foundation.

Harry F. Mariani
President and COO
Banfi Vintners

Why did we donate a teaching dining room to Johnson & Wales University?

Because of a family business, I had experience with imports. I decided to go out on my own, moving from the retail side of the business to the institutional market. Therefore, in 1957, my wife, Helena, and I started our own import business.

In the course of our travels in the late 50s and throughout the 60s, we found the "eyes" of the culinary world had shifted to America. Many chefs decided to seek their fortune in the United States, bringing with them culinary knowledge from their individual countries. Many chefs asked us to import certain products that they felt were needed to round out their classical cuisine endeavors, and we continued to import products that were in demand. As we expanded our business, we became aware of the Johnson & Wales University and its commitment to the classical cuisine with an emphasis on creating unique contemporary plates.

We felt a facility such as a dining room with bar and other teaching facilities would be a fitting atmosphere for the training of students on a daily basis. It is very gratifying to know that now hundreds of students use this facility to learn every day. The Tosi dining room is also used by world-renowned chefs, who are invited to demonstrate the culinary achievements that made them famous.

Ernest A. Tosi
President
E. A. Tosi & Sons Company, Inc.

REFACE

The Johnson & Wales University, College of Culinary Arts, Volume I—*Food: The Fundamentals,* Volume II—*Food: The Social Experience,* and Volume III—*Food: The Recipe* are the University's commitment to excellence in education. This new edition will enable the college to be on the cutting edge as a trendsetter, introducing new ideas, procedures, and technologies to our students and to the foodservice industry.

Each volume will be used as a reference tool for faculty and students to teach and learn from. These textbooks will emphasize theory and practical applications in nutrition, sanitation, cost control, and marketing.

Volume II: *Food: The Social Experience,* explains to the student how to serve the guest. The student will be exposed to front-of-the-house operational procedures, customer relations, preparing the dining room for service, and various styles of service. An in-depth study of French, American, German, Italian, and Australian wines is also presented. The mixology component will examine the procedures for opening and closing a bar, how to properly make cocktails and mixed drinks, and the regulations of liquor liability.

Educational Task Force

Acknowledgments

The College of Culinary Arts, Volumes I, II, and III—*Food: The Fundamentals, Food: The Social Experience,* and *Food: The Recipe*—have been written by people who truly love culinary arts. I wish to thank all the faculty, administration, and friends of the University for their support and participation in this tremendous undertaking. Their collective work represents their dedication to educating students who will keep the flame of culinary inspiration alive for future generations.

Thomas L. Wright
Dean, College of Culinary Arts
Johnson & Wales University

Paul J. McVety
Project Manager

Bradley J. Ware
Assistant Project Manager

Educational Task Force

Dorothy Jeanne Allen
Steven Browchuk
Bill Day
Dorothy DeLessio
Peter J. James
Lars Johansson
Laird Livingston

Jack McKenna
Robert M. Nograd
George O'Palenick
Louise R. Phaneuf
Felicia Pritchett
Robert Ross

The Educational Task Force would like to extend its heartfelt appreciation to Robert M. Nograd and Jean-Michel Vienne, whose efforts in compiling these volumes have been invaluable.

Providence Faculty and Support Staff

Mauritz Adolfsson
Pauline Allsworth
Frank Andreozzi
Soren Arnoldi
Adrian Barber
Richard Bonin
Drue Brandenberg
Peter Cady
Victor Calise
Carl Calvert
Gerianne Chapman
Jack Chiaro
Ricardo Comparini
Richard Coppedge
Jean-Luc Derron
Claire Desmarais
Raymond Desmarais
Susan Desmond
John Dion
Rene Dionne
Rita Dionne
Reginald B. Dow
Thomas Dunn
Ernest Fleury
James Fuchs
Joseph Gagne
Nancy Garnett-Thomas
James Griffin
Bernd Gronert
Fred Haddad
Steve Harrison

Claudia Hinsley-Berube
James Holden
Helene Houde
J. Jeffrey Howard
Linda Kender
Walter Kosior
Barbara Kuck
Hector Lipa
Michael Marra
Dale Mowery
Theresa O'Brien
Sean O'Hara
Divino Osmena
Robert Pekar
Pamela Peters
T. J. Provost
Bonifacio Quicho
Cynthia Salvato
Steve Scaife
Louis Serra
Alice Smith
Christine Stamm
Louis Szathmary
Adela Tancayo-Sannella
Frank Terranova
Segundo Torres
Michael Trainor
Suzanne Vieira
Gary Welling
Laurinda Willis

Fellow

Marty Kahler

Branch Campuses Administration and Faculty

Charleston

Paul W. Conco
Executive Director
Karl J. Guggenmos
Director of Culinary Instruction
Jeffrey Brown
David Hendricksen

Andrew Hoaxi
Michael Koons
Louis Leichter
Steve Nogle
William Wilroy

Teaching Assistants

Todd Hogan
Victoria Romero

Norfolk

Debra C. Gray
Executive Director
Tim Cameron
Director of Culinary Instruction
Susan Batten

Desi Colon
Cindy Groman
Bob Higgins
Steve Sadowski

Culinary Advisory Council

Scott Allmendinger
Christian DeVos
Paul Elbling
John D. Folse
Pierre Franey
Ira Kaplan
George Karousos
Emeril J. LaGasse
Gustav E. Mauler

Franz Meier
Roland Mesnier
Keith Morrow
Stanley J. Nicas
Robert Nyman
Hans J. Schadler
Louis Szathmary
Ernest Tosi
Martin Yan

Distinguished Visiting Chefs

Hans J. Bueschkens
Michel Bourdin
Stanley J. Nicas
Paul Elbling
Gerhard Schmid
Wolfgang Bierer
Siegfried Schaber

Michael L. Minor
Noel Cullen
Carolyn Buster
Madeleine Kamman
Warren LeRuth
Johnny Rivers
Milos Cihelka

Hans J. Schadler
Emeril J. LaGasse
Roland Mesnier
James Hughes
Martin Yan
Marcel Desaulniers

Johanne Killeen
George Germon
John D. Folse
Gustav E. Mauler
Keith Keogh

Special Friends

John J. Bowen
Joseph P. Delaney

Socrates Inonog
Franz K. Lemoine

Companies

Automatic Sales, Inc.
Bertolli USA, Inc.
Comstock-Castle Stove Company
F. D. Dick
Diversey Corp.
Garland Commercial Industries, Inc.
Hallsmith-Sysco
Hobart Corporation
InterMetro Industries Corporation
McCormick & Company, Inc.
The L. J. Minor Corporation
Moët Chandon
John Morrell & Co.

Morris Nathanson Design Incorporated
Nabisco Brands, Inc.
Paramount Restaurant Supply
   Corporation
Pepsi-Cola Company
Procter & Gamble Company
Quaker Oats Company
Ralph Calise Fruit & Produce
Rhode Island Distributing Company
Servolift/Eastern Corp.
E. A. Tosi & Sons Company, Inc.
Villa Banfi
Vulcan-Hart Corporation

CONTENTS

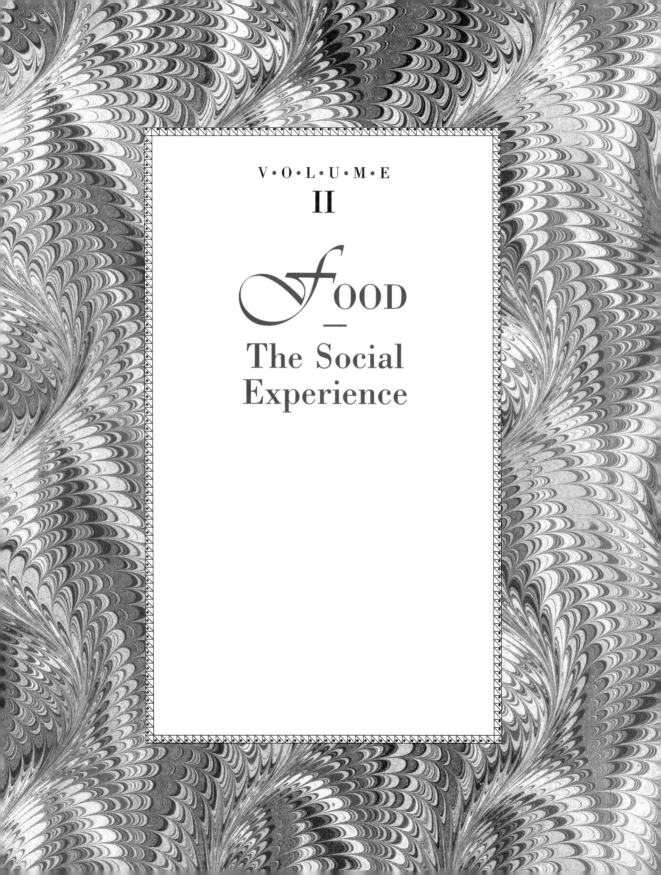

V·O·L·U·M·E

II

*F*OOD
—
The Social
Experience

C·H·A·P·T·E·R

1

THE SERVER

Service is a by-product of sales, which is a by-product of recognizing the needs of the guest. That statement illustrates the relationship between meeting the needs of the guest and the sales that are the result. Without those two ingredients, service would not exist.

Servers must realize that without a deep concern on the part of each person in the front of the house, all effort made by others, from the owner to the prep cook, would be in vain. It is said that all the expense and time taken from the initial conception of a gastronomic idea to the final product can be made ineffectual by a serviceperson's attitude, unprofessional manner, or unintentional mistake.

For a guest to experience a totally satisfying respite within a restaurant or lounge, the individual efforts of many must blend into one effort—ensuring the guest's satisfaction and enjoyment.

Table service itself is a major factor in the guest's enjoyment of a meal. It is important to remember that table service is not only the placing of an item before a guest, but also the grace or polish with which the service is performed.

There are few pleasures in life we find as blissful as the sharing of conversation and nourishment with someone special in our lives. To personally contribute to another's enjoyment should be the goal and satisfaction of all service personnel.

It is important that servers understand the importance of their role in providing service, information, and hospitality to their guests. From the restaurant's point of view, the server provides sales and goodwill, which are essential to its success. To themselves, servers provide personal income proportional to the level of sales and quality of service they render. Quality service does not happen by chance. It is a combination of education, planning, and refinement through practice. The professional server practices all three.

The professional server performs the following roles for the restaurant: (1) representative, (2) salesperson, and (3) skilled server.

REPRESENTATIVE OF THE RESTAURANT
· · · · ·

Servers have the most direct contact with the guest of any restaurant employee and must conduct themselves as ambassadors of the restaurant. The server is directly responsible for setting the mood in the dining room. By demonstrating good interpersonal skills, the server can create a pleasant dining experience for guests. The professional server is responsible for making guests feel welcome, relaxed, and secure in knowing that they will be well cared for.

SALESPERSON
· · · · ·

Servers can increase not only their own personal income, but the overall income of the establishment. By being confident and assertive, and by using suggestive selling techniques, the server can increase sales of both food and beverages, thereby increasing revenue. In addition, the confidence displayed by the serviceperson will result in a high quality of service, thereby ensuring repeat business.

A useful technique for selling in the dining room is called **highlighting.** This is where a particular item is emphasized so as to leave a lasting impression on the guest. It can be used to promote the sale of both menu items and specials of the day. By being enthusiastic and using appropriate adjectives when describing an item, the server helps to create a visual image for the guest. Highlighting draws attention to items and is effective when used during the order taking or selling process. It can also be used to persuade the guest to order those items requiring less preparation time by the kitchen staff. This can help facilitate orders through the kitchen during busy periods when table turnover is desired.

SKILLED SERVER
· · · · ·

Paying close attention to the precise details of proper service will help ensure that the needs of the guest are met. By practicing the highest level of sanitation in handling equipment and food products, the server contributes to maintaining a healthy and wholesome environment for the guest. Quality service will contribute to the success of an establishment and will result in having a satisfied customer who is likely to return. Poor service, however, will tend to disappoint guests and drive them away.

FOUR QUALITY FACTORS DESIRED OF PROFESSIONAL SERVERS
· · · · ·

To be a successful and competent professional, one must possess the following qualities:

1. Positive attitude.
2. Good appearance.
3. Thorough job knowledge.
4. Good communication skills.

Employers will look for these qualities when selecting servers.

Positive Attitude

Maintain a very positive attitude at all times when dealing with the public. There is no room whatsoever for allowing one's personal problems to interfere with one's performance while on the job. The golden rule is give 100 percent of yourself 100 percent of the time. Accepting the proverbial *bitter* with the *sweet* should be kept in mind. Every day in the dining room will not be perfect or without difficulties.

The professional should arrive in plenty of time to do a share of **side work,** never offering excuses for tardiness. Doing one's fair share of preparation is imperative in the successful operation of any establishment.

Behavior at the table is another top priority. Be sure to smile as you greet your guests, addressing them by last name, if known, with proper titles—Mr., Ms., and so on. Do not call guests by their first names unless invited to do so. Avoid common terms like *buddy, pal,* or *honey.* In short, be polite yet not overly familiar. Learn to respect your guests. In this way, they will learn to respect you.

Appearance

Appearance is important. By making a successful first impression, guests will be eager for you to serve them, knowing that you maintain high standards of grooming and sanitation. Being sloppy in appearance has a negative impact on clients, who expect the very best. Be sure to maintain the highest degree of neatness and politeness. Any shortcoming in this area will result in a negative reaction on the part of the guest. Always do your best to appear absolutely flawless in appearance.

Whether tuxedos are worn for formal dinners or casual attire for poolside lunch, uniforms should meet health and safety standards. Uniforms should be kept neat, clean, and well pressed. Long hair must be restrained. Fingernails should be neatly trimmed and clean. Hands should remain clean, which requires frequent washing when handling food and beverages. Washing hands after use of the restroom is required by law and must be observed.

Wearing jewelry or using cologne to excess should be avoided. Fresh breath should be maintained at all times when dealing with the public.

Servers must also be conscious of their physical mannerisms and observe the following:

- No smoking, eating, or chewing gum except during breaks.
- No carrying napkins or utensils in jacket or trouser pockets.
- No slouching or leaning.
- No touching hair, mouth, nose, or ears in view of guests.
- No standing around with hands in pockets.
- No wiping brow or nose on jacket sleeve or sneezing into bare hands or service towel.

Job Knowledge

Servers should not be permitted to represent the establishment without having a complete knowledge of the menu, wine list, and other products offered by the restaurant. Servers must be able to answer questions concerning each food and beverage item being offered. Failure to do so is very embarrassing and unprofessional. Having a thorough knowledge of menu items also enables the server to alert guests to those items that contain ingredients to which the guest may be allergic or which they may not desire.

In addition to having knowledge of the restaurant, a server should be prepared to offer guests additional information about local events, directions to theaters and airports, and so forth.

Communication Skills

Successful servers must have the ability to communicate with guests. Expressing themselves clearly helps to create the rapport necessary for good guest relations. Having good verbal skills enables the server to describe food and beverage items so that guests will want to order them. There is a positive correlation between a server's communication skills and level of sales. Good verbal skills also enable the server to tactfully handle situations that may arise, such as guest complaints, taking reservations, and special requests. Making eye contact while speaking with guests is crucial to developing good communication skills.

PREPARING THE DINING ROOM FOR SERVICE

QUALITY SERVICE

· · · · ·

Quality service begins with properly preparing and placing all equipment needed for service so as to ensure a smooth and efficient operation. Each establishment will have clearly defined duties for each servicemember to perform prior to opening the room. These duties are commonly referred to as side work. Though side work may vary by restaurant, typical side work includes:

1. Setting tables for service.
2. Cleaning and refilling salt and pepper shakers.
3. Refilling sugar bowls.
4. Cleaning and refilling oil and vinegar **cruets.**
5. Folding napkins for service.
6. Polishing flatware and glassware.
7. Stocking side stations for service.

SETTING THE ROOM FOR SERVICE

· · · · ·

Service personnel must handle all equipment, utensils, china, and glassware in safe and sanitary manner—**flatware** and cups by the handles, plates by the rim, and glassware from the base. Under no circumstances should fingers be placed inside glasses (clean or dirty), as this is dangerously unsanitary and is a health violation. Napkins and flatware should not be placed on the seats of chairs even temporarily, as this is also an unsanitary practice.

All items set on the table must be clean. Glassware and flatware should be neatly aligned and free of spots. Salt and pepper shakers should be full and not feel greasy from the previous use. This requires detailed inspection by the server. Service personnel should strive to maintain the highest levels of safety and sanitation in handling food and all dining room equipment.

TABLE SETTINGS

· · · · ·

Whether setting with paper goods or fine **linen,** one must be sure that not only the tabletop is clean, but also chair seats, benches, and the area under and around each table. Continual inspection is necessary before and especially during service when tables are being reset.

When using place mats, whether paper or vinyl, place the mat at the center of the **cover,** or guest's position, about 1 inch (thumbnail) from the edge of the table. A napkin, paper or cloth, may be placed to the left side of the mat or in the center. Place all flatware accordingly, 1 inch from the lower edge of the mat. Remember that the placement of flatware, vases, **condiment** trays, and so on should be consistent on each table.

When placing a cloth on the table, make sure that the sewn seam is on the down side. Place the cloth so that it falls evenly on all sides. Ideally, cloths should not fall below the cushion of each seat.

Cloths that are stained, torn, frayed, or contain burn holes should be sent for repairs or torn into rags. Never attempt to hide stains or holes by placing such things as vases or ashtrays over them. Even these unused cloths should never be rolled into a ball but refolded neatly. Wrinkling linen only adds to maintenance costs. Rolled cloths not only require mending but re-pressing as well.

Cloth napkins should be placed in the center of the setting unless a **showplate** is utilized. A showplate is a decorative plate used to make the tabletop more attractive. Covering showplates with napkins defeats the purpose. In this case, the napkin can be placed above the setting or to either side. This general rule applies to showplates containing a logo.

Setting a Round Table

When setting a round table with four legs, as opposed to a round table with a pedestal, the tablecloth should be laid to allow the corners of the cloth to hide the legs of the table. Chairs and place settings should then be placed to allow the corners of the tablecloth to fall between chairs. Although this may not be possible on large tables with more than four settings, it should be used as a general guide for setting round tables with one to four place settings.

Setting for Even Numbers

If a round table is to be set with an even number of settings, each setting should align with the setting directly across the table. The table is divided into an even number of wedge-shaped sections. Figure 2–1 illustrates a round table set with an even number of settings. When setting a table for two, called a **deuce,** the settings should be directly across from each other.

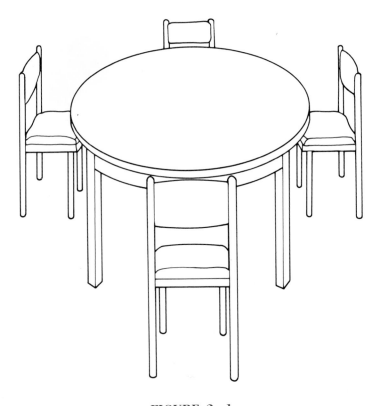

FIGURE 2–1

• • •

Setting a round table with an even number of settings

Setting for an Odd Number at a Round Table

Setting a round table with an odd number of settings requires that each place setting align directly between two place settings across the table. Figure 2–2 illustrates this setting. It is important that care be taken to ensure equal distance between settings to maintain uniformity.

FIGURE 2–2

• • •

Setting a round table with an odd number of settings

Numbering Guest Positions

Number guest positions counterclockwise. The number-one position is that seat that is closest to a predetermined dining room focal point (see Figure 2–3).

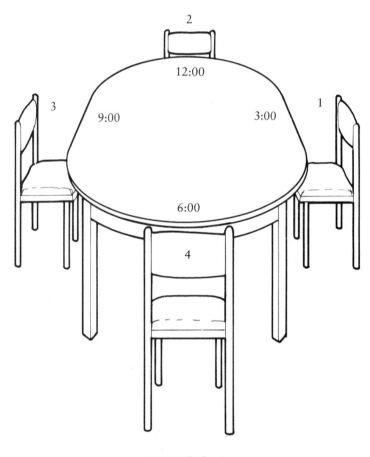

FIGURE 2–3

• • •

Numbering guest positions

TABLE SETTINGS: FLATWARE

· · · · ·

Whether setting flatware for breakfast, lunch, dinner, or **banquet** service, it is useful to remember certain rules (see Figures 2–4 and 2–5).

1. Forks are set on the left.
2. Knives and spoons are set on the right.
3. Bread and butter plates are set on the left, beside or above the forks.
4. All flatware is set from the outside in, following the sequence of use—first course farthest out from plate, and so on.
5. The water glass is set above the tip of the dinner knife. Wine glasses set from the outside in following the sequence of use—first glass used is set above the tip of the dinner knife, and so on.
6. If several wine glasses are preset in a **flight,** or row, the water glass may be set directly above the place setting or off to the right.
7. Coffee and tea cups are preset to the right of the knives and spoons, with handles at the 4 o'clock position.
8. China, flatware, and glassware should not touch.
9. On rectangular, square, or round tables with an even number of settings, all flatware items on one place setting should align with those on the opposite side in a straight line.
10. The place setting itself should allow for the placement of the largest **service plate** in the center without requiring the need to move utensils when serving.
11. In some countries, forks are set with the prongs facing down and knives are set upon **rests,** equipment that keeps the cutting end of a knife off the tablecloth.
12. Knives are always set with the cutting edge toward the center of the place setting.
13. Each restaurant will modify the settings to suit its own needs or the menu.

Dinner settings would include:

1. Salad fork *or* dinner fork
2. Dinner fork
3. Napkin
4. Dinner knife
5. Teaspoon
6. Bouillon spoon
7. Bread and butter plate
8. Butter knife
9. Water glass

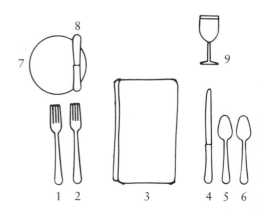

FIGURE 2–4

· · ·

Lunch and dinner setting

À la Carte

When guests are to be served **à la carte,** a basic table setting is prepared in advance (see Figure 2–5). The guest chooses each desired food item from the menu, and the appropriate silverware is brought to the table using a **serviette,** a napkin-covered plate.

1. Showplate
2. Napkin
3. Dinner knife
4. Dinner fork
5. Bread and butter plate
6. Butter knife
7. Wine glass

Silverware is brought as needed.

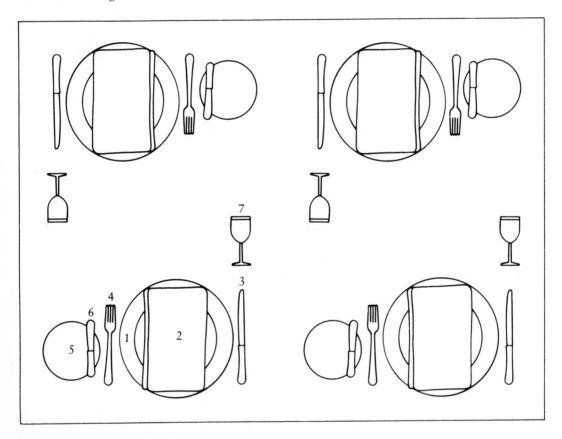

FIGURE 2–5

· · ·

French table setting, à la carte

Preset Menu

A preset menu is serving a meal to a group of persons who have determined the menu and the time of service in advance. The table setting will be according to the particular menu. One example is illustrated in Figure 2–6. Figure 2–7 shows a banquet preset menu, and Figure 2–8 shows a continental breakfast.

1. Showplate
2. Napkin
3. Bread and butter plate
4. Butter knife
5. Bouillon spoon — Consommé Royale
6. Dinner knife — Chateaubriand

7. Dinner fork — Chateaubriand
8. Salad fork — Salade de Champignons
9. Dessert spoon — Pomme Bonne Femme
10. Dessert fork — Pomme Bonne Femme
11. Wine glass — 1969 Château Calon-Sequr

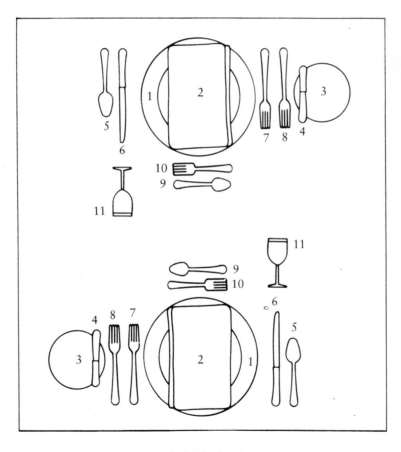

FIGURE 2–6

• • •

Preset menu table setting

1. Bread and butter plate
2. Bread and butter knife
3. Salad fork
4. Main course fork
5. Dinner knife
6. Coffee spoon
7. Coffee cup and saucer
8. Wine glass
9. Water glass
10. Dessert spoon
11. Dessert fork
12. Napkin

FIGURE 2–7

• • •

Banquet preset menu

1. Napkin
2. Bread and butter plate
3. Bread and butter knife
4. Coffee cup and saucer
5. Coffee spoon
6. Cream and sugar
7. Juice glass
8. Water glass

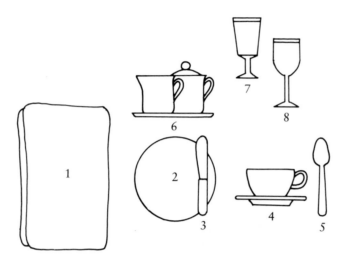

FIGURE 2–8
• • •
Continental breakfast

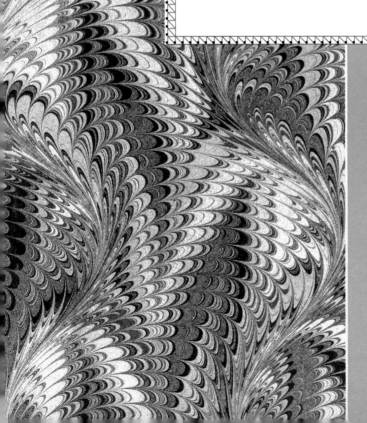

C ·H ·A ·P ·T ·E ·R

3

SERVING THE GUEST

Although each restaurant will vary or adjust the service sequence to suit its needs or the needs of its guests, the following sequence is most commonly used in many of today's restaurants. Quality service is achieved when each step is performed correctly from the time the guest arrives until the time the guest departs.

BASIC SEQUENCE
· · · · ·

1. Greeting upon arrival by maître d' or hostess. Assistance with coats.
2. Seating and menu presentation.
3. Greeting by wait staff.
4. Taking and serving the beverage order.
5. Discussing the menu (selling); order taking.
6. Transferring order to the kitchen (computer, communication).
7. Wine service.
8. Flatware adjustment.
9. Food service.
10. Guest satisfaction.
11. Clearing the table.
12. Crumbing the table and changing ashtrays.
13. Dessert service.
14. Hot beverage service.
15. After-dinner drinks.
16. Check presentation.
17. Guest departure.

Step 1: Greeting Upon Arrival

- Guests are to be greeted at the door by the host or hostess, **maître d',** or manager.
- Greet the guest with a warm smile.
- Make eye contact.
- Act friendly, relaxed, pleasant, and courteous.
- Make the guest feel welcome, important, and special.
- The guests' first impressions are vital to the success of their dining experience.
- Maintain eye contact while speaking to guests:
  a. "Good morning/afternoon/evening."
  b. "How many people are in your party?"
  c. "Do you prefer a smoking or nonsmoking area?"
- If a **reservation** system is used, the host or hostess would inquire if the guest has made a reservation and make the appropriate notation in the reservation book.

Step 2: Seating and Menu Presentation

- Invite the guests into the dining room.
- Treat each party as special; for example, say, "*Your* table is right this way."
- Use the guests' surnames whenever possible.
- Slowly lead the guests to their table.
- Assist the guests into their seats.
- Present menus and wine list after guests have been seated. When presenting the wine list, make reference to it; for example, "Here is our wine list."
- Menus should be presented to ladies first, host or hostess last.
- Take time while seating guests; avoid rushing to return to the front door.
- Relay any special information to the wait staff, such as cake service or special requests made prior to seating.

Step 3: Greeting by Wait Staff

- Give the guests a moment to adjust to the environment before approaching.
- The guests' first impressions often contribute to their view of the entire service.
- Make eye contact while speaking to each guest. Stand erect, look at the guests, and smile; greet them pleasantly: "Good morning (afternoon/evening)."
- It is sometimes appropriate to introduce yourself by name.
- Do not rush or appear flustered or anxious.
- Determine who the host or hostess is, if possible.
- Determine guests' comfort level, whether relaxed or intimidated.
- Determine how formal or casual they are.
- Adjust your behavior to suit their situation or preference.

Step 4: Taking and Serving the Beverage Order

- Server must have knowledge of common drinks, available brands of liquor, and types of beer and house wines.
- It is essential that cocktail service be performed correctly, since it is the first product served.
- Ask:
  a. "Would you care for a cocktail or beverage before your meal?"
  b. "Would you like to begin with a cocktail?"
  c. "What can I get you from the bar?" (assumptive method)
- Take the beverage order from ladies first, host or hostess last.
- Write the order down using seat numbers to ensure the proper distribution when returning to serve.
- Clarify each beverage with guest regarding on the rocks or straight up, garnish or no garnish.

- Whenever possible, serve beverages from the right side, with the right hand, right foot forward.
- Avoid reaching across people to serve.
- Observe proper handling of glassware.
- Check back for a second round of beverages when drinks are approximately two-thirds consumed.
- The procedure for reordering beverages is the same. Refer to the original order to avoid reasking what each guest is drinking.
- Ask if guest is finished with a glass *before* attempting to remove it.

Step 5: Discussing the Menu (selling)

- Servers must know the price structure in case they are asked by a guest if items are à la carte, table d'hôte, or prix fixe.
- The server must know the menu, including ingredients and preparation.
- Discussing the menu is known as **verbal selling.**
- Once the guests have opened their menus, explain the specialties or additions to the menu.
- Mention if certain items are not available.
- When describing menu items, use appetizing adjectives that will enhance the items and stimulate the appetite.
- Aid the guests' decisions through detailed descriptions of each dish being considered.
- It is understood that guests will probably order a main course. Therefore, the server should create interest in soups, **appetizers,** and pastas through description to increase check averages.
- Be prepared to answer any questions concerning the menu. If guests are confused or intimidated by the menu, they will order less from it.
- Determine if guests are prepared to place an **order;** for example, notice if their menus are closed.
- Accurately record each individual's order using seat numbers.
- Be sure to check with the kitchen regarding special requests.
- Servers determine the pace of the meal by controlling the timing of courses served.
- Servers should pace each course equally to avoid rushing the guests.
- Breakfast and lunch service is generally quicker than dinner due to time limitations; adjust the pace accordingly.
- Take into account the workload of the kitchen when timing the order.

Step 6: Transferring Order to the Kitchen

- Transfer order to kitchen production areas either manually or by computer system as determined by each restaurant.
- Double-check order for accuracy.
- Clear up any potential confusion with the kitchen concerning the order.

Step 7: Wine Service

- Servers must be familiar with the wine list in order to guide customers toward their preference.
- Be aware of wines not available.
- Take the wine order from the host or hostess either by name of wine or bin number.
- Check the wine label and vintage for accuracy before presenting the bottle.
- Deliver wine glasses and wine bucket as needed.
- Handle the wine glasses by their stems only.
- Determine who will be having wine.
- Present the bottle to the host or hostess for verification.
- Determine when to serve by asking.
- Open red wine immediately to **breathe.** To breathe a wine means to allow air to come in contact with it. This will improve the taste of the wine.
- Follow correct opening procedures.
- Pour 2 ounces to the host or hostess for tasting. Be prepared to explain this procedure if the host does not understand. If satisfactory, pour ladies first, host or hostess last. If the wine is refused, excuse yourself to inform the manager.
- Avoid reaching across the table to pour.
- Delicately pour for each person from the right side with your right hand, right foot forward.
- Return the bottle to the wine bucket or onto the table with the label facing the host or hostess.
- Avoid overpouring wine. Fill wine glasses no more than half full.
- Frequent repouring or *topping up*, draws attention to the wine, which will increase consumption and sales.
- Be sure to pour the end of the bottle to the host or hostess so that he or she is aware it is empty. Pause and wait for a possible reorder.
- If guests switch to a different wine, bring fresh glasses.

Step 8: Flatware Adjustment

- Adjust flatware to suit the food order before the arrival of the first course. Adjustment may include adding or removing silverware or placing a **waste plate** for bones or shells.
- Readjustment may be necessary after the appetizer or salad course, as guests may use the wrong utensil. Correct the flatware without calling the guest's attention to the error. The guest should use the outside piece of flatware first and work to the inside with each course.
- Use a serviette to carry flatware through the dining room during service.
- Avoid placing flatware on plates containing food or hot beverage saucers.
- Do not carry flatware in your bare hands during service.

Step 9: Food Service

- Bread and butter is usually the first food item served.
- Present each course in order as required by the guests or as determined by the service of the dining room.
- The placement of plates from the left or right sides varies for different service (American, French, Russian, etc.).
- Each dining room will have predetermined how food service will be conducted.
- Serving from a particular side of the guest by all servers in a dining room regulates the presentation of food items.
- Serving food as soon as prepared is the number-one priority of service. *Cold dishes must be served cold and hot dishes must be served hot.*
- Check for completeness and accuracy of the food before serving.
- *Present* each dish in front of the guest; do not simply *deliver* it.
- Handle plates only on the edges. Note the top and bottom of each dish. The **entrée** is usually at the 6 o'clock position or as determined by the chef.
- Serve guest of honor first, children next, then ladies, men, and host or hostess last.
- Present correct menu item to each guest using seat number ordering system. Avoid asking the guest who is having which item.
- Replenishing the bread and butter and water, changing of ashtrays, and crumbing the table is done as needed at any time during the course of the meal. However, performing these tasks is best done between courses so as not to interrupt guests while they are eating.

Step 10: Guest Satisfaction

- Promptly check back with the guest to ensure satisfaction of products served.
- If guest is dissatisfied, attend to the problem immediately.
- *Listen* attentively to the guest's complaint.
- *Clarify* the problem with the guest.
- *Agree* with the guest regarding the problem. The guest is always right. Do not get into an argument.
- *Resolve* the problem. Management will usually assist in rectifying the situation.
- Be sure to notify the dining room manager of any problem regarding food or service.

Step 11: Clearing the Table

- Clear courses from the table when *all* guests have finished eating.
- Observe tables regularly to determine if all are finished before clearing any dish.
- If unsure, ask if everyone is finished eating.
- Clear from right side with right hand whenever possible.
- Avoid reaching across the table when clearing. Walk around the table. Keep dishes in left arm to the outside of table, away from the guests. Your arm level is at the guests' eye level.

- Avoid noise or clumsy clearing.
- Avoid stacking too much on the left arm at one time. Use discretion. Organize dishes on the tray to make carrying the tray easier, safer, and to make breaking it down or emptying the tray quicker.

Step 12: Crumbing the Table and Changing Ashtrays

Crumbing

- **Crumbing** is a procedure used to remove crumbs and food particles from the table.
- Crumbing should be done between courses as needed.
- The server should move any glass or utensil as necessary to ensure that the cover, or place setting, is entirely cleaned.
- Crumbing should be done from either side of the guest so as not be to an inconvenience.
- Crumbers can be in the form of a small dustpan and brush, a pocket-sized bar similar to a tongue depressor, a self-contained unit resembling a lint brush, or the server may use a **service towel** folded into a small square.
- Crumbs are swept onto a small plate.
- The server should crumb toward the center of the table, away from the guest, and then diagonally to an open corner. Crumbing directly across the cover may result in crumbs falling into the guest's lap.

Changing Ashtrays

- Ashtrays should be changed as needed; don't allow an excessive number of cigarette butts to accumulate.
- Invert clean ashtray and place over soiled ashtray before removing to prevent ashes from flying around.
- Place clean ashtray on table.
- Empty dirty ashtray and clean for future use.

Step 13: Dessert Service

- Present dessert menu either verbally, by printed menu, or by pastry cart or tray.
- Dessert order is taken along with the hot beverage order.
- Flatware is again adjusted to suit the order.

Step 14: Hot Beverage Service

- Be sure all condiments, flatware, and china are presented prior to pouring hot beverages.
- The coffee cup and saucer are placed to the guest's right side with the handle at the 4 o'clock position.

- Use an **underliner** for coffee pot to catch drips while pouring.
- Pour from the right side.
- Offer refills before being asked.

Step 15: After-Dinner Drinks

- Offer after-dinner drinks using a printed menu, verbal suggestion, or display cart or tray.
- Serve after-dinner drinks from right side, using a beverage tray.

Step 16: Check Presentation

- Clear all dessert dishes and flatware *before* presenting check.
- Anticipate the request for the guest check by preparing it early.
- Verify that all items are correct.
- Reprint soiled or illegible checks.
- Accurately total the check.
- Write *thank you* and your name.
- Present the check to the host or hostess or in center of the table.
- Collect payment.
- Guests should not be interrupted for payment.
- Never ask if guests need change; always return change.

Step 17: Guest Departure

- Try to be present when guests depart.
- Assist them out of their chairs.
- Assist them with coats.
- Thank guests for their patronage.
- Wish them well.

C·H·A·P·T·E·R

4

STYLES OF TABLE SERVICE

There are many styles of table service, each offering a varying degree of elegance. The common thread that links all styles of service is that customers expect courteous and knowledgeable servers who are well groomed and possess the skills necessary to run an efficient **station** while making them feel welcome and comfortable. Regardless of the type of service being used, there are common rules of protocol that need to be observed when serving the guest.

1. Safety and comfort of guests is of primary consideration.
2. Serve children first, then women, then men.
3. Serve the guest of honor first and the host last.
4. Serve and clear beverages from the right side of guest using the right hand, with the right foot forward.
5. Clear soiled dishes from the guest's right side, using the right hand, with the right foot forward.

There are traditional rules of service protocol, unique to each style of service, that should be observed when possible. These rules will be outlined with each style of service. Servers must realize that not all rules of protocol can be observed at all times and should therefore recognize situations that require adjustments. For example, if the server cannot safely reach the right of a guest to serve a cup of coffee, then the coffee should be served to the left.

MODERN AMERICAN PLATE SERVICE
· · · · ·

The most prevalent style of service is referred to as American plate service, American in origin but now used internationally. This service is popular because it requires fewer and less extensively trained dining room personnel than classical French service. The food is completely prepared, plated, and garnished in the kitchen. The servers do no tableside cooking or plating; therefore, service can be streamlined to allow for speed and efficiency. Servers can usually service a larger station and more guests. The net effect is an overall savings in labor cost that is desirable to both management and guest, as cost savings can be passed on to the guest in the form of reasonable menu prices.

Service Rules

1. Solids and solid foods are served from the left with the server's left hand, left foot forward.
2. Soups are served from the right with the right hand and the right foot forward.
3. Clearing is performed from the right with the right hand and the right foot forward except for items placed to the guest's left.

CLASSICAL FRENCH SERVICE

· · · · ·

Classical French service is the most elegant and elaborate style of service. Classical French service is used internationally, when a fairly high degree of formality is desired. More complex and involved than American service, it is also more labor-intensive and time-consuming. The employees involved must be highly skilled and possess in-depth knowledge of all facets of food preparation and fine dining service. Successful French service is in the hands of not one but a number of service employees, each one responsible for specific duties, all of whom must strive to create a dining experience of the highest quality.

Because tableside preparation is an integral part of this style of service, special equipment is required. The act of preparing special dishes in full view of the guest calls for the employee to possess a high degree of skill that is absolutely flawless, allowing no room for the slightest error. The entire staff must all work as one, with a commitment to excellence, to achieve the common goal of satisfying the customer.

In contrast to other styles of service, classical French differs in a variety of ways. First, not all food items are necessarily prepared in the kitchen, or plated there. Main menu items may be prepared and plated at the table, either on a **service trolley** or **side stand. Accompaniments** may be plated directly onto the guest's plate from a small service platter by the server. The table captain, or chef de rang, may prepare a number of different main food items at the same time, or two items may be prepared at the table while two are prepared in the kitchen.

If an order requiring tableside plating is to be served with items that require no plating, then the commis de suite, or back waiter, must deliver those items requiring tableside plating to the captain first. This delivery would also include the plates to be used for the item and any sauces or utensils. The commis de suite would then return to the kitchen to pick up the plated items and deliver them directly to the guest who ordered them.

During this time, the captain would have completed the tableside preparation and plating. The objective is to have all items served simultaneously. This requires constant planning and communicating on the part of the entire brigade. Communication and anticipation are essential to ensure that all meals for each party be completed and served at the same time. Timing, therefore, is of utmost importance. When completely prepared, items may be plated and served *sous cloche,* under an elegant domed plate cover.

Special flatware may be required for uncommon or exotic menu items. Since such menu choices cannot be anticipated, the flatware they require cannot be preset; it is set just prior to the arrival of each course. Examples include fish knives and forks, snail tongs and forks, lobster tongs and picks, pastry forks, parfait spoons, and expression spoons—spoons served with **demi-tasse** cups—for coffee. Communication is required to furnish each guest with the proper utensils for each food item.

Elegant service also includes the use of show plates and service plates. The first are used as a part of the cover for purposes of decoration only, and they are removed once the guests have ordered. These are replaced by service plates, which serve as underliners for all courses except the entrée. If removed and reset, service plates must be clean. One may think of them as very expensive place mats. Napkins should not cover a logo, but should be placed at the side of each cover.

Service Rules

1. All clearing and beverage service is performed from the right of the guest.
2. All food items are placed before each guest from the right, with the exception of bread, butter, and sauces.

BRIGADE

· · · · ·

Chef de Service

The **chef de service,** or chef de salle, is the dining room manager. The director of service has total responsibility for the dining room. He or she must be in close contact with every department and know all aspects of the business: dining room, banquet facilities, service bar, front bar, kitchen, dishwashing area, and the front office. Responsibilities are to:

- Hire and train dining room personnel.
- Solve problems.
- Ensure proper setup of dining room.
- Request necessary supplies.
- Supervise reservation charts.
- Schedule dining room staff.
- Open and close the dining room each working day.
- Inventory all dining room equipment.

Chef de Rang

The **chef de rang,** or table captain, has the responsibility of supervising and organizing all aspects of the classical French service in his or her station. This requires knowledge of the ingredients and the preparation of the food to be served and its proper service, and the ability to carve meat or fowl, remove fish bones, and prepare and cook before the guest.

The chef de rang must be informed, relaxed, friendly, and attentive to all verbal and nonverbal communication from guests when taking cocktail orders, presenting the menu, and answering any questions that guests may have. When the food order has been taken and prepared, the chef de rang may portion appetizers, salads, entrées, desserts, and flaming coffee. The chef de rang concludes by totaling each check and collecting payment. The final duty is to be certain the station is in perfect order.

Commis de Rang

The **commis de rang,** or front waiter, assists the chef de rang when serving the food. The commis de rang should be able to perform all duties in the absence of the chef de rang. Responsibilities also include serving all cocktails, plated food, and cordials, as well as cleaning after each course.

Commis de Suite

The **commis de suite,** or back waiter, brings all food ordered from the kitchen to the service area. This person is the sole communication link between the brigade and the kitchen staff. Other responsibilities include:

- Presenting platters to guests.
- Assisting in the cleaning.
- Providing ingredients for each table (cold salad plates, hot dinner plates, serving forks, spoons, carving sets, doilies, etc.).
- Possessing knowledge of ingredients and methods of preparation, garnishes, and proper service of food items.
- Being aware of the stage of service of each table.
- Placing and picking up orders.
- Coordinating efforts with the chef de rang and the commis de rang.

Commis Débarrasseur

Responsibilities of the commis **débarrasseur** (busperson) include serving bread, butter, and water, and replenishing these items when necessary, cleaning the table after each course, and changing the ashtrays when needed. When the guests have departed from the table, the commis débarrasseur completely cleans each table (**débarrassage**), resets each table, makes sure that a supply of clean tablecloths and napkins are on hand, and performs duties necessary to keep the dining room in order.

Sommelier

In fine establishments, the **sommelier** (wine steward) is in charge of the wine. This function demands extensive knowledge of wines. The sommelier sells and serves bottled wines and assists guests in making wine selections based on their selection of menu items. The sommelier supervises the wine inventory, helps the maître d' prepare the wine list, and establishes prices.

DINING ROOM EQUIPMENT
· · · · ·

The dining room staff must have knowledge of the equipment used to provide proper service. The following equipment is commonly found in restaurants that perform classical French service. Equipment should always be kept in a clean and well-maintained condition.

Guéridon (service cart)

A **guéridon** is a service cart or trolley (see Figures 4–1 and 4–2). It is used for all tableside preparations including portioning, cooking, finishing, and plating. A guéridon is essentially a portable workstation that can be wheeled from table to table. French service requires the use of a guéridon.

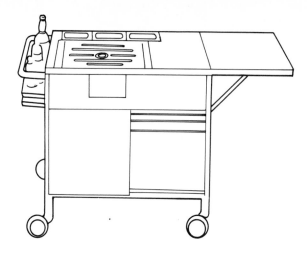

FIGURE 4–1

• • •

Guéridon with built-in réchaud

FIGURE 4–2

• • •

All-purpose service trolley

The top shelf of the guéridon is used to hold the **réchaud** or stove. The réchaud should always be placed on the left side. All spirits and liquors for flambé should be placed at the opposite side of the réchaud. The top shelf is also used for food preparation, salad making, carving, deboning, or cooking. The middle shelf is used to store underliners, napkins, condiments, and service forks and spoons. The lower shelf is used to store the carving board and sets. The linen on each shelf of the guéridon should be neatly folded so that it does not drape or hang over the sides of the shelf.

Guéridon work can be a strong confidence builder for guests, since everything that goes into the dishes they will eat or everything that is to be served is clearly seen and obviously freshly prepared. Guests being served are usually impressed by the skills demonstrated by the chef de rang, and the interest of other guests in the restaurant may be aroused, promoting sales. Above all, the flickering réchaud on the guéridon can substantially enhance a restaurant's atmosphere and create ambience.

Réchaud (stove)

A réchaud is a small appliance designed to cook, flambé (flame), or keep food warm (see Figures 4–3, 4–4, and 4–5). Heat sources used are propane gas, alcohol, or sterno. The following are safety rules for using a réchaud for cooking and flaming:

1. Maintain a safe distance from guests and self.
2. Place liquor bottles at the opposite end of the guéridon, away from the réchaud.
3. Remove the pan from the top of the heating surface (plate) before adding spirit or liquor.
4. Never add liquor to an already flaming pan.
5. Do not allow the tablecloth to hang over the guéridon.
6. Never leave a lit réchaud unattended.

The person handling the réchaud or preparing mise en place must be certain that the réchaud is clean, supplied with fuel, and properly aerated.

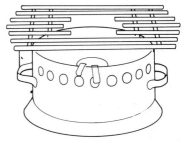

FIGURE 4–4
• • •
Réchaud (alcohol/gel)

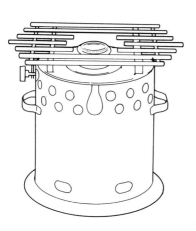

FIGURE 4–3
• • •
Réchaud (wick/fuel)

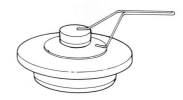

FIGURE 4–5
• • •
Fuel reservoir with flame control lever and extinguisher cap

Chauffe-Plats (Hot Plates)

Chauffe-plats consist of heat-retaining panels that may be stacked in a small battery at a convenient service point inside the dining room and brought to the guéridon for use as required. These panels are used for keeping foods warm when tableside plating is performed or when a direct flame is to be avoided.

Chafing Dish

A chafing dish is a deep dish with a lid and is made precisely to fit its own individual heating unit. The chafing dish was originally designed for dishes requiring techniques other than quick sautéing and flaming. The chafing dish consists of three principal parts:

1. The frame or stand in which a pan with water is placed.
2. The heating unit.
3. The inserts that hold the food.

Blazer-Type Pans

Blazer pans may be oval, rectangular, or round (see Figures 4–6, 4–7, and 4–8). The oval blazer-type pan should be made of copper or stainless steel. Copper, a more efficient conductor of heat, provides an even spread of heat throughout the pan relatively quickly. Copper has more aesthetic value and is thus preferred. The shape of the pan is generally designed to suit particular items; however, its use is not restricted to those items.

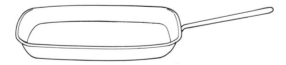

FIGURE 4–6
• • •
Oval blazer pan, commonly used for trout and sole

FIGURE 4–7
• • •
Rectangular blazer pan, commonly used for duckling

34

FIGURE 4–8
• • •

Round blazer pan, commonly used for crêpes Suzette and cherries jubilee

Crêpes Suzette Pans

Crêpes **Suzette** pans are copper-plated shallow pans, normally ranging in diameter from 9 to 16 inches. They are used primarily for tableside dessert items, particularly crêpes Suzette.

Plating Food

When performing tableside plating, it is essential that the serviceperson realize the aesthetics of both the performance and the finished plate. This is the primary factor that makes French service so elegant. Plating should be performed by using a **service set,** the service fork in the left hand and the service spoon in the right. The main item ordered should be placed at 6 o'clock on the guest's plate and all vegetables and starches placed around that area. The food should not extend beyond the inner circle of the plate. Foods being plated must create an impression of palatability for the guest. The addition of a sprig of parsley or watercress in the proper location can make a great difference.

French Casserole Service

In this type of casserole service, plating of the casserole is completed beside the guest's table, usually on a guéridon or, if unavailable, from a tray on a stand. If the starch and vegetable are preplated in the kitchen, the server merely transfers the entire contents of the **casserole dish** to the guest's plate using the service set. After plating the entire casserole, the plate is placed before the guest from the guest's right with the server's right hand.

RUSSIAN SERVICE

• • • • •

In Russian service, used internationally for very formal banquets, food items are completely prepared and portioned in the kitchen, then placed on platters, in tureens, or on a service plate. One server is involved. Items are served to the left of each guest, the server standing with left foot forward. Service proceeds in a counterclockwise direction. The server holds the platter in the left hand and the service set in the right.

Service Fork and Spoon

While in the dining room, service personnel may never touch food items with their hands. Food may only be manipulated with the use of proper service utensils, the most commonly used being the service fork and spoon. These utensils appear similar to a meat fork and soup spoon but are slightly larger. Professional service personnel must be able to use the service fork and spoon with the same dexterity with which they command their hands. The proper position for grasping the service fork and spoon is shown in Figure 4–9.

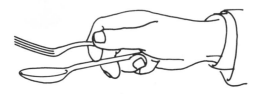

FIGURE 4–9

• • •

Positioning for Russian-style service

Note the position of the first finger, which is inserted between the spoon and fork, giving initial leverage and allowing the food to be firmly held. The spoon is supported by the second finger. Handles of both spoon and fork rest in the center of the palm as if they were hinged. The service set is held with the spoon below the fork and the tines of the fork facing up, so as not to pierce the food item.

Russian Casserole Service

Place the dinner plate containing the starch and vegetable before the guest from the guest's right with the right hand. Holding the casserole dish in the left hand by the underliner, and using a service set in the right hand, serve the entire contents of the casserole onto the guest's plate at the 6 o'clock position. The service set is held Russian style.

When performing either Russian or American casserole service, place the casserole dish as low and as close to the guest's plate as possible. This will help prevent spilling or dripping onto the linen or the guest.

All items are removed from the right of the guest with the server's right hand. Beverages and empty hot plates, soup bowls, or salad plates are placed before the guest from the right.

Russian Banquet Service

Russian banquet service is a very formal service generally utilized at affairs of state. It usually involves a team-type service with each server being assigned to a specific task. To simplify the sequence of service:

- All food is prepared in the kitchen and placed in soup tureens, bowls, or in silver service platters.
- All service vessels—for example, bowls and plates—are preset on the table from the right side, right hand, in a clockwise direction.

36

- All food, including liquids, is served from the left side, working in a counterclockwise direction around the table.

Proper Execution

Russian service can be done as a controlled service in a very precise, paradelike manner. Each server stands at the same place at each table, or the servers can line the perimeter of the dining room. On a given signal from the head waiter—for example, a nod of the head—the wait staff leaves the dining room in unison and files into the kitchen, where each server picks up the bowls or plates and the food item for the first course. The entire staff returns to the dining room in a line together, not individually.

Service begins when the head waiter again gives the signal. Presetting of china begins at each table. In a team service, one server would set the soup bowl, for example, followed by a second server who would then ladle the soup. Likewise, one server would preset plates, while a second would serve the starch and vegetable from a large platter. Still another would follow, serving the entrée. Where staffing is a problem, two waiters may work together, combining presetting the china and serving food items.

FAMILY SERVICE
· · · · ·

Family-style service is used when a casual atmosphere needs to be created. Guests serve themselves and pass the food around the table. This service creates an atmosphere of eating dinner at home with the family. All food items are completely prepared in the kitchen and placed on platters, or into bowls or casseroles, and placed in the center of the table. A service spoon or fork is placed in or beside each food item, and guests pass each food item to the next person after serving themselves. Beverage service, empty plate placement, and clearing are performed from the right by the serviceperson.

BOOTH AND BANQUETTE SERVICE
· · · · ·
Booth

A booth is a table that rests against or is attached to a wall. It generally has high-backed, benchlike seats. A booth has only one focal point—at the end of the table. Guests must be served from that focal point and the server must address all guests from that same location.

Service

1. Serve people seated in the back first, using the right hand to serve guests seated on the left and the left hand to serve guests seated on the right.
2. Clear soiled tableware from the people seated in the front first, using the proper hand as described in step 1.

3. For beverage service, *do not* switch hands. The beverage tray should always remain in the left hand. Serve with the right hand.

4. For coffee service, place the cups for the front guests in front of them. Place the cups for the back guests at the focal point. Pour all coffee first, then pass the cups from the focal point back. While this seems contrary to the rules, it is safer to have less coffee in the pot on the serviette while concentrating on passing the coffee.

5. Always keep hands as low to table level as possible.

6. Never hand an item to a guest; always place it on the table.

Banquette

A **banquette** is a type of seating arrangement in which guests are seated facing the serviceperson with their backs against the wall. This arrangement is generally used to minimize space in a small restaurant.

Service

1. Treat both ends of the banquette as if serving at a booth. While standing at the focal point at the right of the banquette, the guest who is seated center is served first, followed by the person seated nearest the server. The left hand is used. While standing at the focal point at the left of the banquette, the guest who is seated center is served first, followed by the person seated nearest the server. The right hand is used.

2. Clear tableware from the guests seated nearer the server first, using right and left hand as described in step 1.

3. Beverages are served with the right hand, with the tray in the left hand. Stand with the right hip against the table and the left hand in the aisle.

ORDER TAKING AND TIMING THE SERVICE

TAKING THE ORDER
· · · · ·

When ordering, the customer is in a decision-making mode and is usually receptive to suggestions made by the server. A service staff possessing in-depth knowledge of the menu can be confident in their recommendations. Verbal suggestions usually can result in additional courses being sold. When taking the order, the server should approach each guest individually and receive the entire group of menu selections, including appetizer, soup, entrée, and choice of salad dressing. The guest's menu is then removed and the server proceeds to the next guest, repeating the procedure until all guests have placed their orders. If at any time the server is unsure of a guest's selection, the question should be resolved before the server leaves the table. The following techniques will make order taking easier and more productive:

1. Stand erect.
2. Make eye contact with the person who is ordering.
3. Speak clearly and use appropriate adjectives when describing menu items.
4. Smile.
5. Listen attentively.
6. Record each order on an order pad with the correct seat or position number.

Orders are generally taken on a small notepad and then transferred to a restaurant check or entered into a computer system. It is important for the server to encode each item with the seat number to eliminate the server having to ask guests what they ordered during service. Number guests counterclockwise. The number-one position is the seat closest to a predetermined dining room focal point (see Figure 5–1).

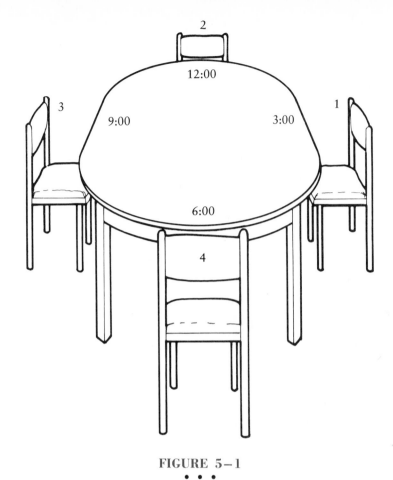

FIGURE 5–1

• • •

Numbering guests positions

Following this numerical sequence, the server would then proceed as follows: Divide the notepad according to the number of guests at the table; allow enough space for recording the complete order for each guest; then number each space on the pad according to the guest's position at the table. Figure 5–2 illustrates this method.

Example 1   Example 2

1. *Tomato soup* (#51) *Salad, O & V* *Veal*	*Tomato* *Salad, O & V* *Veal*	_____ *Salad, French* (#51) *Sole*
2. *Chowder* *Salad French* *Sirloin R*	1	4
3. *Mushroom soup* *Salad It.* *Chicken*	2	3
4. _____ *Salad French* *Sole*	*Chowder* *Salad French* *Sirloin R*	*Mushroom* *Salad It.* *Chicken*

FIGURE 5–2
• • •
Sample orders

Yet another way to take an order is to divide the pad, listing all choices according to the sequence of the course. An example of a server's order pad is shown in Figure 5–3.

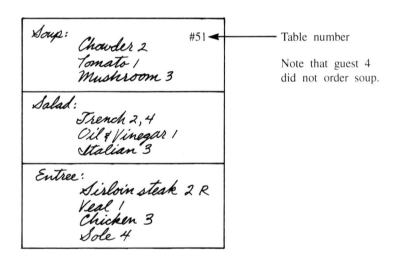

— Table number

Note that guest 4 did not order soup.

FIGURE 5–3
• • •
Order pad, divided by course

42

Notice that the seat number of each guest is listed to the left of each selection. For example, guest number 2 selected the chowder, salad with French dressing, and sirloin steak, rare.

Remember to take the entire order from each guest before moving to the next guest. If a guest should order for someone else, simply write the selection in the diner's number position; for example, a parent at position 2 who orders for a child in position 4—write the child's order in the number-4 position and the parent's selection in the number-2 position. In this way, orders are kept separate and confusion is avoided. When transferring orders from the notepad to the guest check, food items must be grouped according to the sequence of consumption. That is, all appetizers together first, followed by soups, salads and dressings, entrées, and so on (see Figures 5–4 and 5–5).

Be sure to fill in the information at the top of each check in the boxes provided for date, server number or initials, table number, and number of guests. In the column on the far left, list the quantity of each item ordered. To the upper right of each order, write the number of the guests' positions.

TIMING THE SERVICE
· · · · ·

Once the check has been properly filled out, the server should then proceed immediately to the kitchen. The top copy, or dupe, of the check is then given to either the chef or the expeditor or coordinator. This person will then call orders to the appropriate station personnel such as the sauté cook, broiler cook, or salad maker, who will then verbally acknowledge that they have heard the order and will proceed accordingly. The expeditor is also responsible for proper plate presentation and portion and quality control. The expeditor also ensures that each dish leaves the kitchen with proper accompaniments and garnishes.

Some plating, portioning, and garnishing may be done by the servers when picking up the order. They may also be required to provide condiments such as salad dressings, mustard, sour cream, and steak sauce.

In some establishments, servers are required to fire, or begin cooking, certain items that require extra preparation time. This provides lead time for the kitchen staff and eliminates the server's having to wait at the pickup line for such food items. The server would fire ahead of time so the dish is ready to be served along with other items that can be prepared more quickly.

Never serve a course until all selections are ready to be served to an entire group. Servers should never serve two dishes to a party of four while waiting for the other two selections. Food items for an entire group should be brought to the table simultaneously. The server should never serve a partial order and then return to the kitchen for the remainder. If unable to furnish all items at the same time, the server should recruit the assistance of a fellow server or busperson. At the time of pickup, the professional server must make sure that all items are collected and all side dishes, accompaniments, and condiments are included.

The chef or expeditor should be notified of any discrepancies. Menu knowledge is of utmost importance. If and when problems occur in the kitchen, they should be rectified at pickup, without regard to who is at fault, the kitchen or the server. Long-winded arguments accomplish nothing. Remember, it is the guest who suffers while precious time is being wasted in quarreling. By consulting the chef or expeditor, the server can prevent an improperly prepared item from

DATE	SERVER	TABLE NO.	PERSONS	CHECK NO.
				128940
1				
2				
3				
4				
5				
6				
7				
8				
9				
10				
11				

G-4797-3

GUEST RECEIPT

DATE	SERVER	TABLE NO.	PERSONS	CHECK NO.
				128940

REQUISITION

FIGURE 5–4

• • •

Blank guest check

DATE 10·15·91	SERVER 5B	TABLE NO. 51	PERSONS 4	CHECK NO. 128941
1	1	*Tomato soup* [1]		
2	1	*Chowder* [2]		
3	1	*Mushroom* [3]		
4				
5	4	*Salads* [1] O.V. [2] FR. [3] IT. [4] FR.		
6				
7	1	*Veal* [1]		
8	1	*Sirloin* [2] Ⓡ		
9	1	*Chicken* [3]		
10	1	*Sole* [4]		
11				

G-4797-3

GUEST RECEIPT

DATE	SERVER	TABLE NO.	PERSONS	CHECK NO. 128941

REQUISITION

FIGURE 5–5

• • •

Sample order on completed guest check

being served to a guest. Order mixups sometimes do occur and should be corrected by all involved. Both the **front of the house** and the back areas must function like spokes on a wheel if the establishment is to run properly. Never take sides as to who is at fault. The emphasis must be on quality and consistency. This simple philosophy separates the successful restaurant from the mediocre.

When the order has been filled and double-checked, the server should stack the tray by placing each plate in a position that coincides with the guests' positions at the table. This eliminates any fumbling or plate shuffling while at the table. A systematic manner of stacking and removing should be established by the server to eliminate any confusion. This is done by consulting information recorded on the notepad or guest check. When picking up an order, the server should organize the food or beverage tray so that there will be no hesitation or interruption in service in the dining room.

Establishing priorities in serving is essential. The server should never be busy with other duties if food and beverage items are ready to be collected and served. Thinking ahead in an organized fashion provides for an organized system. Anticipating guests' needs enables the server to stay on top of things without rushing or scrambling at the last second, which in turn makes for quality service and satisfaction on the part of the guest. By thinking ahead and establishing priorities, the server can function with peak efficiency at all times. Never wait to ask, *"What do I do now?"* Rather, ask, *"What can I do for later?"* Be aware of economy of time and effort; for example, avoid excessive trips to the bar, pantry, or kitchen if one trip will suffice. Expending energy needlessly can only result in a waste of time and tax the physical and mental capability of the server. Before you make your next move, *stop and think*.

C·H·A·P·T·E·R

6

BEVERAGE SERVICE

Beverage service is the serving of liquids other than foods and is generally grouped into two categories:

1. Cold beverages, including spirits, cocktails, and soft drinks, milk, and juice.
2. Hot beverages, including coffee and tea.

Each establishment will vary the presentation of beverages. The following represent standard procedures that must be followed:

1. All glassware, cups, saucers, and utensils must be clean.
2. With the exception of coffee and tea, a clean glass must be given with refills and reorders.
3. If spills over the rim of the glass occur, whether due to accident or overfilling, the used glass should be removed, a new glass presented, and the beverage repoured.
4. A hot cup should be used with hot beverages. Cold glasses should be used with cold beverages.
5. Under *no circumstances* should ice be scooped using a glass.

COLD BEVERAGE SERVICE
· · · · ·

When serving both soft drinks and liquor, the glass suited to the beverage should be used. The glass should be filled to no more than ½ inch from the rim of the glass. Overfilling only results in spilling by the server or guest and displays sloppy service.

When serving beverages that require garnishing, the garnish should appear fresh and wholesome. Otherwise, it should not be used. Many establishments require the server to garnish cocktails. This requires knowledge on the part of the server of appropriate garnishes and alternative garnishes. For example, a Manhattan is garnished with a cherry or a twist of lemon.

When no tablecloth is being used, a cocktail napkin should be placed under the beverage glass. It is not necessary to use a cocktail napkin when a tablecloth is in use.

HOT BEVERAGE SERVICE
· · · · ·
Coffee

Depending on the meal service, coffee cups may be preset on the table as part of the cover or brought out when ordered by a guest. At breakfast, it makes sense to preset cup and saucer, spoon, sugar, and sweeteners. Cream should be *kept refrigerated* and brought to the table with the hot coffee, since cream is highly perishable.

If lunch or dinner is to be served, coffee cups and saucers may not be preset, as this discourages the sale of other beverages such as cocktails and wine that the establishment wishes to sell. When a guest orders coffee, the server must bring all the items necessary to serve the coffee. If no teaspoon is set as part of the cover, a teaspoon must be brought with the cup, saucer, cream, and sugar. The cream and sugar are placed on a convenient part of the table and the cup and saucer are assembled and placed to the right side of the guest. The server should carry all items on a beverage tray in the left hand and place all items with the right hand. Particular attention should be given to the position of the handle on the coffee cup. It should be situated so as to give easy access for the guest.

The table is now ready for the coffee to be poured. If individual coffeepots are to be used, the pot may be brought at the same time as the coffeeware. Once poured, it may be left on the table to be used for refills. When pouring coffee from a large pot, the server needs to make two separate trips. The first trip is to bring the coffeeware to the table. The second trip is to bring and serve the coffee. Bringing a large coffeepot on a tray with the coffeeware could result in spillage and the possible burning of guests. Remember, cups should be hot when delivered to the table. It may be necessary to pour hot water into the cups in the kitchen for a moment to warm them. Also, if coffee is to be transferred to a serving pot, the serving pot should also be heated in the kitchen before it is filled with coffee.

The role of coffee service is certainly an important one. Most guests have coffee as their last course and may very well be paying the check at this time. Therefore, the coffee and its service is critical as the *lasting impression* of the meal and service.

It is interesting to foodservice professionals to know a brief history of the coffee plant, the proper purchasing of coffee, and the preparation and service of a good cup of coffee. The word *coffee* refers to the roasted, ground beans of the coffee plant as well as the drink made from the *beans*, sometimes termed *seeds*. Coffee is the most important caffeine beverage plant grown. The coffee tree, whose foliage forms a rough pyramid, is native to Arabia and has more than 25 known species. As a self-pollinating evergreen, it produces fruit called cherries or berries. These take from seven to eight months to ripen from green to red. Each contains two coffee seeds or beans. The coffee plant matures in 4 to 6 years and can be expected to be productive for approximately 40 years.

Varieties

There are two commercial varieties of coffee, Arabica and Robusta. Each has characteristics that should be considered in deciding which to purchase.

Arabica   Constituting 75 percent of the world's coffee production, this variety is predominantly grown in Central and South America and eastern Africa. It grows at an altitude of 2,000 to 6,000 feet. Its characteristics are a sweet, aromatic flavor and a low yield due to susceptibility to several diseases. Because of the latter fact and the high elevation needed to grow it, Arabica is expensive.

Robusta   Grown predominantly in Africa and Indonesia, this variety grows at altitudes of 2,000 feet above sea level. It also thrives in wet valley lands and humid tropical forests. Its characteristics are a heavy, earthy taste and high yield because of its resistance to diseases and insects. Low cost is the result of ease of growing and harvesting. Robusta has an industry application as an economical blender.

Harvesting and Processing Methods

Selective This method is used for individual picking made necessary by cherries that do not ripen simultaneously. The processing is called the wet method and is used primarily for Arabicas. During this process, a machine breaks away the outer pulp to expose the parchment-covered beans. These are then soaked in tanks and allowed to ferment to remove mucilage coating. Then the beans are washed and spread in the sun for two to three days. Next, a hulling machine removes the silver skin and remaining parchment and the beans are ready for roasting.

Mechanical This method has limited application because it requires relatively level terrain and long, even rows of shrubs for efficient operation. The machine agitates the shrubs, knocking cherries onto conveyor belts. The processing for mechanical harvesting is called the dry method and is used for Robusta. This process begins with the cherries being sun-dried with frequent turnings for approximately two to three weeks. A hulling machine then removes the dry pulp and the bean is ready for roasting.

Classifications

The dried green beans are classified as to botanical variety, processing method, and altitude of growth.

Colombian milds These are grown principally in Colombia, Kenya, and Tanzania. They constitute 16 percent of world production and are graded principally on bean size. Coffee produced from these beans will be sweet in taste and high in aromatics, with a thick body.

Other mild Arabicas The majority of other Arabicas are grown in Central and South America. They account for 26 percent of world production and are graded by altitude, density, color, and number of defects. The taste is typical of medium-altitude–grown coffee (2,000 to 4,000 feet), winy to sour, with a moderate level of aromatics and a smooth body.

Brazilian and other Arabicas Grown in Brazil and Ethiopia, these beans constitutes 37 percent of global coffee production and are graded by growing area, which determines taste characteristics and number of imperfections. The finished product is typical of Brazilian natural-processed Arabicas grown at low to medium altitudes (sea level to 4,000 feet) and has a winy to sour taste with a moderate level of aromatics and a smooth body.

Robustas Produced primarily in Africa and Southeast Asia, Robustas account for 21 percent of total coffee produced and are graded on density and size, as well as number of defects. Characteristics are a neutral to sharp taste with pungent aromatics and a heavy body. However, Robustas are generally priced from 10 to 40 percent below Arabicas, making Robustas an attractive filler.

Roasting the Beans

It is necessary to roast the coffee beans in order to bring out their full flavor and aroma. Beans are roasted at a temperature of 500° F for varying amounts of time to achieve the desired level of caramelization.

Green coffee beans contain moisture and roasting reduces that moisture. Darker roasted beans contain less moisture, are lighter in weight, and require more beans per pound. The higher price of darker roasted coffee is attributed to this fact.

As beans are roasted, the level of acidity in the beans is reduced, while the level of bitterness is increased. This inverse relationship must be closely monitored by the roaster in order to control the outcome of the product. Coffee roasters provide many levels of roasted beans for specialty use. However, most commercially available roasts fall into three main categories, and only these three will be discussed.

1. Medium—highly caramelized.
2. Heavy—heavily caramelized.
3. Dark—heavily caramelized, becoming carbonized; slightly burnt.

Full city   Full city is considered a medium level of roasting. It is widely accepted by the bulk of American coffee drinkers and is, therefore, the most common degree of roasting used by commercial coffee companies. The words *full city* will generally not appear on the label.

French roast   French roast involves heavy roasting to provide a very full flavor with noticeable bitterness and a strong, distinctive flavor and aroma. Whole beans will display a slight oily coating, as extended roasting expels the natural oils contained in the beans. In the southern part of the United States, the French roast is often called New Orleans roast, due to the large French population in that region.

Italian roast   The Italian roast is the darkest and last stage of roasting. Beans become carbonized, with a coating of carbon, and secrete a noticeable amount of oils. This contributes to the very strong flavor of the coffee. Italian roasts are usually reserved for making espresso coffee.

Espresso   *Espresso* is an Italian word meaning *fast cup*. It is a process by which a combination of steam and boiling water are quickly passed through finely ground coffee beans. Espresso coffee requires a special espresso machine that produces only one or two cups at a time. However, the brew process takes only about five seconds to complete, which enables the coffee to be brewed to order. Espresso is traditionally served in half cups called demi-tasse and not in the usual coffee cup used for other coffee.

Cappuccino   Cappuccino is made by combining one-third espresso with two-thirds steamed milk. The espresso is made in the standard-sized coffee cup, while the milk is steamed using a special steam nozzle on the espresso machine. The steamed milk is then poured directly into the cup of espresso. The finished cup should have a foamy topping of steamed milk on which ground cinnamon or cocoa may be sprinkled. Extreme caution should be taken when making cappuccino. The steam generated from the nozzle is extremely hot, 275–325° F, and can inflict severe burns to the operator.

Decaffeinated Coffee

Caffeine is a nitrogen compound found in many plants, including coffee beans. Though research has shown that caffeine can quicken the heart rate and cause sleeplessness and other side effects, its long-term effects remain inconclusive.

The increased demand for decaffeinated coffee has led to the availability of numerous types of decaffeinated coffee products. The public no longer has to settle for poor-quality coffee sold as instant powders. Decaffeinated coffee, or decaf, can be purchased in ground or whole-bean form alongside caffeinated coffee. Brewed decaf can be obtained in most restaurants today. The brewing process for decaffeinated coffee is the same as for caffeinated coffee. Currently, two general processes are used to remove caffeine from coffee.

Water method	The green coffee beans are soaked in water for several hours.
Chemical method	The green coffee beans are soaked in a solution containing methylene chloride, which absorbs the caffeine. This method requires less time, which reduces the cost of the process.

Preparation and Service

The quality of coffee depends on the aroma released during preparation. To release that aroma, the beans must first be roasted. Best results are obtained from coffee that is ground and served immediately after roasting. Darkness of coffee depends on the level of roasting. Overroasted coffee results in a bitter, burned-flavored aftertaste that overpowers the coffee aroma.

The following steps will ensure a quality cup of coffee that will result in a positive lasting impression:

1. Select equipment designed for proper coffee making and be aware of the importance of proper maintenance.
2. Match the grind of coffee to the brew cycle time of the brewer.
   a. Fine grind will require two to four minutes.
   b. Drip grind will require four to six minutes.
   c. Regular grind will require six to eight minutes.
3. Always match the portion of coffee to the brewing capacity. For most commercial equipment, 2.5–3.2 ounces is recommended.
4. Ensure that the coffee brewer operates between 195 and 205° F for proper brewing temperature.
5. Ensure that the coffee brewer operates with the proper turbulence, or agitation, of the water in contact with the coffee grounds.
   a. Spray head must be in place and not clogged by coffee or water residues.
   b. Brew basket must be of proper size so height of the coffee bed is 1 to 2 inches.
6. Always use clean, cold water for brewing.

7. Allow brew cycle to conclude before removing beverage.

8. Do not combine old and new coffee.

9. Never hold coffee for more than 30 minutes.

When properly serving coffee, provide utensils and condiments for all guests prior to service. Pouring of the coffee should always take place at the table and never in the back kitchen area. Just before pouring, swirl the coffee gently to ensure that all layers of the coffee have been combined.

Tea

In most restaurants today, the service of tea has been lost. Very often, when a guest asks for tea, the service of that tea is treated with much less importance than that of coffee. It is not unusual for a guest to receive a tea bag floating in a glass of warm water.

The earliest written reference to tea is in a Chinese dictionary of A.D. 350. The tea plant, *Thea sinensis,* was growing naturally in India and was brought to China by a proselytizing Buddhist monk. In the 16th century, it was brought by the Dutch to Europe.

Knowing the correct service of tea is as important to the restaurant owner or manager as it is to the serviceperson and guest. For profits alone, the service of tea over coffee should be recommended. In the following section, you will learn the basic types of teas, how tea is produced, and most important, the correct procedure for serving a proper cup of tea.

Tea Growing

The shrub: *Thea or Camellia sinensis*   The methods of culture of the shrub vary from one country to another. Chinese farmers follow an old pattern, sowing tea seeds first in nursery beds and later transplanting the young plants. The young shrubs are set out in rows about 6 feet apart and cultivated for leaves. The leaves are suitable for tea when the bushes are three years old. The shrubs are kept in a bushy form by pruning to a height of no more than 5 feet so that the plant will expend its strength in producing leaves rather than height, and pickers can reach every branch. The shrubs grow in warm climates and flourish at elevations of up to 6,000 feet. Large plantations are usually sited in hilly country. It is thought that leaf quality is improved by clouds, snow, and a misty atmosphere.

Since all tea comes from the same plant, and since there are 1,500 different grades and 2,000 different blends, quality and difference in taste are due to the location in which the bush grows; the time of year at which the leaves are harvested; the position of the leaves on the bush; whether the leaves are picked high or low on the bush, which is very important; whether or not the leaves are broken in handling; variations in climate and soil; the way the leaves are prepared before packing; and the way the infusion is made.

Manufacturing processes   Tea is divided into three categories:

1. Fermented black tea (fermented-oxidized). The leaves are spread on a screen and are dried either by the sun or by a gentle current of hot air. Next, they are carefully rolled to expose and oxidize the juice, then left to wilt on cool tables made of stone, glass, or

metal. The leaves are then heated until they are thoroughly dry. They come out of the process a dark, coppery red color.

2. Unfermented green tea. The leaves are steamed in cylinders or boilers until soft, then rolled on mats. The process is repeated until the leaves are crisp after rolling; then they are given a final drying.

3. Oolong (semifermented). The leaves are partially fermented before drying. The name means black dragon.

Pouchon is called *scented tea*. The leaves are mixed with jasmine and gardenia blossoms. Lapsang-Souchong is a smoked black tea from Hunan, China. Its leaves are smoked over charcoal. Darjeeling is grown in the high foothills of the Himalayas in India.

Tea Brewing

Most establishments use a commercial grade of bagged tea. Packaged in individual servings gives convenience to the service. However, higher-quality loose teas are available and should not be overlooked as an alternative. Whether bagged or loose, there is only one proper way to brew and serve tea in a foodservice establishment. Brewing and serving tea is a simple procedure, but certain points should be observed in order to provide a quality product.

The tea leaves or bag should be immersed in boiling water, 212° F, or near boiling water, 190° F, and left to steep for two to five minutes in order to allow the flavor to be extracted from the leaves. This requires some specific equipment. The equipment needed to serve a portion of tea is:

1. Teacup and saucer.
2. Teapot or **tea hottle** (a pear-shaped bottle).
3. Tea ball or bag containing tea.
4. Tea strainer, if loose tea is used.
5. Underliner for teapot, hottle, and strainer.
6. Condiments such as lemon, milk, and sweetener.

Serving bagged tea is achieved by placing a tea bag into a teapot or hottle, then pouring boiling water in the pot and letting it steep, with the teapot or hottle covered. The teapot is then placed on an underliner plate along with the teacup and saucer to the right of the guest. When the tea is steeped to the guest's liking, the guest can remove the tea bag and place it on the underliner to keep the tea from overbrewing, which will result in a bitter cup of tea.

ŒNOLOGY

HISTORY OF WINE
· · · · ·

The oldest known record of grapes being grown for the sole purpose of wine production is 2000 B.C. in Mesopotamia. Much speculation exists among experts as to the origin of wine. Most experts agree, however, that as the human species appeared, so did wine.

The Greek references to wine, a thousand years before the birth of Christ, were many. Bacchus, the god of wine and fertility, was better known to the Greeks as Dionysus, a nature god, especially of the vine and of wine, the son of Zeus and Semele, the earth goddess. But the Greeks also called him Bacchus and his symbol was the thyrsus, a staff wreathed with ivy and grape leaves and surmounted by a pine cone. Many legends about this god exist in Greek literature. The Roman counterpart was Liber, but the banquets in his honor were referred to as bacchic rites (bacchanalia). These celebrations were stopped in Rome around 186 B.C. because of excessive celebrations. In Egypt, Bacchus took the name of Osiris. Whatever name Bacchus took, the people of ancient times praised their god for his gift of wine.

The Roman Empire played a major role in the cultivation of vines. As the troops moved, they planted vines. When they conquered Gaul (now known as France), the Romans planted vineyards still present today.

The wine consumed in ancient times was usually sweet and young. Little aging took place because most wine was stored in ceramic or wood barrels. Exceptions did exist; for example, in the year 121 B.C., Opimius served wine that was 125 years old at his Roman banquet.

Little was accomplished with regard to increasing the quality of wine produced, but the cultural significance of wine was widespread. The Old Testament refers to wine 155 times and the New Testament about 10 times. The use of wine by Christ is probably the most significant.

Throughout the centuries of the Dark Ages and into the Middle Ages, the cultures of Europe modified the arts. One art was wine making. Most important to the development of wine making were the monasteries.

The 17th century represents the beginning of modern wine production as we know it. In this century, the British increased trade with Portugal and Spain. An overland route was taken through France to the city of Bordeaux, where merchandise was loaded onto ships bound for England. Because of this trade route, the French noticed wines from Portugal using cork bark stoppers. Seeing that cork sealed the bottle better than wooden pegs or oil skins, the French began importing cork for their bottles. Today in France, most cork is still imported from Portugal. The introduction of the cork throughout most of Europe revolutionized the wine industry because cork gave wine makers the ability to age wine.

Near the end of the 17th century, a monk, the cellar master of the Abbey of Hautvillers, perfected a method of making sparkling wine. His name was Dom Perignon. The English and Italians claim to have invented sparkling wines, but neither could produce consistency or prevent large losses. In Champagne, Perignon perfected the blending of wines to make his sparkling beverage. This was, and is, referred to as the cuvée of champagne. Because of the pressure created by the second fermentation, Perignon developed a more efficiently shaped cork that was held with a restraining wire.

To further reduce the literal "blowing up" of bottles, Perignon ordered heavier gauge glass bottles with a concave bottom (punt). In honor of his developments, the company of Moët & Chandon names its "super-luxury wine" in his honor.

The next major event took place almost two centuries later. In 1855, to prepare for a World's Fair in Paris, the brokers of Bordeaux decided to rate what they considered to be the best wines of the world. This classification placed various wineries in Cru (growth) classes, determined by the consistency of quality over the years. The Médoc red wines were the only ones considered, with the one exception of a white Sauterne. Even though biased and political, this classification was very accurate. Thus began the merchandising of wine. Prices would be determined for all time using this method.

Napoléon III, ruler of France, was troubled with the amount of wine spoilage. He requested the top scientists of the day to find a solution. Louis Pasteur's studies in 1863 primarily centered around the effects of oxygen on wine. Pasteur found that a "vinegar bacteria" was present in all wine. When air came in contact with this bacteria, the wine would deteriorate to vinegar. Very slight amounts of air over a long period of time, however, would make the wine mature.

Pasteur offered two solutions to Napoléon. First, place the wine on its side. This would keep the cork moist and swollen, allowing only a small quantity of air into the wine. Second, if the wine were brought to a temperature of 142–145° F for 30 minutes, all bacteria would be destroyed. This process was termed *pasteurization,* a process that is also used in milk. Pasteur was only one of many scientists to study wine. In 1866, A. Julien published the figures for the alcoholic strengths of recent vintages. However, while scientists were busy studying wine, the wine makers were simply trying to survive. In 1870, the Blight of Europe was at its peak. The blight was an infestation of a native New England insect called *Phylloxera vastatrix.* The *Phylloxera* was imported by accident to France, when importing *Vitis lambrusca* Concord grapevines. The American vines were imported because the native European vine *(Vitis vinifera)* had not developed heavy enough roots to survive severe winters like its American counterpart. Insects, once introduced to France, devastated most of Europe's vineyards by boring through the thin-walled roots in the *vinifera* vines. The solution was simple; return to America and take the roots from American plants. Once the roots had settled, the European vines were grafted to them. Today, in Europe, most vines have American roots. The vines are still classified as *vinifera,* but only a few obscure areas have true *vinifera* vines.

California was also severely affected by the blight. It was not until 1890 that wine production there returned to normal.

Another "blight" was about to take place in America: prohibition. Maine first ratified state prohibition in 1846. In 1920, the Volstead Act was passed, stating no alcoholic beverages could be produced, sold, or consumed. Wineries continued some production for sacramental uses, but many closed. Those that did remain open reported an evaporation rate of up to 70 percent instead of 1 percent, the extra losses "evaporating" into stills for illegal brandies.

The 21st Amendment—repeal—was passed in 1933, leaving to state governments the control of liquor consumption. Today, 17 states have state liquor control boards. The greatest effect of prohibition is the still prevalent attitude of European dominance in regard to superior wines and liquors. In many blind tastings, these attitudes have been proved wrong. The American wine industry is young but more consistent, versatile, and most of all, sanitary.

GRAPE GROWING
· · · · ·

Many large wineries today buy ripe grapes rather than grow vines themselves. Smaller wineries, concerned with quality rather than quantity, would prefer to care for the grapes themselves. Producing a good vintage is half luck and half hard work. Growing seasons will vary with climate and geographic location. The following schedule applies to temperate climates in the northern hemisphere.

During the winter months, vines must be pruned, so growth in the spring will concentrate on grapes instead of vine growth. In March, plowing is done to aerate the roots. April 1 begins the season and within 10 days, the budding of the stalks, leaves, and tendrils is obvious. Late in May, frost is most damaging, and small stoves of flame throwers are used. In June, the vines start to flower. Weather is critical—the warmer and calmer, the better. Spraying against oidium and mildew must be done with powdered sulfur.

The baby grapes form in July and change to normal color in August. Temperature is very important at this point. The higher the temperature, the greater the sugar in the grape. This could result in a sweet wine or a grape harvested with the proper amount of sugar but not ripe in flavor.

Rain is preferred prior to summer. Too much rain in the summer bloats the grape with sugar content that is measured with an instrument called a refractometer. Sugar content is the key factor in determining harvest time, usually in late September through the end of October.

Prior to the harvest, grapes may be sprayed with sulfur dioxide to neutralize the natural yeast. Natural yeast, which lives on the skins of grapes, is not always preferred because of the unpredictability of fermentation. Purchased or cultivated yeast is added after pressing.

Once the grapes are harvested, they are transported to the winery where they may be removed from the stems. The grapes are now ready for pressing. The oldest method of pressing is to place grapes in a large container, stand in it, and constantly squash with your feet. This method is still practiced today in some areas in Europe.

The following are three modern methods for pressing grapes:

1. Macerate grapes in juice by use of a basket press.
2. Press and filter by use of drag screens or macerate and centrifuge liquid.
3. Crush (not press) and ferment free runoff liquid by use of a horizontal or balloon press.

Once liquid is produced, it is termed a **must.** The must is next placed in a fermenting vat. The containers may be made of concrete, glass, or be ceramic lined, but the most popular material is stainless steel. Yeast is added, and fermentation is about to start. Vats are not filled because of seething resulting from the release of carbon dioxide and heat. If the temperature should exceed 100° F, the result is a *stuck fermentation.* To avoid this and produce a better-quality wine, temperature of fermentation is controlled between 65 and 85° F. The best quality white wine is fermented at a lower range, while red is fermented at a higher limit.

FERMENTATION
· · · · ·

Fermentation is the process by which sugar is transformed into alcohol and carbon dioxide and by which grape juice becomes wine. It is the work of living organisms with the aid of zymase, the enzyme of yeast. Today, in most good cellars and wineries, fermentation is carefully controlled by regulating the temperature of the fermenting must. The fermenting rooms of Champagne and Burgundy are warmed, and the must itself is generally cooled in California.

Some other practices involve the sterilization of the must or grape juice with sulphur dioxide and the introduction of special strains of yeast. In some instances, white wines are now fermented under pressure in glass-lined steel tanks. Red wines are fermented with their skins on, white wines without. Fermentation normally continues until all or practically all of the grape sugar has been converted. It can be stopped at anytime, as in the making of Port, by adding brandy or high proof spirits; even without such addition, it will tend to slow down and stop as 14 or 15 percent of alcohol by volume has been attained.

CHAPTALIZATION
· · · · ·

Chaptalization is the process of adding sugar to the must or grape juice before fermentation. This is not done to make a sweet wine but to give the wine the proper minimum alcoholic content. It is used in cooler countries and in poor years. This process is rarely authorized in Bordeaux and only in very poor years; always, but within very strict limits in Burgundy; and not at all in California, where it is illegal and considered unnecessary.

The cheaper German wines use this process but never those marked *kabinett* or *spätlese*. Many New York State and Ohio wines are made with the addition of sugar as well as water. This brings the alcoholic content up to par and reduces the wine's final total acidity, which might otherwise be excessive. This also greatly increases the amount of wine that can be made from a given tonnage of grapes. Truly superior wines are never made this way.

TANNIN
· · · · ·

Tannin is a group of organic compounds existing in the bark, wood, roots, and stems of many plants. It is also in wine, red wine especially. To the taste, it is astringent and makes the mouth pucker, particularly the better young red Bordeaux wines of good years. It is especially pronounced in wines that have not been *égrappé,* or separated from stems before fermentation. Some additional tannin is certainly picked up by wines stored in oak barrels, especially new oak barrels, and this often improves them greatly. Tannin forms part of the normal sediment that fine red wines throw as they grow older. A mature wine has less tannin than a young wine because the tannin expends itself as it ages. Some grape varieties give wines far higher in tannin than others, and these generally are the wines that improve with age. Tannins suppress the bacterial growth that ages wine. The longer the duration in wood, the longer the wine will last in the bottle.

PRODUCTION PROCESSES FOR BASIC WINE
· · · · ·

Figure 7–1 illustrates the flow of processes used to make wine.

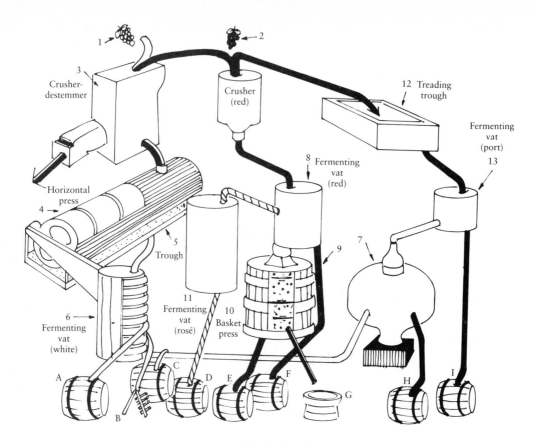

FIGURE 7–1

• • •

Wine production flowchart

Step 1: Pressing or Crushing

White

1. Grapes are put into a destemming machine *(égrappoir)*, which separates the grapes from the stems and presses the grapes to release the sugar.

2. The grape juice is pumped into a fermenting vat.

Red

1. The grapes, along with the stems, are placed into a crushing machine to break or bruise the skins, releasing the tannins and coloring matter.

2. The crushed grapes and juice are pumped into a stainless steel fermenting vat.

3. The grape juice before and during fermention is now called a *must*.

4. The amount of natural sugar will determine the alcohol content of the wine. If needed, natural sugar can be added to raise the alcohol content to 14 percent.

5. SO_2 (sulfur dioxide) may be added to stop the natural *flor* (flower or crust) from reacting with the must.

Step 2: Fermentation

Yeasts

Yeasts are unicellular microorganisms, some of which bring about fermentation in grape juice through the agency of an enzyme, zymase, and turn it into wine. There are many selections or cultures of yeast, some capable of working at lower temperatures than others or having other advantages. In most modern wineries, the yeast cultures are chosen with great care.

The strain of yeast used in fermentation is *Saccharomyces*. There are many different strains. Other compounds, called *esters,* help to develop bouquet and flavor. Yeast and sulfur dioxide are added to start the fermentation. For white wine, the fermenting temperature is between 10 and 21° C (50–70° F). For red wines, the fermenting temperature is 18–30° C (65–85° F) for a shorter time than for whites. The high temperature is needed to extract the tannins and color from the skins.

The two by-products from sugar and yeast are alcohol and carbon dioxide. To avoid too much exposure to oxygen, carbon dioxide may be floated on the fermenting must. The fermentation process is violent. The skins and stems float to the top to form a hat, called a *chapeau.* The chapeau must be broken to release the gas (CO_2) and heat.

Fermentation will stop:

1. When all the sugar is eaten by the yeast.
2. When 14 percent alcohol content is achieved.

If the natural means of yeast dying is not desired—for example, to stop fermentation so that some residual sugar remains in the finished wine—various artificial methods may be followed:

Fortification	The addition of brandy or neutral spirits, raising the alcohol content above the lethal range for yeast.
Pasteurization	Raising the temperature to 61–63° C (142–145° F) for 30 minutes. Once pasteurized, the bacteria are also neutralized, producing a stable, nonmature wine recognized by a metal cap.
Sulfurization	The addition of sulfur dioxide to the fermenting must. This procedure, if performed correctly, stops fermentation without any noticeable taste.
Filtration	Sometimes performed, filtration is not accurate because of the size of the yeast particles (10 million on the skin of one grape).

Once fermentation is completed, which may be four days to six weeks, the wine is stored to allow it to settle.

Step 3: Racking and Fining

The sediments in wine that fall to the bottom of the wine cask are called *lees*. The lees consist principally of cream of tartar, yeast cells, coloring, and other proteins. The heavier solids precipitate because of their weight to form the lees. A few lighter particles may remain suspended in the wine.

The three processes used to remove lees are:

1. Racking: Process of moving liquids to new casks, leaving the solids behind.
2. Fining: Clarifying process using gelatin or egg whites mixed with the wine—causes a raft effect.
3. Dégorgement: Freezing the solids in the neck of the wine bottle in a brine freezing solution and shooting the plug—letting the gas inside the bottle push the plug out when the cork is removed. This process is used only in the Champagne method, discussed in the Sparkling Wine section of this chapter.

Racking

Racking is the drawing off of clear young wine from one vat, cask, or barrel to another, leaving the lees and sediment behind. This operation, which is essential in wine making, involves the loss of 2 or 3 percent of the wine's volume. All well-made wines are racked at least twice, and some of them four times, before bottling.

When red wine is ready for racking, the wine is pumped into oak casks. The solids (lees) are moved to a hydraulic basket press—to press what liquids are left in the skins. Some pressed wine is usually mixed with free-run wine.

To clear and leave the wine bright, it must go through a fining process.

Fining

Fining is the process of clarifying the wine. A small amount of gelatin or egg white is mixed with a little wine and poured into the cask. This mixture coagulates the solids in the wine into a heavy film that acts as a filter for all extraneous matter, leaving the wine in a brilliant condition for bottling. The fining process takes one to two weeks and is completed twice before bottling.

During this period, *malolactic fermentation* may take place. Bacteria converts the malic acid present into a weaker lactic acid and carbon dioxide. This is desired in cool climates, where the natural acids are too high and need to be softened. In hot climates, malolactic fermentation makes the wine too weak in acid content and should be avoided.

Step 4: Aging and Blending

1. During the first few months the wine is in wood, there will be an air space (ullage) due to evaporation. To prevent this, the cask is refilled with sound wine twice a week for the first two months, then every two weeks until the wine becomes clear, five or six months later.
2. During this period, the wine will throw off impurities and superfluous solid matter that fall to the bottom of the cask, requiring racking.

3. Blending of wines will also take place at this time.

4. Centrifuging the wine may take place to further remove sediments. Before bottling, the wine may be fined again to remove lees. A final filtering through paper may be completed for greater purification. This removing of sediments is not always practiced, for some believe sediments should be present.

5. Once bottled, as a precaution against oxidation, the neck may be filled with carbon dioxide to stop air from entering.

6. The wine bottle is stored on its side so that the cork stays moist.

7. In red wine, lees will also develop after bottling.

For Cognac production, the wine is pumped to a chaudière for the distillation process. The basic wine is not aged or blended.

Wine is aged in wood (oak cooperage) because the wood:

1. Affects the color, depending on the type of cask used. Casks are made of oak, new or used, charred or uncharred.

2. Affects the flavor. The type of oak cask used will also determine how tannic the wine will be.

3. Removes impurities through ullage and mellows the harshness.

Modern wineries will also finish their wine. *Finish* refers to correcting the wine if it is found to be out of balance. It is done by adjusting sweetness and acidity through the use of biological chemicals. This is done after a chemical analysis and balancing where deficient. The bottling of wine today is very advanced—the average machine can fill 55 bottles per minute.

SPARKLING WINES
· · · · ·

If sparkling wine is desired, the unbottled finished wine is just the beginning. Three methods are used to make sparkling wines: the Champagne method, the Charmat method, and impregnation.

The Champagne Method

The Champagne method is simply a second fermentation in the bottle. The process begins the blending, or cuvée, of table wine. Some yeast and sugar is diluted in some of this wine to form the liqueur de tirage. The tirage is then added to all the wine that will undergo a second fermentation. The wine is bottled as soon as this new yeast is added, so this fermentation will take place within a restrained atmosphere and the gases can't escape.

Once fermentation is completed, the bottles are placed in racks, neck down, to move the sediments in the bottle gently and slowly to the cap. This is done by twisting and turning the bottles periodically. Wine makers call this riddling, or remuage. The duration of time spent on the racks will vary; generally, the better-quality wines age longer.

The next step is to remove the sediment that has carefully moved down the bottle. *Dégorgement* is completed by dipping the neck of the bottle in a freezing solution. This will freeze about an inch or two of wine, trapping the sediments within the frozen cylinder. The bottle is then refilled with similar wine or Cognac. If dry wine is added, the wine will stay bone dry (brut). All Champagne is produced brut. The *liqueur d' expedition* with which the bottle is refilled, may contain a dosage of sugar, which provides us with sparkling wines of various sugar levels.

The Charmat Method

In the Charmat method, the second fermentation takes place in large vats rather than in the bottle. Due to production in quantity the cost of making this sparkling wine is considerably less, and so is the quality.

Impregnation

The lesser quality and priced sparkling wines are made by a simple impregnation of table wine with carbon dioxide. No yeast flavor exists, nor does the carbonation have the same sensory effects.

The various sweetness levels of sparkling wines available today are:

Nature or Brut Sauvage	The epitome of dryness.
Brut	Bone dry, no sugar added.
Extra Sec	Fairly dry, no noticeable sugar.
Sec	Slightly sweet.
Demi-Sec	Sweet.
Doux	Very sweet.

GRAPE TYPES
· · · · ·

The *Vitis vinifera* is considered to be the wine vine. There are as many as 5,000 types named, but only 50 or so are of concern to the wine lover. Within each grape type are further separations of style. For example, there are about 150 clones of Pinot Noir alone. The following is a description of some of the more popular grapes grown. The grape is the common denominator among the wines of the world. To recognize the grape is to know the general characteristics of the wine.

White

1. Reisling. 80 percent of Germany's plantations are Riesling, best known as the primary German grape. There, it produces various wines of leveled sweetness with a honeyed character. Delicately flower scented, it may be slightly spicy. It is affected by the mold *Botrytis cinerea,* called *noble rot.* The mold shrivels the grapes and dehydrates them so that their sugar is concentrated. In Alsace, France, it is almost always made dry. Best suited to cooler climates.

2. Chardonnay. The grape used for the white Burgundies: Chablis Montrachet, Meursault, and Pouilly-Fuissé for example. It gives a firm, full, strong wine with scent and character. In chalky soils, it becomes almost luscious without being sweet. Chardonnay ages well and is usually made dry. It is also used in Champagne for Blanc de Blanc and secondary blending. It produces the best wine of Napa and Sonoma in Northern California.

3. Sauvigon Blanc. The chief white Bordeaux grape with Sémillon and Muscadelle to make dry Graves with an earthy, gravely characteristic. In the Loire, it makes an interesting, clean, lighter wine where it is used alone. It may have a smokey or flinty taste. In California, Sauvignon Blanc may be called Fumé Blanc. It is best in the Livermore and Santa Clara valleys.

4. Chenin Blanc. The white grape of Anjou and Touraine on the Loire, it gives nervy, intense wine. It is honeylike when very ripe, but always high in acidity. Its finest wine is Vouvray. It is fruity with sugar and acidity, sometimes slightly or half sparkling. In California, Chenin Blanc may be called Pineau de la Loire, and mistakenly White Pinot.

5. Gewürztraminer. Makes up 17 percent of plantings in Alsace. Also used in Germany. Somewhat lacking acidity, it produces a spicy specialty. It is the most pungent table wine grape, with rather small crops ripening early in the season. In California, it is usually made the German way, with some noticeable sugar.

6. Other white varietals:
   a. Sémillon (Sauterne and Barsac). Sweet *Botrytis* style; smooth, noble, and ages well.
   b. Sylvaner (Germany and Alsace). Ripens early with a big crop; slight flavor and lacking acidity.
   c. Müller-Thurgau (German). Highly aromatic, rather soft, and lacking acidity.
   d. Palomino or Listan (Spain). The sherry grape, it produces a big crop; it is a neutral wine, with low acidity, and oxidizes easily.
   e. Seyval Blanc (alias Sèyve-Villard). One of the most successful of hybrids between French and American vines, it is hardy and fruity. It was banned from the AOC areas of France.

Black

1. Gamay. Makes the first class wine of Beaujolais. It is light, delicate, and fruity; some sugar may be noticeable. It is best consumed young (one to seven years). Because it is delicate, it can be slightly chilled. Gamay is best adapted to soil with a high granite concentration.

2. Cabernet Sauvignon. Gives the distinctive red wines of Médoc and Bordeaux. Blended with Merlot and Malbec. In St.-Emilion and Pomerol, its lesser cousin, Cabernet Franc, is used. Cabernet Sauvignon produces full-bodied wine with finesse, dry with slight amounts of noticeable acid. It ages very well, 10 to 20 years on the average. It produces the finest quality red wine of northern California.

3. Pinot Noir. The single red grape of the Côte d'Or area of Burgundy. It produces some of the best wine in the world if planted in the right area. At best, the scent, flavor, body, and texture are all profound pleasures. It is used as the primary grape to produce the Standard Cuvée (blend) of the great champagnes. It does not transplant well, and it is not producing excellent quality in California.

4. Grenache. High-sugar grape with character but not much color. It is used in a blend to make Châteauneuf-du-Pape. The wine produced is medium-bodied with slightly noticeable acidity and a subtle character. It ages somewhat.

5. Sirah (Petit Syrah). The best red grape of the Rhône. It makes dark, tannic, long-lived Hermitage and Côte Rôtie wines. If blended properly, it produces a well-bodied wine without harsh acidity. It has a very good future in California.

6. Merlot. Used primarily in Pomerol and St.-Emilion. It is a softer, fleshier wine, maturing sooner than Cabernet. It is good in New England and the cooler areas of California.

7. *a.* Zinfandel. Unknown place of origin, probably Italy. It is a highly concentrated, heavy wine; noticeable acid may take up to 50 years to smooth out. It likes a dry, cooler climate.

   b. Carignan. The most common grape grown in France. It produces large quantity of harmless, dull red wine, low in acidity, extracts, and tannins. It is best for blending.

   c. Catawba. Native American grape. It gives fruity, foxy wine, some white or pale red. Not as full flavored or sweet as the Concord.

   d. Concord. North American grape, *Vitis labrusca*. It gives a fruity, foxy wine that typifies the *labrusca* species. *Jam and jelly* bouquet and taste.

8. Other red varietals:

   a. Sangiovese. Used in Tuscany, Italy, for Chianti. It has a deep color, good acid balance, and a pleasant flavor. One strain, the Brunello, produces heavier wines that age forever.

C·H·A·P·T·E·R

8

VARIOUS CLASSES OF WINE

TABLE WINE
·····

Table wine generally is dry to semidry and consists of 10–14 percent alcohol. The must generally stops fermenting when all of the sugar has been consumed. White table wine can be made from white grapes or black grapes with the skins removed. Red wine must be made from black grapes and the skins must be present during fermentation. The skins contain the pigments that give wine its color and they are only fully released if present during the heat transfer of fermentation. Rosé wine is generally made by allowing the skins to remain during the first half of fermentation, then removing them during the second half.

DESSERT WINE OR LATE HARVEST
·····

Dessert wines are made from grapes that have more than 30 percent sugar content. Three factors will determine high sugar content:

1. Grape variety—naturally sweet at harvest.
2. Late harvest—allowed to vine ripen longer.
3. Presence of *Botrytis*—a mold that dehydrates the grape and increases sugar content (examples: Sauterne and Trockenbeerenauslese).

SPARKLING WINE
·····

Sparkling wine is allowed to ferment a second time within a restrained atmosphere. The carbon dioxide given off by the yeast cannot escape; therefore, pressure rises in the container. This carbonates the wine, producing an average pressure six times normal atmosphere at sea level (85 lbs. per square inch). All sparkling wines are produced dry. In the final stages of bottling, artificial sugars may be added in various dosages.

Three methods are used to make sparkling wine: Champagne, Charmat, and impregnation. These were described in Chapter 7.

FORTIFIED WINES
·····

Brandy or neutral spirits are added to the wine, raising the alcohol content to 18–22 percent. This is done either to stop fermentation, to retain sugar, or simply to increase alcohol content.

Port Wine

Port wine originally came from northern Portugal. Port is made by filling a barrel already a quarter full of brandy with the partially fermented red wine. The brandy stops the fermentation, leaving the mixture both strong and sweet. The juice from the grapes is extracted by maceration and not crushing. Crushing the grapes would also crush the pits, resulting in a bitter wine.

Vintage Port

Vintage port usually comes from a wine harvest that promises great distinction. A certain proportion is selected and kept in wood for two to three years. It is then sent to England where it is fortified, bottled, and left for 10 to 40 years to mature, or as long as the owners can afford. For the first 8 years, the wine is raw, but after 10 years, it is palatable, gaining each year thereafter.

The other ports are ruby, tawny, and crusted. Tawny and ruby mature in wood, but crusted port is a good substitute for vintage port. Only port wine produced in Portugal does not need to show the country of origin; other port producers such as California, South Africa, Australia, and so on must so indicate.

Production of Port

To make port, the grapes are pressed, then stored as previously mentioned. This noble wine cannot be moved with impunity. Port, because it has to absorb so much brandy, not only gives a heavy sediment but also a crust inside the bottle. Vintage port has a white paint mark on the bottle; always keep the bottle in the same position with the white mark to the top. It takes a long time for the wine to throw a crust, which, if broken or disturbed, takes a long time to settle down. The bottle should be carried in a cradle. It should be decanted with a candle or light bulb in back to see the sediment, and then poured slowly through a fine filter.

Port is usually served with dessert. It should be served clockwise around the table, as the sun rotates—this is traditional.

Madeira

Originally, Madeira was made on the island of Madeira. However, today other countries—including the United States—produce Madeira. Madeira has a close relationship with port and sherry and is both an apéritif and dessert wine. The four types are: Sercial, Verdelho, Bual, and Malmsey, named after the types of grapes used. Sercial and Verdelho are lighter in body than the other two.

Madeira is usually fermented in wine lodges (production facilities) for two to four weeks, at which time it is known as clear wine. It is then fortified with brandy distilled from Madeira wine. Next, it is moved to a hot room called an *estufa*, where it is stored at a temperature of 130° F. This temperature is set and enforced by the government.

The length of time that the wine remains in the estufa determines the temperature of the room. The shorter the stay, the higher the heat necessary. If the government seal is broken by overheating, the wine is confiscated by the government because overheated wine appears older than it is and is considered a fraud.

After the wine is heated, it is allowed to rest for 18 months to two years, then blended into fresh casks and additionally fortified to 20 percent. It is now ready to mature, which can take many years. It is the longest living of all wines and some 150-year-old Madeira is still excellent.

You may find a date of Solera on a bottle. This is a definite guarantee of longevity only if the wine is produced in Madeira.

Marsala

Marsala takes its name from the city of Marsala in western Sicily, around which it is produced. It was originally made during the latter half of the 18th century by a few English families, Woodhouse and Ingham being two of the original houses.

The Grillo, Caterratto, and Inzolia grapes are used in making Marsala. Marsala is a dry wine brought up to 17–19 percent alcohol content by fortifying it with high-proof grape brandy, and then to the desired degree of sweetness by adding an extremely sweet concentrated grape juice. Marsala is also aged in oak, giving the wine some of its color.

Aging and Types of Marsala

1. Fine or Italia Paricolare—17 percent alcohol by volume, aged four months, normally sweet.
2. Superior—18 percent alcohol, aged two years, can be sweet or dry, with a strong caramel flavor.
3. Vergine—18 percent alcohol, aged five years, dry, with more barrelwood flavor.
4. Speciali—18 percent alcohol, a strange aberration, Marsala blended with eggs or even coffee.

CALIFORNIA DESSERT WINES
· · · · ·

Dessert wines are generally considered fortified wines; *fortified* has long been and is still used to describe wines that have brandy added to them for the purpose of arresting fermentation, or simply to increase the alcohol content above the level at which wines will normally stop fermenting. However, the word *fortified* cannot legally be used in the United States, a rule in effect since 1939, when Regulations No. 4 relating to Labeling and Advertising of Wine (Bureau of Alcohol, Tobacco, and Firearms of the U.S. Treasury Department) were adopted. The regulations include the statement that no advertisement for wine, label, wrapper, container, and so on, can contain: "any statement, design, device, or representation which relates to alcoholic content, or which tends to create the impression that the wine has been 'fortified'."

California dessert wines include all the rich, sweet, full-bodied wines that were formerly known in the trade as sweet wines. Their alcohol content is usually under 20 percent, the minimum being 17 percent for sherries and 18 percent for port, Madeira, Muscatel, and Angelica, the upper limit being 21 percent. They range in taste from medium to very sweet and include both white and red wines. If the wine name is preceded by the word *light,* the alcohol content can be as low as 14 percent.

SHERRY

· · · · ·

Spanish Sherry is produced only from grapes grown in the triangle formed by the towns of Jerez, Sanlúcar, and Puerto de Santa María. The two main types of Sherries are Oloroso and Fino. Fino, which includes Manzanilla and Amontillado, is pale in color, rich, and dry in flavor and bouquet.

Oloroso

Oloroso is sweet and heavy except for Amorosa, which is medium dry and sweetened before being sold.

Brown and Cream Sherries

These are Olorosos, the flavor is full-bodied, and their bouquet is slightly less fragrant. Golden Sherry is similar to Cream Sherry but a little lighter.

Fino

Finos are the driest of Sherries and should be served cold since they are better when chilled. The best known are Tio Pepe and La Ina. *Tio* means uncle.

Amontillado

Amontillado is produced from grapes grown in the Montilla area. It is a pale dry white wine with a high alcoholic content. *Amontillado* means "in the manner of Montilla."

Amontillado is darker and stronger than the Finos; Amontillados obtain their depth of flavor from aging. Although they can be made with the same dryness as Finos, Amontillados are more often found in export markets in a medium-dry style.

Production of Sherry

The Palomino grape used for Sherry is picked, then laid out on grass mats for 24 hours so that some of the moisture can evaporate before pressing the grapes. Gypsum, a form of calcinized essence from the white soil, is added to increase the acidity and then left in the casks to ferment. *No* brandy is added to halt fermentation; the casks are not completely filled. The casks are left in the open air (solera—sun—system) and fermentation will last about three months. After fermentation, the casks may have a different taste, bouquet, and body, even though they were filled the same day with identical wine from the same vineyard. After the wine has been racked into new casks, it develops a flor (flower) or soft white crust, which is essential in giving Sherry its unique character. Those with a thick heavy flor become Finos and those with scanty or no flor become Olorosos. This flor occurs only in South Africa and Spain. The barrels or casks are checked in December when they are rated by skilled tasters and the barrels are marked with white chalk: one stroke for the best; two strokes for medium; three strokes for lesser, and so down the line, which are then distilled into brandy.

The graded wines are drawn into fresh casks and fortified with Spanish brandy—not French. The Finos will be brought to 15 percent alcohol, while the Olorosos to 18 percent. The extra brandy in Oloroso kills the flor, while the flor in Fino continues for 18 months or more. The wines are tasted and graded and left for two more years to develop. They are left out in the solera system and the casks are replenished from others to cover the evaporation. The youngest wine is on the top, with the oldest at the bottom of a three-barrel pyramid. Each cask is filled from the one above. There is no vintage in Sherry, but age is a factor in that in the older soleras, a certain amount of residue is in the casks and adds character to younger wines.

When the Sherry is finally drawn, it is completely free of sugar. It is then clarified or refined with egg whites, which gather the sediment and sink to the bottom. Sweet Sherry is sweetened by a heavy sweet wine made from the Pedro Ximénez grape that has been left out in the sun to develop noble rot, and not by sugar. As Sherry is a blended wine, consistency can be controlled. Sherry may contain wine that has matured in 15 or more soleras.

How and When to Serve Sherries

Pale Dry Sherries (Finos)

Manzanilla	Very dry, very pale, and light bodied.
Fino	Very dry, very pale, and medium bodied.
Amontillado	Dry, pale to light gold, full bodied, and nutty.

The finos are ideal apéritifs. Serve chilled or on the rocks. Serve them before meals with hors d'oeuvres, with soup, or at any time, afternoon or evening.

Dry and Medium Sherries (Olorosos)

Oloroso	Usually sweet, deep golden, full bodied, and nutty.
Cream	Sweet, deep golden, full bodied, and nutty.
Brown	Very sweet, dark brown, full bodied, and nutty.

Some Olorosos may be served, like the drier wines, at room temperature; or they may be served slightly chilled or on the rocks. It is a matter of personal taste. The richer Oloroso or brown wines are too full bodied to be chilled and should be served at room temperature. They make delightful drinks to serve with dessert or after dinner.

Because Sherry is fortified and has a higher percentage of alcohol than table wine, it is sturdy, and does not suffer from travel. It is also an inexpensive wine; once the bottle is opened, especially Oloroso, it does not deteriorate and will keep indefinitely either in the bottle or in a decanter. A Fino is more delicate and may oxidize if held too long. Finos should not be kept too long, a few months to a year at most.

Olorosos on rare occasions may deposit some sediment. This is cream of tartar, which is natural to the wine. Stand the bottle up for an hour and the deposit will settle to the bottom so that clear wine may be poured.

APÉRITIF WINES
· · · · ·
Introduction

An apéritif wine is usually known as a quinined wine since it has quinine, aromatics, and bitters added to it. Apéritifs are sipped before a meal because of the stimulating effects on the digestive system. They can also cleanse and stimulate the sense of taste before eating. The addition of quinine to wine was reinforced by the Armed Forces trying to battle malaria. By disguising the quinine in wine and spices, soldiers took the antidote more readily.

The purpose in serving apéritifs is to stimulate the guest's appetite. Suggest an apéritif to guests in lieu of a cocktail. Most cocktails retard the appetite and in some cases may burn the taste buds in the mouth, causing a decrease in the appreciation of the food served. It is the serviceperson's obligation to ensure that guests are totally satisfied with their dining experience.

European Types

The term *vermouth* comes from the German term *wermut,* which means wormwood (an herb). This term was first used in 1786 in a commercial sense to market sweet vermouth. Vermouth is available in two types: dry and sweet.

Production Process

After the Gerault and the Mistelle wines have been matured and blended, a special blend of aromatics and flavorings is steeped in. This end product of steeping is called an infusion. The infusion's ingredients and their proportions are in accordance with strict family secret or house formulas. It is the formula that gives each vermouth its characteristic bouquet. Some of the aromatics include nutmeg, coriander, cloves, cinnamon, rose leaves, Peruvian quinine bark, hyssop, marjoram, angelica root, orange peel, elder flowers, and Bengal rose petals. The infusion is added in a ratio of 1:5 with other wines, and sometimes brandy is added to raise alcohol content to 19 percent.

After blending, the wine is placed in glass-lined vats and brought almost to the freezing temperature, to ensure proper blending and to help avoid the later crystalization of the cream of tartar. Vermouth darkens as it ages, but this coloring neither adds nor detracts from the wine. By French law, vermouth is bottled and matured three and one-half to four years before shipping.

Dry vermouth   Dry vermouth was originally produced in France. It was developed around 1900 by Louis Noilly. Noilly used wines from the Gerault region as the basis of his invention. Gerault wines are considered light, thin, and characterless, thus providing an excellent base for future improvisation.

By French law, the base wine must have at least 10 percent alcohol and cannot exceed 80 percent of the finished product. These wines are made from the Clairette grape. Alcohol and sugar can both be added to fortify the base wine, but then the alcohol content cannot exceed 19 percent. The other 20 percent of the vermouth is referred to as Mistelle. This is created by adding alcohol to unfermented must. The amount of alcohol is determined by what percentage of alcohol the must would have produced if it fermented. The must is usually made of Granache and Muscat grapes.

Sweet vermouth   Sweet vermouth was originally made in Italy. It was first commercially introduced in 1786 by Antonion Benedetto Carpano. Like dry vermouth, sweet vermouth is also made from white wines, especially ones from Piedmont and Muscats. These whites are sweeter and fuller than the whites of Gerault.

Again, the characterless wines are infused with different botanicals and some quinine. They are allowed to mature, then drawn off, fortified to 17 percent, and filtered. After filtering, some sugar and caramel coloring are added. The base wine, by Italian law, must be at least one year old, and the phase between infusion and the final filtering is also one year; so it takes about two years to make sweet vermouth.

Another type of apéritif wine is Cynar, also known as artichoke brandy, as the name and taste denote artichokes. Cynar was developed by the ancient Romans, who believed this "elixir" helped to keep the liver young and to prevent liver sickness. Now it is distilled in France using Jerusalem artichokes. Cynar is distilled from white wine and obtains its dark color from caramel. It should be served with a slice of lemon. Cynar, like vermouth, has only 17 percent alcohol.

A third type of aromatized wine is Campari. This apéritif is listed under bitters fit for beverages because it contains stomachics or aids to digestion. It is considered a premixed beverage bitter from Italy and is said to have a slight orange flavor. Campari is also infused and distilled from white wine, but the Mistelle content is almost 50 percent. This apéritif is called the most bitter of all beverages, due to its quinine content. Aside from its bitterness, it also has a high alcohol content—24 percent.

Campari can be served straight, on-the-rocks, with soda as a highball, or with gin and vermouth in an American or Negroni cocktail. Classically, it is served with a horse's neck—the skin of an orange, peeled and studded with cloves—but sometimes just a twist of lemon is used.

Other Types of Apéritifs

When the apéritif is white, the basic wine used is white; when red, the basic wine is red. The variation in taste—the sweetness, bitterness, or aromatic flavor—results from the use of the different formulas that are trade secrets of each producing house.

The principal apéritif wines sold in the U.S. market are:

1. Dubonnet.
2. St. Raphaël (only red is sold in the U.S.).

3. Byrrh (red only).
4. Lillet.

St. Raphaël is slightly sweeter than Dubonnet. Byrrh and Lillet are slightly drier.

How and When to Serve Apéritifs

Apéritif wines are widely used by themselves. Most are served well chilled. The classic ways to drink them are neat, on the rocks, or with a splash of soda and a twist of lemon added. Lillet, however, is enhanced by a zest of orange rind. Both sweet and dry vermouths are often mixed together, half and half.

Other uses for these wines are over fruit and in cooking. Because it combines wines and savory herbs, vermouth provides an easy-to-use blend of some of the world's most prized seasonings. French vermouth, for instance, can often be substituted for dry white wine in recipes calling for wines and herbs, and the amount of herbs can then be reduced.

Apéritif wines are increasing in popularity in the United States. Since spirits before dinner tend to dull the palate, many people have found that a wine apéritif is the best prelude to a wine-accompanied dinner.

C·H·A·P·T·E·R
9

PURCHASING WINE

Prior to purchasing wine, a few factors should be carefully considered. What food will this wine accompany? Who will be sharing it with you? Is this wine meant for a special occasion? If this wine is meant to be "laid down," is there a space provided to age it properly?

First, let us think about food and wine affinities. The old guide was to serve light wine with light meat and dark wine with dark meat. This type of thinking is for the individual who needs one rule to follow and one only. Many white wines are heavy enough to be compatible with heavier foods, and some light red wines with more delicate foods.

For example, veal is a light meat for which white wine is often preferred. Yet, many Italian dishes with veal would overpower white wines. What is most important in selecting wine is having compatible flavor intensities of food and wine, not matching colors of meat and grape.

Foods can be categorized into various flavor intensity levels: light-delicate, light-medium, medium-full, full, and heavy full-bodied. Wine may also be classified the same way. If the food has a stronger flavor than the wine, the wine will not be appreciated. The opposite will have the same effect.

Other concerns beside flavor intensity are acids, sugars, spices, and other characteristics of food and wine. Try to match the various flavors and intensities, so that both food and wine will be enjoyed. Don't force guests to approve of the food only because it compares well to inferior wine—or vice versa.

Another factor is the occasion. Wine serves to accent the event. Select your wine to suit a picnic or an anniversary. Be aware of who will be sharing this bottle. Various people have various tastes. Will all involved appreciate this particular wine with their food?

WINE LABEL IDENTIFICATION
· · · · ·

Reading the wine label is mandatory when purchasing better-quality wine. You should be aware of the various terms and what they represent. Always follow one basic rule: *buy the best quality for the money.* This does not necessarily mean the highest price.

There are basically three items of information of concern on a label (see Figure 9–1):

1. Place of origin.
2. Bottled at the estate.
3. Vintage (year).

Place of Origin

Place of origin of the wine is guaranteed by the state or control board of each country. It is the only item government will stand behind. No quality is guaranteed, but it is a guide to better quality. Along with place of origin of the grapes, most areas also enforce regulations on grape variety, minimum alcohol content, maximum yield per acre, vine-growing practices, and wine-making practices. Guidelines are set forth by the control boards but are difficult to enforce.

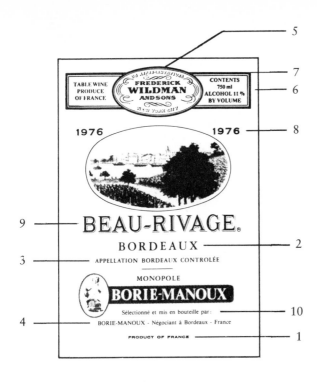

1. The wine is a product of France.

2. The region in which the wine was produced.

3. The appellation for which the wine qualifies, accompanied by AOC or VDQS.

4. The name and address of the shipper, except in the case of champagne, where the house is also the shipper.

5. The name and address of the importer.

6. The alcohol percentage by volume.

7. The net contents of the bottle.

The following information is considered optional:

8. Vintage

9. Brand name or château.

10. "Estate bottled," "Château bottled," or similar phrase.

FIGURE 9–1

• • •

Wine label identification

California

California only regulates the use of 100 percent California grapes. If the grape varietal name is stated, the wine has to be made up of at least 75 percent of that grape. No additional sugar may be added to wine, allowing only natural grape sugar to be used. A federal appellation controlling all states began in 1983.

France

France has three levels of wine produced:

1. Vins de Pays is the country wine, usually regional.
2. Vins Delimités de Qualité Supérieure (VDQS) are the wines of limited superior quality. The wines may be of superior quality but not usually consistent.
3. Appellation d'Origine Contrôlée (AOC) makes up the bulk of French wine obtainable in the United States. The word *d'origine* will not appear on the label, but rather the designated place of origin. The more specific the designation, the more it will serve as a general guide of better quality.

Italy

Italy also has three levels of wine produced:

1. Denominazione Semplice is Italy's simple country wine.
2. Denominazione di Origine Controllata (DOC) is the class of wine most available in the United States. Unlike its French counterpart, the AOC, no specific designation of origin is needed. If this phrase appears on the bottle, the government will guarantee the style of wine stated is from the appropriate area.
3. Denominazione di Origine Controllata e Garantita (DOCG) are simply DOC wines with a higher quality standard, not easily obtainable in this country.

AMERICAN WINE LABELING
· · · · ·

To identify any type of wine, it is necessary to become familiar with the ways in which wines are labeled in the United States. Just as in Europe, American wine labelers must adhere to certain laws, which serve to ensure quality and product identity.

Varietal Labeling

Varietal labeling is considered to be the top of the line. The established regulations, as of January 1, 1983, state that a varietal designation label for *Vitis vinifera* grapes must be composed of 75 percent of that specific grape type. However, *Vitis labrusca* may still be only 51 percent, due to palatability.

Eighty-five percent of the grapes used must come from the exact area stated on the label. For example, California Chardonnay must contain 75 percent Chardonnay, 85 percent from California; Napa Valley Chardonnay must contain 75 percent Chardonnay, 85 percent of which comes from the Napa Valley.

Ninety-five percent of the identified grape must be grown in one single year if the wine is to qualify for a vintage label.

Generic

There are 14 generic labels in all. These wines are made to resemble, or be in *the style of,* a wine from a very famous region or a world-famous type of wine. The legal generic names are:

- Burgundy (France).
- Chablis (France).
- Champagne (France).
- Chianti (Italy).
- Claret (France).
- Hock (Germany).
- Madeira (Portugal).
- Malaga (Spain).

- Moselle (Germany).
- Port (Portugal).
- Rhine (Germany).
- Sauterne (France).
- Sherry (Spain).
- Tokay (Hungary).

Generic wines are usually jug or low-price category wines. Customers do not have to be informed as to what is actually in the bottle as to grape types, areas of origin, ratio, and so on. Two Chablis from different wineries may be entirely different in taste due to makeup. There is no law to regulate control of grape types. In brief, the client does not know what he or she is drinking other than the fact that it is red, white, blush, fortified, or sparkling wine, all imitations of world-class examples from which each takes its name.

Proprietary

Proprietary or name brand wines are easy to identify due to efforts in advertising to promote client familiarity with the label. A gimmick might be used, either name, label feature, bottle shape, or whatever, to permit and promote easy identification. Due to media promotions, the buyer risks no embarrassment when trying to interpret foreign wine labels and terminology.

Aimed at providing a perpetually consistent product, proprietary wine makers make no claim to greatness nor do they attempt to compete with or create world-class products. Their only goal is to produce a drinkable, ordinary wine of sufficient quality. As in the case of generic wines, the buyer never knows anything about the grapes used, the area of origin, or the ratio of blends. These wines are usually jug quality, mass-produced, and inexpensive.

LABELING TERMS
· · · · ·

The following are labeling terms used by France, Germany, Italy, and the United States.

France

Mise en bouteille dans nos Caves	Bottled in the cellars.
Mise en bouteille par le Proprietaire	Bottled by the grower.
Villages	From selected parishes of the region.
Récolte	Vintage.
Negociant	Shipping house.
Château	Estate.
Supérieur	Indicates wine is 1 percent over minimum alcohol percentage.

Cuvée	Blend.
Cremant	Half sparkling.
Brut	Bone dry.
Extra Sec	Dry.
Sec	Slightly sweet.
Demi-Sec	Sweet.
Doux	Very sweet.

Germany

Rotwein	Red wine.
Weissherbst	Pink wine from red grapes.
Schillerwein	Pink wine from red and white grapes.
Schaumwein	Sparkling wine.
Sekt	Sparkling wine under controls.
Trockenwein	Fully dry wine.
Eigenu Abfullung	Bottled by the producer.
Weinkellerei	Wine cellar.
Winzergenossenschaft	Wine growers' cooperative.

Italy

Vendemmia	Vintage.
Riserva	Wine held for three years.
Classico	From best area of region.
Imbottigliato	Estate bottled.
Bianco	White.
Rosso	Red.
Nero	Very dark red.
Rosato	Pink or rose.
Secco	Dry.
Dolce	Very sweet.
Spumante	Sparkling.
Gradi	Followed by a number; alcohol percentage.
Vino Liquoroso	Fortified.
Cantina Sociale	Wine growers' cooperative.
Stravecchio	Very old, ripe, mellow.

United States

Vintage wine	95 percent of grapes must be of that year.
Estate bottled	100 percent of grapes must come from the winery.
Produced and bottled by	75 percent of grapes must be crushed and fermented at the winery.
Bottled by	Wine purchased and then bottled at the winery.
Cellared and bottled by	Wine purchased, blended, and then bottled at the winery.
Varietal	At least 75 percent of that grape.
Generic	Specific region of origin.
Alcohol content	Allowed a leeway of 1 percent in either direction.

SERVING WINE

TEMPERATURE

· · · · ·

Before the opening of a wine bottle takes place, the wine should attain a temperature that will enhance its characteristics. Disregard the color of some wines and be more concerned with how delicate or heavy a wine is. More wines should be chilled or slightly chilled rather than remain at room temperature. These are the ranges of temperature for various types of wine:

40–45° F	Dessert wine.
45–50° F	White and rosé table wine and sparkling wine.
55–60° F	Light-bodied red table wine.
Room temperature	Full-bodied red table wine.
Room temperature	Fortified wine.

Red wines should be opened 20 minutes to one hour prior to consumption, or as soon as ordered, to allow for a breathing period. This is needed to release the initial amounts of tannic acids present. Some older red wines may also be **decanted** to allow for more oxidation and to remove the wine from undesirable sediments. Decanting may be done with immature wines to speed the aging process, but the end result will not be as smooth as a wine that has properly aged in the bottle.

Do not allow chilled wines to return to room temperature, and do not keep wines chilled indefinitely. When serving a chilled wine, it is desirable to pour it into an empty glass. Otherwise, the wine being poured will be warmed slightly by the wine remaining in the glass.

White wines should be opened just prior to the course that they accompany, or whenever a guest prefers them opened. Rosé wines should be treated as white wines for service purposes. Sedimented wines should be decanted.

When a red wine is requested to be served chilled, chill the bottle in a wine bucket with cracked ice. When ice cubes are requested for the service of red or white wines, serve ice cubes separately (this does not apply for apéritif wines requested on the rocks). Do not give a customer a wet wine glass. Do not chill wine glasses in wine buckets. Wine glasses should not be chilled. Always handle wine glasses, clean or used, by the stem.

Large, clear glasses are a prerequisite in the evaluation of wine. A glass for tasting should have a capacity of at least 8 ounces, preferably 10 or more. It should be tulip-shaped, or at least have sides that slope inward near the top, so that the wine can be swirled around inside without spilling. The glass should be only half filled to facilitate the swirling, an action that thrusts the bouquet upward. The swirling also helps to aerate the wine, which tends to accentuate its flavor as well as its aroma.

Despite the beauty of cut or etched glasses, such glass interferes with the evaluation of wine. In order for a wine's appearance to be examined thoroughly, the glass should be absolutely clear, with no designs or frosting or coloration that might disguise how the wine looks. The most useful wine glasses tend to be the simplest, although variations in shape are appropriate for different types of wine served on the same table. The different shapes enable both the pourers and the tasters to avoid confusing the wines.

Avoid selling bottled wines by the glass, unless you have the volume of business to allow it. Pasteurized wines are best sold by the glass. They come in gallon or half-gallon jugs but should be transferred to a decanter for service in the public view.

Do not wrap the wine bottle in a napkin when pouring wine. Do not recork a wine if sold by the bottle. A wine portion should be no less than 3 ozs. and no more than 4 ozs. The glass should be at least twice the size of the portion served. *Note:* The above does not apply to cocktails made with wines; for example, a spritzer (Rhine wine, club soda, and zest of lemon).

Due to variables in all wine, it is wise to have the guest approve each bottle of wine separately. Even though two bottles may be identical in all details, they may not be the same.

To open a bottle of sparkling wine, no corkscrew is necessary. Be aware of the dangers of this bottle; it is under pressure and rather unpredictable.

SEDIMENT
. . . . .

Sediment is the deposit or precipitate of crystals and other solids that most wines tend to throw as they are aged in bottles. It is as natural a part of an old wine as the peel is part of a lemon. It should never be confused with cloudiness or haziness or lack of clarity, all of which are grave faults and often indicate that a wine is not fit to drink. Sediment, on the contrary, is not a defect in any sense; it is a sign of bottle age, and a fine red wine that claims to be old and has no trace of sediment may well be regarded with suspicion.

In the case of white and rosé wines, sediment usually takes the form of colorless crystals of cream of tartar, which is the base of baking powder. These are tasteless and harmless and will often disappear if the wine is shaken and then left for a week or so in a warm room. If white and powdery rather than transparent, some pectins and albumens from the grape are probably also present. Red wine sediment is more copious and more complex and sometimes forms a mask or crust over the inside of the bottle. It is composed of tannins, pigments, and minute quantities of the mineral salts normally present in wine.

In any case, sediment should settle fairly rapidly if the bottle is not disturbed and should simply be left in the bottle when the clear wine is poured off. Certain very full-bodied red wines throw so heavy sediment that they must often be decanted before they are served.

OPENING PROCEDURES—RED WINE
. . . . .

1. Present the wine bottle from the right side, label up to host.
2. Place the bottle on the table or gúeridon with the label facing the guest.
3. Cut lead seal with a wine screw blade above the lip of the wine bottle. Remove the top piece of the seal.
4. Insert the wine screw into the center of the cork.
5. Place the lever on the lip of the bottle and break the seal by pulling the cork out just slightly, making sure that while pulling, the motion of the hand is up and away rather than toward you. Make one additional turn of the screw into the cork and return the lever to its previous position. Pull the cork completely out of the bottle slowly, with as little popping sound as possible. *Note:* Bottles from some wine

regions such as Bordeaux use longer than average corks. In removing these corks, merely using the lever may not be enough.

Upon breaking the cork seal and screwing the opener further into the bottle, do not assume the cork can be removed in one pulling motion. It may be necessary to grasp the exposed portion of the cork with your fingers and, while holding it against the screw itself, pull it slowly straight out of the bottle.

6. While the cork is still attached to the screw, make a wiping motion around the neck of bottle with the cork itself.

7. Remove the cork from the screw and with a clean service towel wipe the top of the cork (portion of cork exposed when lead seal was removed).

8. Inspect and present the cork to the guest. Presentation should be on the right side of the taster's glass. The cork should also be placed on the same small plate the bottle of wine will be placed on after serving.

9. Pour a small taste (approximately 1 ounce) for the host and obtain approval.

10. Pour for the other guests, ladies first, and return to the host last. Do not pour more than half a glass at one pouring.

11. Place the bottle on a plate with the cork, the label facing the guest.

Note: During the service of all wines and champagnes, the lip or any part of the bottle should not touch the rim of the glass.

OPENING PROCEDURES—WHITE AND ROSÉ WINES
· · · · ·

Procedures for opening these bottles follow closely those of red wine.

1. Present the wine bottle, label up to the host, from the right side.

2. Place the wine bottle in the wine bucket.

3. Holding a service napkin around the neck of the bottle and while it is still in the bucket, remove the top of the seal in the same fashion as used for red wine.

4. Insert the screw into the center of the cork.

5. Place the lever on the lip of the bottle and break the seal by pulling the cork out just slightly, making sure that while pulling, the motion of the hand is up and away rather than pulling toward you. Make one additional turn of the screw into the cork and return the lever to its previous position. Pull the cork completely out of the bottle, slowly and with as little popping sound as possible. (*Note:* Bottles from some wine regions, such as Bordeaux, use longer than average corks. In removing these corks, merely using the lever may sometimes be not enough.)

Upon breaking the cork seal and screwing the opener further into the bottle, do not assume the cork can be removed in one pulling motion. It may be necessary to grasp the exposed portion of the cork with your fingers and, while holding it against the screw itself, pull it slowly straight out of the bottle.

6. While cork is still attached to the screw, make a wiping motion around the neck of the bottle with the cork itself.

7. Remove the cork from the screw and, with a clean service towel, wipe the top of the cork.

8. Inspect and present the cork to the host or hostess. Presentation should be on right side of taster's glass.

9. Holding the service towel in the right hand, remove the bottle from the bucket with the left hand. Place the bottle in the palm of the right hand with the label facing the host or hostess.

   The portion of the towel below the bottle should be lifted up and around the side of the bottle so that the label is still visible. That portion of the towel is held under the server's thumb.

10. Pour for the other guests, ladies first, and return to the host or hostess last. Never pour more than half a glass at one pouring.

11. Place the bottle back in the ice and fold the service towel across the top of the bucket.

OPENING PROCEDURES — CHAMPAGNE
· · · · ·

1. Present the wine bottle from the right side, label up to the host or hostess.

2. Hold the wine bottle at chest level and at a 45° angle.

3. With the service towel wrapped around the neck of bottle, locate the wire cage (underneath the foil covering) by touch. After locating the small ring where the wire is twisted tightly, untwist the wire and loosen the foil around the top of bottle. Hold the cork in place with the thumb of the other hand.

4. Twist the *bottle* while holding the cork firmly with the other hand, and remove the cork. Make sure gas is expelled slowly so as to make as little noise as possible.

5. Holding the service towel in the right hand, remove the bottle from the bucket with the left hand. Place the bottle in the palm of the right hand with the label facing the host or hostess.

6. Serve ladies first, starting from the right of the host or hostess, making sure that once champagne has started flowing from the bottle into the guest's glass, it is a continual flow until the glass is approximately three-fifths full. To accomplish this, the flow of champagne must be very slow and the bottle held extremely steady. The host or hostess is last to be served, whereupon the bottle is placed back in the bucket and the service towel is folded and placed across the neck.

WINE TASTING
· · · · ·

In order to become skilled at tasting wine, it is necessary to realize that memory or retention plays an important role. Once having experienced a certain wine, one must catalog all the important aspects of color, body, aroma, flavor, and aftertaste mentally. All of the characteristic attributes of each wine must be recognized, identified, and stored for further reference.

For example, when one is tasting a Chardonnay, certain elements regarding *style* —color, body, flavor, and so on—should immediately become evident to the taster. These elements allow distinction of an American wine from a French, for example. The ability to make these distinctions is only possible by years of tasting various wines and by becoming familiar with the varied styles and characteristics of the grapes from which each wine is made.

A certain amount of research is necessary to understand the different soil and climate conditions of wine-making regions of the world, and obviously to learn the different grapes that are grown in each region. Because of influences such as weather, soil, and wine-making traditions, wines from different regions, or even from the same region made from the same grape, may show obvious differences in bouquet and taste.

It is advisable to the novice that one grape be isolated and many wines made from that grape be sampled in order to gain an insight as to the innate highlights of taste and smell. That is, one should taste many Chardonnays from California. When the taster has pinpointed these highlights, then Chardonnay from other areas such as Burgundy can be tasted. Obvious individual traits that allow the taster to distinguish between each should become relatively evident for each wine.

One can note, for example, that wines from certain areas or countries display certain definite qualities of color, body, smell, and taste that separate them uniquely from all others. This same experiment can also involve the wines of the same grape from two or more areas of the same wine region; for example, wines made from the same Chardonnay grape can be compared from the different areas of Mâcon, Pouilly, and Meursault. With experience gained from extensive solo and comparative tastings, the taster will be able to expand personal knowledge and educate the palate.

The taster should make every effort to retain what is learned from each wine. Good notes should be taken when tasting, and personal comments as to the attributes of each wines' many facets should be recorded. Special attention should be paid to the taster's own experience with the wine. The taster should not necessarily expect to find the same specific highlights as others do. Since we all see, smell, and taste differently, the taster should not find it strange or disappointing not to recognize certain tastes and aromas that others do.

For example, a wine company might claim that their wine has a bouquet suggesting apples. If the taster detects scents other than apples, he or she should not feel a failure but should realize that sensory evaluation is a personal experience. When dealing with the intangible aspects of taste and smell, only be concerned with personal impressions. When tasting with others, do not expect to agree with their comments. No one is right or wrong, and trying to experience what others do will only serve to frustrate and disrupt the taster's own concentration.

The Tasting Experience

Some things to remember when presenting a wine tasting:

- Make sure that glassware is absolutely clean and free from odors imparted by detergents. Glasses should be examined for cleanliness and foul odors ahead of time and cleaned anew if necessary.
- Use oversized glasses that will permit the taster to swirl the wine sampled without risking spillage.
- Place a piece of paper under each glass and number each selection accordingly so as not to confuse the wines to be sampled.

- Pass each wine bottle individually, making sure that the taster can register the proper number of each, avoiding any confusion as to which wine is being tasted.
- Provide logbooks so each taster can register personal comments concerning each wine.
- Remind tasters beforehand to avoid using toothpaste, chewing gum, smoking, or eating foods that are heavily spiced before a wine tasting. Also caution them against wearing heavy perfume, cologne, or aftershave.

Also recommended:

- Pour wines into glasses immediately and allow ample time for breathing—at least one-half hour.
- Serve all wines at room temperature. This allows tasters to get a better idea of the wines' attributes. Chilling can serve as a detractor.
- Serve water at room temperature as a palate cleanser. Caution tasters against eating or drinking anything else while tasting.

The Six Ss of Tasting

The six *Ss* of wine tasting are see, swirl, sniff, sip, swallow or spit, and savor.

See

1. Examine the color and clarity of the wine, holding the glass up to a light. By viewing the wine through the bowl of the glass, the taster can personally describe the color and record it in the log.
2. Tilt the glass so that the wine is thinned out all the way to the rim. Examine the color of the meniscus, or edge, and record. Much can be learned by the individual hues of each wine with respect to grape variety and age. For example, young red wines display youthful pinkish-purple colors, while older wines may turn orange or brick red. White wines from different grapes will show different tinges of yellow.
3. Return the glass to the upright position and examine the *legs* or the way in which the wine sheets run down the glass. This will give an indication of the wine's body or fullness. If the wine sheets off slowly, one can expect the wine to be rich and full. If the wine runs off in rivulets, expect the wine to be weak and thin.

Swirl

Swirling oxidizes the wine or allows it to breathe. As the wine is exposed to air, it will begin to open up, developing the aroma and allowing the taster to experience a variety of aromas. Ample breathing time is a must since inspecting the bouquet of a newly opened bottle can result in a *closed nose,* or bouquet. Premature evaluation cheats the sampler of experiencing the true highlights of the smell. On the other hand, overoxidation can result in a flat or stale wine.

Sniff

Examine the aroma and bouquet of the wine for distinct qualities and register these in the log. Tasters should remember not to limit themselves to things organic but rather to open up their minds to just about any sensation including synthetic, material, chemical, and the like. Keep reactions personal. Take short sniffs and don't inhale deeply, as this tends to quickly numb sensor cells in the brain and prohibits accurate evaluation. Olfaction, the sense of smell, is extremely important, much more important than taste itself. Pinch the nostrils when swallowing and you taste very little. The tongue is sensitive to only four reactions, while the sense of smell can easily identify at least 2,000 comparisons.

Even if the sensation is not a pleasant one, tasters should write it down. It is absolutely necessary to record each one accurately, whatever it may be. The intensity of the bouquet should coincide with the body of the wine as indicated by the legs.

Sip

Take a small amount of wine into the mouth in a slurping fashion. Take in air from the corners of the lips so as to allow the wine to oxidize on the palate. Roll the sample around so that it coats the tongue and all areas of the mouth. Take in more air. Before swallowing or spitting, record reactions of taste in the log. Once again, be truthful and indicate even unpleasant sensations.

Swallow or Spit

Alcohol is absorbed into the system through the capillaries in the tongue; therefore, spitting does not prevent all reactions caused by the alcohol in the wine. If tasters wish to swallow, they should. If not, they should feel free to spit into a provided cuspidor. If swallowed, wine will be absorbed into the bloodstream, resulting in intoxication, which serves to numb all the senses and inhibits serious evaluation.

Savor

Much can be learned about wine from the *finish* or aftertaste. If it is lingering, it is termed long; if the taste quickly disappears, it is short. Before eating or drinking, take time to examine carefully what the wine suggests long after it has been swallowed.

It is now time to reevaluate the wine's overall balance. One should find similarities in body, bouquet, and taste if the wine is to be judged as well-balanced. If any one aspect is not in line with the others, consider the wine as lacking. If all indicators fall into the same area of intensity, or lack of it, the wine is considered to display overall balance. Before advancing to the next selection, it may be necessary to reexamine the wine by repeating the steps one by one.

HOW TO TALK ABOUT WINE
· · · · ·

The following are words that describe the various characteristics of wine.

Aroma	The smell or bouquet of a wine. Used only in a favorable context. An intensely aromatic wine tends to be high in alcohol.
Big	Intensely flavored, full-bodied, and textured. Having a weighty quality that can be sensed in the mouth.

Body	Texture, weight, and flavor intensity.
Bouquet	Smell or aroma; an especially intense, flowery bouquet is called a nose.
Buttery	Having the flavor of butter, evident in some Chardonnays and white Burgundies. Also, creamy.
Complex	Challenging and interesting, with several dimensions.
Dry	Absence of sweetness from residual sugar.
Earthy	Taste of the earth where the grapes grow.
Elegant	Displaying great finesse and balance. Lacking intensity, but complex and interesting.
Fat	Heavy, but lacking in complexity and firmness.
Finesse	Having great balance and harmony.
Finish	Aftertaste, sensation that remains after swallowing.
Flowery	Having an intense aroma of lilacs, honeysuckle, or other flowers.
Forward	Mature before its time, soft and pleasant at a young age.
Fruity	Having the flavor of grapes and sometimes suggesting other kinds of fruit. Erroneously used for sweet.
Green	Young, immature, undeveloped.
Hard	Immature, tannic.
Intense	Having strong, well-defined flavor and texture. Robust.
Light	Low in alcohol, lacking in body, dull.
Nose	Very pronounced bouquet.
Oaky	Aroma and flavor of oak barrels used for aging. Also, woody.
Off	Turned bad.
Oxidized	Deteriorated from exposure to air, often indicated by brownish color and the odor of rotting hay.

STORAGE OF WINE

· · · · ·

Most people take more care in storing a bunch of bananas than they do with wine. The average person buys wine from a shelf next to spirits in a liquor store, and therefore thinks, wrongly, that all liquors may be stored the same.

Distilled products age in wood; wine ages in the bottle. Most distilled products will survive under adverse conditions, wine will not. Most bacteria cannot survive in the high alcohol climate of distillates; in wine, they are alive and doing well.

Wine changes with time because separate flavors and scents in the wine intermingle. Bacteria also changes wine. In wine, vinegar bacteria is present. This bacteria eventually causes the wine to deteriorate and become vinegar. Natural component acids like citric, malic, and tartaric are added to help retard bacterial growth. The best deterrent is tannic acid. Tannins are derived from the oak cooperage during the maturing stage. They are also present in grape skins and stems. This acid slows down the bacteria so it only slowly deteriorates the wine. This process is called *aging*. All wine will turn to vinegar when the bacteria overwhelms the acid content. This also explains why pasteurized wine will not age. All bacteria are killed and until opened and exposed to bacteria present in the atmosphere, the wine does not change.

What we attempt to do in storing wine is to allow present bacteria to deteriorate the wine under our control. To store wine:

1. Locate a roomy, well-ventilated area. Proper air circulation is necessary to avoid a musty aroma in the wine. Some humidity is desired so as not to prematurely dry out the corks. Too high a humidity will allow unwanted molds to grow.

2. The wine storage area should be at a constant temperature. The desired temperature is 55° F. As high as 75° F is acceptable as long as the temperature change is a gradual one. High temperatures accelerate bacterial growth and low temperatures place it in a dormant state where no aging takes place.

3. The area should be away from direct light and free of vibration or agitation. Some of the diseases that affect wine (such as protein cassé, which is a precipitate formed by the presence of protein) react only in the presence of light. Strong light may also "bake" the wine, which will raise the temperature and accelerate bacterial growth. Vibration and agitation may age wine prematurely by a physical stimulation of bacteria, not to mention the fact that the sediment that had settled will now be floating.

4. The bottles should be stored on their sides to keep the corks moist and swollen, allowing only small amounts of oxygen to affect the wine. Wine stored standing usually has a dry, shrunken cork. This allows overoxidation to take place, and the wine will be brown (maderized) and vinegary.

5. To help organize your wine cellar, it is wise to start an inventory book. For each wine, you should record the name, year, price, amount purchased, from whom, date purchased, name of shipper, and any other pertinent information.

C·H·A·P·T·E·R

11

*F*RENCH
WINES

INTRODUCTION TO FRENCH WINES

· · · · ·

Wine is a product of the earth born out of devotion and hard work. France, blessed with an ideal combination of soil, climate, and a long tradition of dedicated wine making, has over the centuries created wines that are the standards against which all other wines are judged. This section is a guide that will help you tour France. You will be introduced to the major wine regions of the country (see Figure 11–1), how wine is made, and how French laws protect the wine consumer.

French Wine Laws

In 1935, France passed the first comprehensive wine legislation, the Appellation d'Origine Contrôlée (AOC). These laws cover every aspect of wine making, from soil and vine to bottle and label. This far-reaching control provides the strongest possible protection to both the consumer and the reputation of France's fine wines. The factors that are controlled by AOC laws are:

- Place of origin. Because soil gives wine its basic characteristics and climate affects its quality, the geographic location of a vineyard is of utmost importance. Thus, only those vineyards located within the defined boundaries of a given area and capable of producing wines that are characteristic of the area are permitted to use that appellation.
- Grape variety. The centuries old wine history of France has shown that the quality of a wine is unalterably bound by two factors—the grape variety and the soil. Under AOC laws, only grape varieties that have proved themselves best for that place are allowed to be grown there and to be used in that wine.
- Minimum alcohol content. AOC rules specify a minimum alcohol content for each wine. This alcohol content is achieved by harvesting only ripe grapes that have developed an adequate sugar content. It is this grape sugar that is converted into alcohol during fermentation. Alcohol helps to preserve wine and helps it to live longer and develop its potential.
- Maximum yield per acre. In order to prevent overproduction and thus maintain high standards, a maximum number of gallons of wine per acre has been established. As an appellation becomes more specific, the number of gallons allowed from each acre usually decreases.
- Vine-growing practices. Both minimum alcohol content and maximum yield per acre can be controlled through the limitation of vines per acre and proper pruning methods. AOC laws place tight controls on these practices in order to promote small yields of high-quality grapes.
- Wine-making practices. Each wine area has developed its own traditional wine-making methods. A large part of a wine's individuality comes from these methods. To be sure that these same methods are continued, all facets of wine production are regulated by AOC laws.
- Controls. The regulations for AOC wines are enforced by the French government. They are constantly being strengthened in order to maintain the two basic purposes of the laws: to uphold the reputation of France's wines and to give the utmost confidence to the consumer.

We will now discuss the major wine regions of France.

96

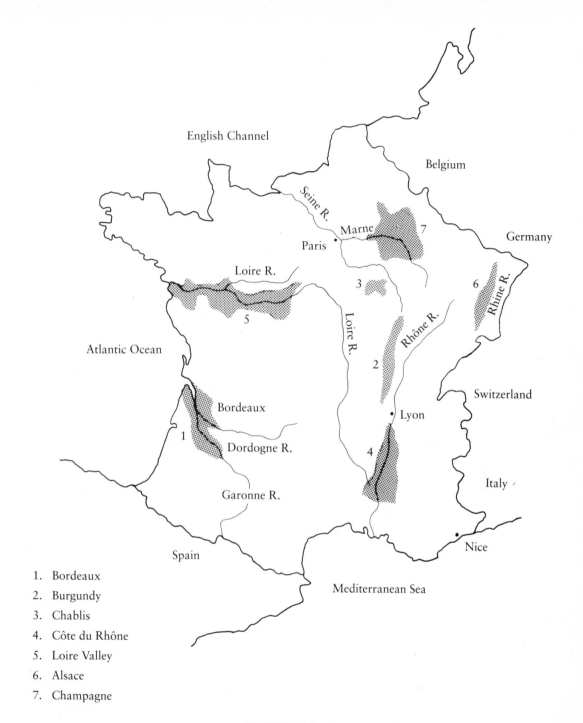

English Channel

Belgium

Germany

Seine R.

Marne

Paris

Loire R.

Loire R.

Rhône R.

Rhine R.

Atlantic Ocean

Switzerland

Bordeaux

Lyon

Dordogne R.

Garonne R.

Italy

Spain

Nice

Mediterranean Sea

1. Bordeaux
2. Burgundy
3. Chablis
4. Côte du Rhône
5. Loire Valley
6. Alsace
7. Champagne

FIGURE 11–1

• • •

Map of the major wine-producing areas of France

BORDEAUX

· · · · ·

Bordeaux is one of the most important wine regions on earth. Located near the Atlantic coast in southwest France, Bordeaux is a region geographically dominated by its rivers (see Figure 11–2). The Garonne and Dordogne rivers meet north of the city of Bordeaux and combine to become the broad Gironde River, which, in turn, flows 50 miles to the Atlantic Ocean. All the great wines of the region come from vineyards close to one of these waterways.

The major grapes grown for Bordeaux red wines are:

Cabernet Sauvignon.

Cabernet Franc.

Merlot.

Malbec.

Petit Verdot.

Cabernet Sauvignon and Cabernet Franc give the wine vigor, tannin, and long life. Merlot gives softness and suppleness. Malbec and Petit Verdot are planted in small quantities and are used to balance the major varieties.

The major grapes grown for Bordeaux white wines are:

Sauvignon Blanc.

Sémillon.

Muscadelle.

Because each grape variety contributes characteristics that balance those of the other grapes, Bordeaux wines are almost always a blend. Only occasionally is a wine of this region made of one grape variety.

There are five categories under which Bordeaux wine is sold.

1. Château. Bottled wine made from grapes grown entirely on the vineyards of one estate and vinified, aged, and bottled on the same estate.
2. Bordeaux shipper. Wines that are made at a château or vineyard and then sold in the barrel to a Bordeaux shipper who bottles them.
3. Regional or communal. Wines that are marketed by their appellation of origin: Médoc, Saint-Emilion, Graves, Sauternes, Barsac, Margaux, Saint-Julien, or simply Bordeaux. They are wines bought by a shipper from vineyards within the area of their appellation. The shipper blends these wines to maintain a consistent quality from year to year.
4. Grape variety. Bordeaux wines sold under the name of the grape variety from which they are made. By law, these wines must be made from 100 percent of the designated variety.
5. Monopole. A wine blended by a merchant shipper and given a brand name. Often the brand name is coupled with a regional or communal appellation. These, too, are regional blends, but their labels emphasize the brand name rather than the appellation of origin or the name of the shipper.

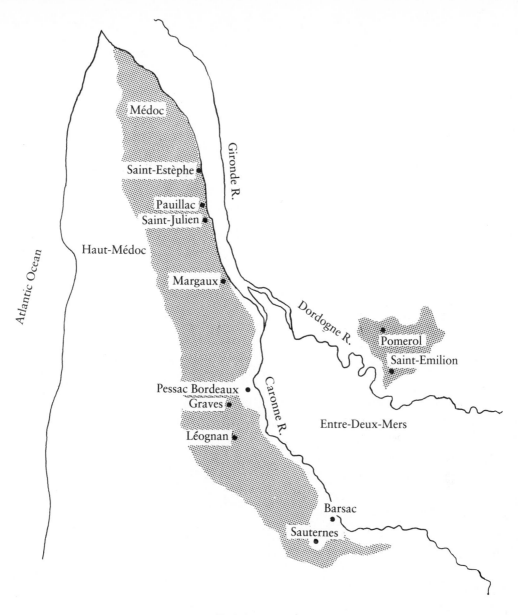

FIGURE 11–2

• • •

Map of the wine-producing regions of Bordeaux

Principal Red Wines

Médoc

An exclusive red wine district, Médoc is divided into two parts: the Haut-Médoc, which is the northern part of the peninsula, and Médoc, which is the southern half.

The Haut-Médoc is home of some of the most famous vineyards in the world. It is itself divided into communes, four of which produce wines of such distinctive and individual character that they have the right to their own appellation.

Going from north to south, the first of these communes is Saint-Estèphe. It is a commune whose wines are deep colored, full-bodied, generous, and attractive. They mature more slowly than other Médoc wines. Saint-Estèphe's best wines are:

Château Cos d'Estournel	Second growth.
Château Montrose	Second growth.
Château Calon-Ségur	Third growth.
Château Lafon-Rochet	Fourth growth.
Château Cos-Labory	Fifth growth.

Pauillac

Pauillac is perhaps the most remarkable wine-growing township in the world. The wines of this commune generally tend to have deep color, great finesse, and opulent bouquet when mature. Within its communal limits are produced a number of the very greatest red wines of France or perhaps of the world.

Château Lafite-Rothschild	First growth.
Château Latour	First growth.
Château Mouton-Rothschild	First growth.
Château Pichon-Longueville	Second growth.
Château Pichon-Longueville Comtesse de Lalande	Second growth.
Château Duhart-Milon	Fourth growth.
Château Pontet-Canet	Fifth growth.
Château Batailley	Fifth growth.
Château Haut-Batailley	Fifth growth.
Château Grand-Puy-Lacoste	Fifth growth.
Château Grand-Puy-Ducasse	Fifth growth
Château Lynch-Bages	Fifth growth.
Château Lynch-Moussas	Fifth growth.
Château Mouton-Baron-Philippe	Fifth growth.
Château Haut-Bages-Libéral	Fifth growth.
Château Pédesclaux	Fifth growth.
Château Clerc-Milon	Fifth growth.
Château Croizet-Bages	Fifth growth.

Graves

The district of Graves derives its name from gravelly soil. It means a specific defined area on the left bank of the Garonne River, largely west and south of the city of Bordeaux.

The best red Graves come from the communes of Pessac, Léognan, Martillac, Talence, and Cadaujac. In character they are close to the Médoc wines and they age well. The grapes that come from this soil give wines that are distinctive and garnet colored.

The vineyards of Graves were last classified in 1959. The top châteaux are all rated equally as Crus Classés, or classified growths. Château Haut-Brion is the exception, having been classified as a first growth in 1855.

Official classifications

Château Haut-Brion	Pessac	First growth.
Château Pape Clément	Pessac	Classified growth.
Château La Mission-Haut-Brion	Talence	Classified growth.
Château La Tour-Haut-Brion	Talence	Classified growth.
Château Haut-Bailly	Léognan	Classified growth.
Château Fieuzal	Léognan	Classified growth.
Château Carbonnieux	Léognan	Classified growth.
Château Malartic Lagravière	Léognan	Classified growth.
Domaine de Chevalier	Léognan	Classified growth.
Chateau Oliver	Léognan	Classified growth.
Chateau La Tour-Martillac	Martillac	Classified growth.
Chateau Smith-Haut-Lafitte	Martillac	Classified growth.
Chateau Bouscaut-Cadaujac	Martillac	Classified growth

Saint-Emilion

The picturesque village of Saint-Emilion is about 20 miles northeast of Bordeaux. Most of the best vineyards are in the township of Saint-Emilion itself. Seven adjoining communes are also entitled to the appellation, and five more areas, or communes, plus a portion of a sixth may add the words Saint-Emilion to their own name on wine labels. The vineyards surrounding the medieval village of Saint-Emilion produce wines that are considered among the fullest of all the red wines of Bordeaux. They are generous, deeply colored, and tend to mature more quickly than other Bordeaux reds.

Saint-Emilion wines, all reds, are classified under four quality designations. In descending order, they are:

1. First classified great growths.
2. Great classified growths.
3. Great growths.
4. Saint-Emilion.

The following are the best first classified great growths of Saint-Emilion:

Château Ausone.

Château Cheval Blanc.

Château Beauséjour-Duffau Lagarrosse.

Château Beauséjour-Fagouet.

Château Belair.

Château Canon.

Château Figeac.

Château La Gaffelière.

Château Magdelaine.

Château Pavie.

Château Trottevieille.

Clos Fourtet.

Saint-Julien

This township is in the very center and heart of the Haut-Médoc; its wines are somewhat lighter. They have harmony and balance, and they mature sooner than Pauillac and Saint Estèphe.

The most famous châteaux of Saint-Julien include:

Château Léoville-Las-Cases	Second growth.
Château Léoville-Poyferré	Second growth.
Château Léoville-Barton	Second growth.
Château Gruaud-Larose	Second growth.
Château Ducru-Beaucaillou	Second growth.
Château Lagrange	Third growth.
Château Langoa-Barton	Third growth.
Château Saint-Pierre-Sevaistre	Fourth growth.
Château Branaire-Ducru	Fourth growth.
Château Talbot	Fourth growth.
Château Beychevelle	Fourth growth.

Margaux

Margaux is one of the best sections of the Haut-Médoc, producing wines remarkable for their bouquet, silky texture, and great elegance. The appellation now covers, in addition to the small township of Margaux proper, most of the neighboring communes—Cantenac, Soussans, Arsac, and Labarde. The finest Margaux wines, of course, carry a château label.

Château Margaux	First growth.
Château Rausan-Ségla	Second growth.
Château Rauzan-Gassies	Second growth.
Château Durfort-Vivens	Second growth.
Château Lascombes	Second growth.

Château Brane-Cantenac	Second growth.
Château Giscours	Third growth.
Château Kirwan	Third growth.
Château d'Issan	Third growth.
Château Palmer	Third growth.
Château Cantenac-Brown	Third growth.
Château Boyd-Cantenac	Third growth.
Château Desmirail	Third growth.
Château Ferrière	Third growth.
Château Marquis-d'Alesme-Becker	Third growth.
Château Pouget	Fourth growth.
Château Marquis-de-Terme	Fourth growth.
Château Prieuré-Lichine	Fourth growth.
Château du Tertre	Fifth growth.
Château Labarde	Fifth growth.
Château Dauzac	Fifth growth.

The following are the best great growths of Margaux:

Château l'Angelus.
Château Balestard-la-Tonnelle.
Château Cadet-Piola.
Château Canon-la-Gaffelière.
Château Cap-de-Mourlin.
Château Corbin.
Château Corbin-Michotte.
Château Curé-Bon.
Château Dassault.
Château Fonroque.
Château Grand-Barrail.
Château Grand-Corbin.
Château La Clotte.
Château La Dominique.
Château La Marzelle.
Château Larcis Ducasse.
Château La Tour-Figeac.
Château Pavie-Macquin.
Château Ripeau.
Château Soutard.
Château Tertre-Daugey.
Château Trimoulet.

Château La Marzelle-Pigeac.

Château Troplong-Mondot.

Château Villemaurine.

Château Yon Figeac.

Château Clos des Jacobins.

Pomerol

Pomerol is the smallest of the famous districts into which the Bordeaux country is divided. Its wines can be even fuller and sturdier than those of its neighbor, Saint-Emilion, and have, in addition, a unique velvety quality; they mature more quickly than the Médocs. No classification has ever been established for Pomerol, but many of its châteaux are outstanding and enjoy a world reputation.

The following list is of the best châteaux of Pomerol.

Château Pétrus.

Château Vieux-Château-Certan.

Château La Conseillante.

Château Trotanoy.

Château Petit-Village.

Château l'Evangile.

Château Lafleur.

Château Cazin.

Château La Fleur Pétrus.

Château Nenin.

Château La Pointe.

Château Beauregard.

Note: Château Pétrus stands apart on a level with the growths of the Médoc.

Other Red Wines

Other Bordeaux red wines come from Blaye, Premières Côtes de Blaye, Côtes de Bourg, and Première Côtes de Bordeaux. These districts make wine that represents the basic Bordeaux taste. Most of them are blended by shippers and sold under Monopole labels as Appellation Bordeaux Contrôlée.

Principal White Wines

The white wines of Bordeaux offer a cornucopia of choice, from the lightest and driest to the most famous sweet wines of the world. All white Bordeaux wines are made from grapes of the Sémillion and Sauvignon Blanc varieties, plus an occasional minor mixture of Muscadelle.

Graves

The Graves district is known mainly for its white wines. The finest white Graves come principally from the commune of Léognan, plus a few exceptions from Talence, Pessac, Martillac, and Cadaujac. Some of Graves châteaux make both red and white wines; others produce one or the other. In the 1959 classification of Graves, the most outstanding whites were rated equally as Crus Classées.

The following are the best classified growths of Graves:

Château Bouscaut.
Château La Tour-Martillac.
Château Carbonnieux.
Château Laville-Haut-Brion.
Château Couhins.
Château Olivier.
Château Haut-Brion.
Château Malartic-Lagravière.
Domaine de Chevalier.

Sauternes and Barsac

Sauternes and Barsac wines are known as luscious golden, unique, sweet wines. The officially delimited district comprises five townships: Preignac, Bommes, Fargues, Barsac, and Sauternes itself. The wine is made by leaving the grapes on the vine beyond the usual harvest time. A combination of fog, humidity, and sunshine encourages the mold *Botrytis cinerea* to develop, which causes their sugar to become highly concentrated. The grapes are handpicked as they are ready, which means the workers must go through the fields as many as six times during the harvest.

Classification of 1855 for Sauternes and Barsac

Château d'Yquem	First great growth.
Château La Tour-Blanche	First growth.
Château Coutet	First growth.
Château Climens	First growth.
Château Lafaurie-Peyraguey	First growth.
Château Guiraud	First growth.
Château Rieussec	First growth.
Château Rabaud-Promis	First growth.
Château Sigalas-Rabaud	First growth.
Château de Rayne-Vigneau	First growth.
Château de Suduiraut	First growth.
Château Nairac	Second growth.

BARON PHILIPPE DE ROTHSCHILD S.A.

MOUTON-CADET

MARQUE   DEPOSEE

BORDEAUX
APPELLATION BORDEAUX CONTROLEE

un vin

Baron Philippe

MIS EN BOUTEILLE PAR

BARON PHILIPPE DE ROTHSCHILD S.A.
NEGOCIANTS A PAUILLAC.GIRONDE

CONT. 750 ml   Imported by   ALC. BY VOL. 11,5 %
THE BUCKINGHAM CORPORATION
RED BORDEAUX WINE   NEW YORK N.Y.   PRODUCT OF FRANCE

TABLE WINE
PRODUCE
OF FRANCE

US REPRESENTATIVES
FREDERICK
WILDMAN
AND SONS
NEW YORK CITY

CONTENTS
750 ml
ALCOHOL 11 %
BY VOLUME

197€   1976

BEAU-RIVAGE.

BORDEAUX
APPELLATION BORDEAUX CONTROLÉE

MONOPOLE
BORIE-MANOUX

Sélectionné et mis en bouteille par:

BORIE-MANOUX - Négociant à Bordeaux - France

PRODUCT OF FRANCE

RED BORDEAUX
TABLE WINE
PRODUCE OF FRANCE

US REPRESENTATIVES
FREDERICK
WILDMAN
AND SONS
NEW YORK CITY

CONTENTS 750 ml
ALCOHOL
12 % BY VOLUME

Château Sénéjac

MIS EN BOUTEILLES AU CHATEAU

1979

CRU BOURGEOIS

HAUT-MÉDOC

APPELLATION HAUT-MÉDOC CONTROLÉE

C. DE GUIGNÉ, PROPRIÉTAIRE – 33290 LE PIAN MÉDOC

Shipped by: WILDMAN & Fils, Wine Shippers at BORDEAUX (Gde) - France

WI5

Château Suau	Second growth.
Château Romer	Second growth.
Château Caillou	Second growth.
Château de Malle	Second growth.
Château Lamothe	Second growth.
Château Myrat	Second growth.
Château Doisy-Védrines	Second growth.
Château d'Arche	Second growth.
Château Broustet	Second growth.
Château Filhot	Second growth.

BURGUNDY

· · · · ·

The region of Burgundy begins about 70 miles southeast of Paris and extends to Lyon (see Figure 11–3). From this 225-mile span comes some of the world's most exalted wines, as well as two of the world's most popular wines: Chablis and Beaujolais.

Geographically, Burgundy is an elongated region of varying soils, separated into a number of major districts. From north to south these districts are Chablis, the Côte d'Or (which is divided into the northern Côte de Nuits and southern Côte de Beaune), Côte Chalonnaise, the Mâconnais, and Beaujolais.

All of Burgundy's major white wine is made from the Chardonnay grape. The reds of the Côte d'Or and the Chalonnais are made from the Pinot Noir grape. The reds of the Mâconnais and Beaujolais are made from Gamay. A regional blend of Pinot Noir and Gamay is bottled under the Appellation of Bourgogne, Passe-Tout-Grains.

In the late 1400s, Burgundy became part of France. It was a common practice to give vineyards to religious orders. By the time of the French Revolution, a good part of Burgundy's best wine land was owned by the monasteries. After the Revolution, the vineyards of Burgundy were taken from the church and divided into small parcels and sold to the people.

Today, over 200 years later, the system of small ownership still prevails in Burgundy, and so while the great vineyards remain intact as appellations, they are divided among many proprietors.

The names of the wines of the Côte d'Or are controlled by AOC laws. They are also classified as Grand Cru, Premier Cru, and Village wines. Grand Cru wines, which are the most distinguished, are identified only by the vineyard name. Premier Cru wines, only slightly less distinguished than Grand Cru, are labeled first with the village or communal name, then with either the vineyard name or the phrase Premier Cru. Village wines, which are far more plentiful than the other classifications, are named simply for the village. Over the years, many villages have added the name of their most famous vineyard to their own.

Red Wines

The red wines of Burgundy begin in the north with the Côte de Nuits section of the Côte d'Or. At their best, the Côte de Nuits reds are full, elegant, and vigorous, with a deep perfumed bouquet.

Chassagne-Montrachet makes a small quantity of appealing red wines, often very good but rarely of absolutely top class. Further south is Santenay, the last wine village of importance in the Côte de Beaune. All of its wine is pleasant and light red. These somewhat resemble the red wines of Chassagne-Montrachet nearby, being rather full and soft, yet with a good deal of tannin and an earthy taste. The best vineyard is Gravières.

Below the Côte de Beaune begins southern Burgundy, an area comprised of the Côte Chalonnaise. The red wines of the Côte Chalonnaise are pleasant and often reminiscent of their neighbors in the Côte de Beaune. Its red wine parishes producing good and well-balanced wines are Givry and Mercurey, the largest area dedicated to one appellation in Burgundy.

The Mâcon district makes some red wine. Red Mâcon is a pleasant, sound wine, less fruity and attractive than good Beaujolais though somewhat firmer and coarser.

Beaujolais, the district of the Burgundy span, produces what is possibly the most famous red wine in the world. For the most part, Beaujolais is light and fruity and should be enjoyed slightly cooled and young. In fact, some of it—Beaujolais Nouveau—is drunk immediately after it is made in the fall. It is a light wine with low alcohol and short life. On the other hand, some of the Beaujolais Cru wines improve in the bottle and are quite enjoyable after several years of age.

There are four grades of Beaujolais. The first, labeled Beaujolais, comes from Bas-Beaujolais, the southern part of the district where the soil is chalkier. Beaujolais Supérieur is essentially the same as Beaujolais except that it must have one degree more alcohol. Beaujolais-Villages comes from 38 designated villages and displays a decided step up in elegance and balance.

The most outstanding and distinctive wine of the region is Cru Beaujolais. It comes from any one of nine villages in the north where the granite soil brings out the best of the Gamay grapes. These wines range from soft, elegant, and light to those that are fuller and longer lived. These Crus are Brouilly, Chénas, Chiroubles, Côte de Brouilly, Fleurie, Juliénas, Morgon, Moulin-à-Vent, and Saint-Amour. These are the only Beaujolais wines entitled to the Burgundy appellation.

White Wines

The village of Chablis, separated from the Côte d'Or by about 57 miles, produces one of the best-known dry white wines of France, if not the world. A crisp, fruity, extremely dry wine with refreshing acidity, Chablis is the product of chalky soil and a short growing season.

There are four categories of wine in Chablis. The first is Petit Chablis. This wine is made from grapes grown farthest from the town of Chablis. It is also the lightest of the Chablis and is at its best when served young. Chablis without any other qualification is the regional appellation. This wine, which accounts for nearly half of Chablis' total production, is green-tinged and flinty. Chablis Premier Cru is usually labeled Chablis with its appellation Premier Cru. In

FIGURE 11−3

• • •

Map of the wine-producing regions of Burgundy

addition, it may also have the name of its vineyard on the label. Chablis Premier Cru is green-tinged, refreshing, and bone dry.

The most elegant wine of Chablis comes from its seven Grands Crus, or growths. Fuller-bodied than other Chablis, Chablis Grand Cru has personality, distinction, and excellent style. Wines of this classification are labeled with their vineyard name. They are Blanchots, Bougros, Les Clos, Grenouilles, Les Preuses, Valmur, and Vaudésir.

Côte de Nuits, the northern section of the Côte d'Or, makes very little white wine. Among its small output, however, is the outstanding Clos Blanc de Vougeot, white Nuits-Saint-Georges, and the big flavorsome Grand Cru and Musigny Blanc.

Côte de Beaune's greatest fame is in its whites. The first of these whites can be found in the village of Aloxe-Corton, where the rare and rich Grand Cru Corton-Charlemagne is located, as well as Premier Cru Corton-Languettes, Corton Pougets, and Corton.

Beaune's best known white wine is Clos des Mouches. Meursault is dedicated almost exclusively to white wine. Generally, Meursault is straw colored, full-bodied, big, soft, round, and very dry. Meursault's leading vineyards, in about this order of quality, include:

Perrières.

Genevrières.

Charmes.

Blagny.

La Pièce-sous-le Bois.

Dos d'Ane.

Poruzot.

Jennelotte.

Boucheres.

Goutte d'Or.

Meursault.

These are white Burgundies of high quality and real distinction; the finer ones are surpassed by only a few great rarities among the dry white wines of France.

Puligny-Montrachet produces what are generally and correctly regarded as the finest dry, white wines of France. It is a village of two Grands Crus, Chevalier-Montrachet and Bienvenue-Bâtard-Montrachet, and parts of two other Grands Crus, Bâtard-Montrachet and the incomparable Montrachet, are generally considered to be the best dry white in the world.

Within the communal limits of Chassagne lie major portions of Montrachet and Bâtard-Montrachet as well as Criots-Bâtard-Montrachet wines. These, however, do not carry mention of Chassagne-Montrachet on their labels and are sold simply under the vineyard name. Almost of equal excellence are Chassagne-Montrachet Les Ruchottes, Cailleret, Chenevotes, Morgeot, and a few others.

In southern Burgundy, the white wines of the Côte Chalonnaise are pleasant, agreeable, and charming. Montagny makes white wine exclusively. Rully also produces white wine.

The Mâconnais produces large quantities of light, dry, crisp, well-balanced white wine. Most of it is wine of good value labeled as Mâcon, Mâcon Supérieur, Mâcon-Villages, or Pinot-Chardonnay-Mâcon. Some carry the name of the wine's village, such as Mâcon-Vire. The best known wine of the region is Pouilly-Fuissé, a very dry white wine that comes from five delimited communes. Similar wines are made in Pouilly-Loché, Pouilly-Vinzelles, and Saint-Véran.

BOUCHARD PÈRE & FILS
BEAUJOLAIS-VILLAGES

APPELLATION BEAUJOLAIS-VILLAGES CONTRÔLÉE

MIS EN BOUTEILLE PAR LA MAISON
BOUCHARD PÈRE & FILS, NÉGOCIANT AU CHATEAU, BEAUNE (COTE-D'OR)
PRODUCE OF FRANCE   RED BURGUNDY WINE
ALCOHOL 13% BY VOLUME   CONT. 750 ML
PRODUCED AND BOTTLED BY : BOUCHARD PÈRE & FILS, BEAUNE
IMPORTED BY : INTERNATIONAL VINTAGE WINE CO. HARTFORD CT.

BOUCHARD PÈRE & FILS
CHABLIS Premier Cru
VAILLONS

APPELLATION CHABLIS PREMIER CRU CONTRÔLÉE

MIS EN BOUTEILLE PAR LA MAISON
BOUCHARD PÈRE & FILS, NÉGOCIANT AU CHATEAU, BEAUNE (COTE-D'OR)
PRODUCE OF FRANCE   WHITE BURGUNDY WINE
ALCOHOL 13% BY VOLUME   CONT. 750 ML
PRODUCED AND BOTTLED BY : BOUCHARD PÈRE & FILS, BEAUNE
IMPORTED BY : INTERNATIONAL VINTAGE WINE CO. HARTFORD CT.

GRAND VIN
DE BOURGOGNE

Mise en Bouteilles
au Château

CHÂTEAU FUISSÉ
Pouilly-Fuissé

Appellation Pouilly-Fuissé Contrôlée

M. Vincent et Fils Prop. Vitic. Fuissé (71)

PRODUCE OF FRANCE   73 cl

Joseph Drouhin

ALCOHOL 12.5 % BY VOLUME   BURGUNDY WINE   750 ML   PRODUCT OF FRANCE

MACON-VILLAGES

APPELLATION CONTROLÉE

MIS EN BOUTEILLE PAR
JOSEPH DROUHIN
Maison fondée en 1880
NÉGOCIANT A BEAUNE, COTE-D'OR

AUX CELLIERS DES ROIS DE FRANCE ET DES DUCS DE BOURGOGNE

SOLE AGENTS   *Dreyfus, Ashby & Co*   NEW YORK, N.Y.

Joseph Drouhin

ALCOHOL 12.5 % BY VOLUME   BURGUNDY WINE   750 ML   PRODUCT OF FRANCE

LAFORET
BOURGOGNE
Chardonnay

APPELLATION BOURGOGNE CONTROLÉE

MIS EN BOUTEILLE PAR JOSEPH DROUHIN
NÉGOCIANT A BEAUNE, COTE-D'OR, AUX CELLIERS
DES ROIS DE FRANCE ET DES DUCS DE BOURGOGNE

SOLE AGENTS   *Dreyfus, Ashby & Co*   NEW YORK, N.Y.

CÔTES DU RHÔNE

· · · · ·

The Côtes du Rhône is a long, narrow strip of wine country that stretches along the banks of the Rhône River (see Figure 11–4). It begins just below Lyon and ends 140 miles south at Avignon, site of the ancient palace of the popes. The climate is hot and sunny and more constant from year to year than most wine regions of France. The soil is rocky, dominated by granite, and in some areas covered with fist-sized stones.

When Clement V became pope in 1305, he made Avignon his residence. From then until 1377, it was the papal seat. A summer castle built north of Avignon by Clement V was called Châteauneuf-du-Pape. Today, the area is the home of the most famous of all Rhône wines.

With their long, intensely hot, and sunny growing season, the wines of the Rhône are generally big, robust, and higher in alcohol than most French wines. In the northern part of the valley, where some of the finest Rhône reds are to be found, the wines tend be full-bodied, long-lived, vigorous, and deeply colored; most of these wines are made from the Syrah grape. Southern Côtes du Rhône wines are usually full-bodied and tend to mature earlier than their northern counterparts. They may be produced from more than a dozen different grape varieties.

Northern Vineyards

Côte Rôtie

This region, with its steep, precipitous, sun-drenched hillsides, produces red wines that are warm, robust, full-flavored, and richly colored. Hard and dark in their youth, they become softer and rounder and develop an excellent bouquet as they age. Côte Rôtie has often been called the best of the Rhône wines.

Hermitage

The red wines of Hermitage are generous and full, with a rich flavor and a full bouquet. They too take well to aging, and with maturity become softer and smoother. The vineyards of Crozes-Hermitage, which are on the lower slopes surrounding Hermitage, are similar although they are slightly less full and intense and usually reach maturity earlier.

Saint-Joseph

The wines of Saint-Joseph are more delicate and less full and flavorsome than Côte Rôtie and Hermitage. Saint-Joseph has a ruby color and a distinctive taste, and it matures more quickly than most northern Côtes du Rhône reds.

Cornas

Like most northern Côtes du Rhône reds, Cornas can live to an old age. Cornas is tannic in its youth and velvety in its maturity.

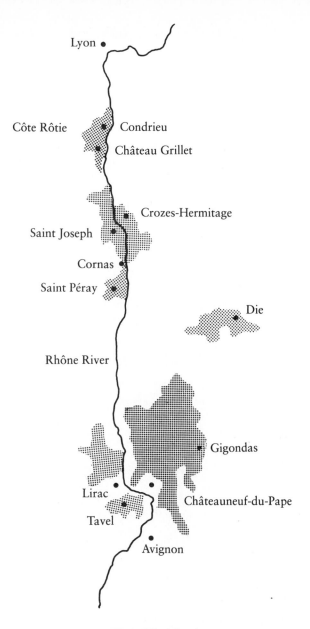

Lyon •

Côte Rôtie • Condrieu
• Château Grillet

Crozes-Hermitage •

Saint Joseph •

Cornas •

Saint Péray •

Die •

Rhône River

Gigondas •

Lirac •

Châteauneuf-du-Pape

Tavel •

Avignon •

FIGURE 11–4

• • •

Map of the wine-producing regions of the Côtes du Rhône

Southern Vineyards

Châteauneuf-du-Pape

The most celebrated of all Rhône wines is Châteauneuf-du-Pape, big, pungent, strong, and deep colored. It can be made from a combination of as many as 13 authorized grape varieties including Syrah, Grenache, and Clairette, and generally matures earlier than northern Rhône wines.

The vines of Châteauneuf-du-Pape grow in soil that is covered with large stones. The sun is reflected off the stones and onto the vines. As a result, the grapes develop an abundance of sugar and thus produce wine that has a high alcohol content. In fact, Châteauneuf-du-Pape has the highest legal minimum alcohol strength of any French wine.

Côtes du Rhône

Wines of the area without the right to more specific appellations are bottled under the appellation Côtes du Rhône. They are produced in great quantities. Almost all of them are red. Those that read Côtes du Rhône with a communal name hyphenated are usually of high quality. The area also produces a few interesting white wines and some fine rosés.

White Wines

The wine of Condrieu, situated close to Côte Rôtie, is golden, and with its intense, almost peachlike flavor, is a highly individual wine. Château Grillet, the smallest appellation contrôlée in France, produces a very small amount of a generous, golden, fragrant white wine. Hermitage, Crozes-Hermitage, and Saint-Joseph produce whites that are also golden tinged.

Rosé Wines

Tavel, the best known rosé of France, comes from the southern part of the Rhône Valley. A very dry and delicate wine made predominately of the Grenache grape, it is orange-tinged pink, medium-bodied, and fruity. Lirac rosé is slightly lighter-bodied than Tavel and considerably less well known. Otherwise, there is little difference between the two.

RHÔNE
RED WINE
PRODUCE
OF FRANCE
750 ML

CONTAINS
SULFITES

ALCOHOL
12,5% BY VOLUME

PRODUCE OF FRANCE

TRADE   MARK

Parallèle "45"

MARQUE DÉPOSÉE

CÔTES du RHÔNE

APPELLATION CÔTES DU RHÔNE CONTRÔLÉE

75cl   **PAUL JABOULET AÎNÉ**

Mis en bouteille par
PAUL JABOULET AÎNÉ, NÉGOCIANT ÉLEVEUR À LA ROCHE DE GLUN-26600 TAIN L'HERMITAGE (FRANCE)

MAISON FONDÉE EN 1865

RED STILL RHONE WINE
PRODUCE OF FRANCE

Côtes du Rhône

APPELLATION CONTROLEE

MIS EN BOUTEILLE PAR

MOMMESSIN

Négociant - Eleveur à Mâcon (S. et L.) France
Alcohol by vol. 13%   NET CONTENTS   750 ML
SOLE U.S.A. DISTRIBUTORS, COSMOPOLITAN IMPORTERS
DIVISION OF RENFIELD IMPORTERS. LTD. N.Y. N.Y

VINTAGE 1978

REGISTERED TRADE MARK

BOUCHARD PÈRE & FILS

CHATEAUNEUF-DU-PAPE

APPELLATION CHATEAUNEUF-DU-PAPE CONTRÔLÉE

MIS EN BOUTEILLE PAR LA MAISON

BOUCHARD PÈRE & FILS, NÉGOCIANT AU CHATEAU, BEAUNE (CÔTE-D'OR)

PRODUCE OF FRANCE   RED RHONE WINE
ALCOHOL 13% BY VOLUME   CONT. 750 ML
PRODUCED AND BOTTLED BY : BOUCHARD PÈRE & FILS, BEAUNE
IMPORTED BY : INTERNATIONAL VINTAGE WINE CO. HARTFORD CT.

═ **Seigneur de Maugiron** ═

PRODUCE OF FRANCE
750 ML

RED RHONE WINE
ALCOHOL 12,5 % BY VOL

Côte - Rotie

APPELLATION CÔTE-ROTIE CONTRÔLÉE

1979

Mis en Bouteille par   DELAS   à Tournon s/ Rhône

SOLE AGENTS   *Dreyfus, Ashby & Co* NEW-YORK N.Y.

LOIRE VALLEY

· · · · ·

The Loire Valley, in west-central France, takes its name from the Loire River, which flows east to west for about 350 miles before emptying into the Atlantic Ocean (see Figure 11–5). The eastern part of the valley is called the Upper Loire. The first vineyards of the area were those of Pouilly-sur-Loire.

The village of Pouilly-sur-Loire produces two white wines. The Chasselas grape produces a wine labeled Pouilly-sur-Loire. The Sauvignon Blanc grape, locally known as the Blanc Fumé, produces Blanc Fumé de Pouilly-sur-Loire, shortened to Pouilly-Fumé, the village and grape name combined. Pouilly-Fumé has a delightful fragrance, rich flavor, and distinctive tang. Pouilly-sur-Loire is an agreeable wine, less distinguished than Pouilly-Fumé, and should be drunk when young.

Across the river is Sancerre, which produces an excellent white wine from the Sauvignon grape and is one of the better known of the Loire whites. It is very dry, full-flavored, delicately crisp, and clean.

Further to the west in the center of the valley is the large district of Touraine. Here, the Chenin Blanc is the dominant white grape, and its most famous wine is Vouvray, generally a soft, fresh, fruity wine. Vouvray is made dry, mellow, or sweet, still, sparkling, and semi-

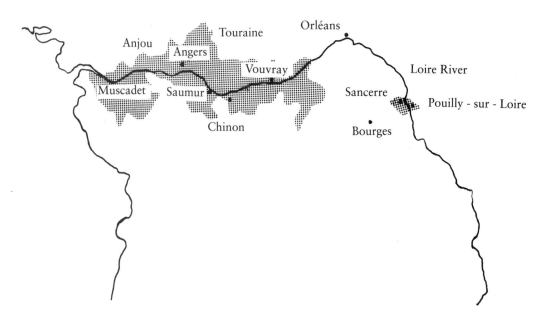

FIGURE 11–5

· · ·

Map of the wine-producing regions of the Loire Valley

sparkling. The Touraine also produces two red wines in the villages of Chinon and Bourgueil made entirely from the Cabernet Franc grape. These two wines combine the tannic character of a light Bordeaux with an appealing fruity taste and a brilliant light ruby color.

The large district of Anjou, Touraine's neighbor to the west, also produces white wines of the Chenin Blanc grape. The village of Saumur produces a charming white wine that is made dry, with a hint of sweetness, both still and sparkling.

The village of Champigny produces a red wine made from the Cabernet Franc grape. It is often listed and sold as Saumur Champigny to distinguish it from the white wine of Saumur. The other white wine—producing areas of Anjou are the Coteaux de la Loire, the Coteaux de l'Aubance, and the Coteaux du Layon, the Aubance and the Layon being tributaries of the Loire River. The Anjou district also produces rosé wines. Rosé d'Anjou is a light, mellow, and agreeable wine made from a lesser grape variety, the Groslot. Another rosé, labeled Cabernet d'Anjou, is made from the Cabernet Franc grape. This wine is generally less sweet and has somewhat more character than does Rosé d'Anjou Muscadet.

The last of the Loire Valley districts produces pale white wine that is dry, light, refreshing, and tart. The grape variety, like the region and the wine, is called Muscadet. The Muscadet grape, brought from Burgundy in the 16th century, was extensively planted and ultimately gave its name to the vineyard region around Nantes. The best Muscadet comes from the Sèvre-et-Maine district and these words will be found on the label.

ALSACE

· · · · ·

Alsace, a region in northeast France, is bordered by the Vosges mountains on the west and separated from Germany by the Rhine River on the East (see Figure 11–6). Between 1870 and 1918, Alsace and the neighboring province of Lorraine were part of Germany. Because the wine strip of Alsace, about 70 miles long and never more than 1 or 2 miles wide, is in the north, it is subject to rigorous weather conditions. Still, many geographic factors conspire to make this climate beneficial to the grape.

The wines of Alsace were granted the Appellation Contrôlée Vin d'Alsace in 1962. The wines are labeled and marketed with the name of a specific grape variety and must be made entirely of that grape.

Ninety-eight percent of all the wines of Alsace are white. The following are among the most important.

Riesling

Riesling is one of the very greatest of white wine grapes, and is a native of the Rhine Valley. Riesling makes clean, graceful wine. It has balance and breed and well deserves to be called the finest wine of Alsace.

Gewürztraminer

Gewürztraminer is the most distinctive and individual of Alsace's wines. *Gewürz* means spicy in German, and this spiciness is the most outstanding characteristic of Gewürztraminer. It is a delicious, fruity wine with a pungent flavor and a highly perfumed and flowery bouquet. It is usually dry.

Sylvaner

Sylvaner is a productive, white wine grape that produces comparatively light, agreeable wines without much distinction. Today, nearly 70 percent of the vineyards of Alsace are planted with Riesling, Gewürztraminer, and Sylvaner. The rest is made up of Pinot Blanc (also known as Klevner), Pinot Gris (also marketed as Tokay d'Alsace), Muscat, Chasselas, and Pinot Noir. The last is used to make a small quantity of Pinot Rosé.

Edelzwicker

Edelzwicker is the only blended wine of Alsace. It is a light, simple table wine made from a blend of noble grapes such as Riesling and Sylvaner, and usually sold under a brand name.

The words Grand Vin and Grand Cru may only be used on wines of superior varieties containing no less than 11 percent natural alcohol by volume.

The Alsatian shipping firms of Hugel, Trimbach, Willm, Dopff, and Irion are the best known. They market about half of the wines of the region. A third is produced by the many cooperative wine cellars, and the rest are estate-bottled and sold by individual growers. Alsatian shippers also buy grapes and make the wines in their own cellars. Since 1972, all Alsatian wines must be bottled within the region.

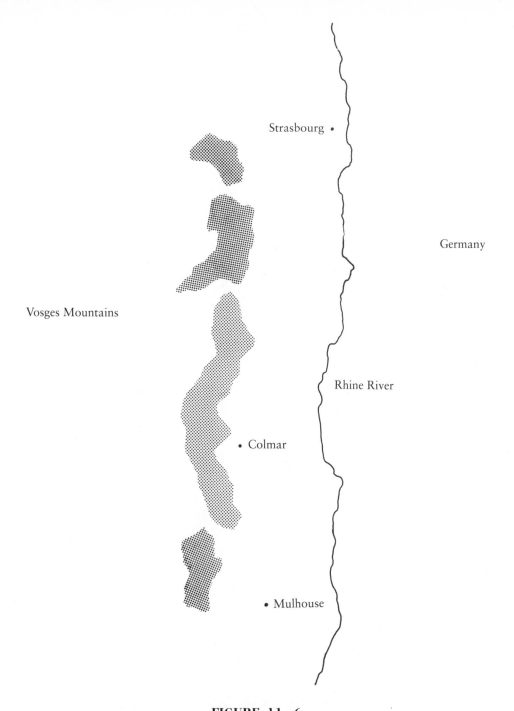

FIGURE 11–6

• • •

Map of the wine-producing regions of Alsace

CHAMPAGNE
· · · · ·

Champagne is a sparkling wine, but not all sparkling wines are Champagnes. Champagne is the most famous sparkling wine in the world. Born in the province of Champagne in northeastern France, it is the only one of the world's hundreds of sparkling wines that rightly bears the name Champagne. Located about 90 miles from Paris and the northernmost appellation contrôlée, wine producers within the region of Champagne make wines that are the product of a chalky soil and an austere climate (see Figure 11–7).

Champagnes were essentially still wines until the 17th century when the cork was introduced, a contribution credited to a Benedictine monk named Dom Perignon. Only then was it possible to keep the magical bubble in the bottle.

The grapes that make this wine are the Chardonnay and two black grapes—Pinot Noir and Pinot Meunier. The juice of the black grapes is separated from the dark skins quickly to prevent their adding color.

All Champagne is blended wine and all great Champagne is the result of the blender's art. Vintage Champagne is a blend of wines from one superior year. Not every year is a vintage year.

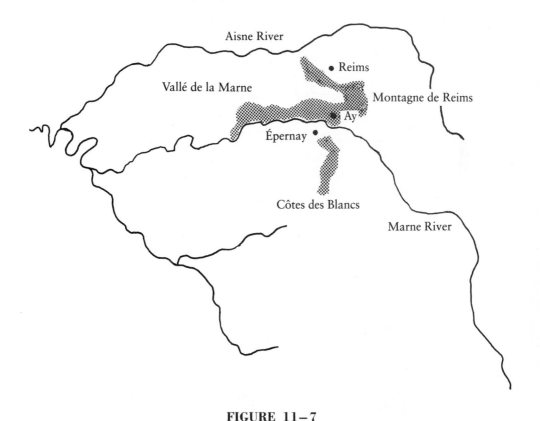

FIGURE 11–7
· · ·
Map of the wine-producing regions of Champagne

121

The blender uses his skills to create the cuvée or Champagne blend by which the firm is known and on which it stakes its reputation.

Soon after the new cuvée is completed, it is bottled with a very small amount of sugar and yeast dissolved in wine and called the *liqueur de tirage*. This solution is responsible for starting the next major step in Champagne making. The second fermentation occurs in the corked bottle, where there is no way for the resulting carbon dioxide to escape. The result is the most important part of Champagne, its bubbles. The bottled wine is stored in the cellar for a period of one to two years. At the end of that time, the wine has undergone its second fermentation; the bubbles are in the bottle, as is the sediment that the fermentation has deposited.

The widow Clicquot made her contribution to Champagne in the early years of the 19th century. She devised a method of removing the sediment without removing the bubbles. She invented a wooden rack in which the mature bottle of wine could be inserted upside down in holes. Each day, skilled workmen would twist the bottle and tilt it farther down to force the sediment into the neck next to the cork. This process is called *remuage*. When all the sediment has been worked into the neck, the wine is ready for its dégorgement. Today, to make disgorging easier, the neck of the bottle containing the sediment is first frozen. When the cork is removed, the gas inside pushes out this plug, leaving perfectly clear wine behind. A slight dose of cane sugar is usually dissolved in wine from another bottle of the same cuvée and then the bottle receives it final cork and is wired.

The amount of sugar to be added to each type of Champagne is determined by the individual Champagne house for its own wines. Brut contains less than 2 percent. Extra Sec or extra dry 2–4 percent. Sec actually refers to a fairly sweet wine in Champagne terminology. Demi-Sec, over 6 percent, is very sweet. Not only does Champagne come in varying degrees of dryness and sweetness, it also comes in a wide selection of sizes.

Split	6.5 oz. or 187 ml.
Half bottle	13 oz. or 375 ml.
Bottle	26 oz. or 750 ml.
Magnum	Two bottles or 52 oz.
Jeroboam	Four bottles.
Rehoboam	Six bottles.
Methuselah	Eight bottles.
Salmanasar	Twelve bottles.
Balthazar	Sixteen bottles.
Nebuchadnezzar	Twenty bottles.

Representative Champagne Houses of Reims

Mumm.
Charles Heidsieck.
Heidsieck Monopole.
Veuve Clicquot-Ponsardin.
Henriot.
Ruinart Père et Fils.

Pommery and Greno.

Taittinger.

Piper-Heidsieck.

Krug.

Lanson.

Louis Roederer.

Masse.

Representative Champagne Houses of Épernay

Moët & Chandon.

Pol Roger.

Perrier-Jouet.

Mercier.

Jacquesson.

OTHER WINE REGIONS

· · · · ·

There are many lesser known wine regions of France whose wines are excellent and often represent unique and interesting discoveries (see Figure 11–8). Many of these wines have been granted VDQS, or the coveted AOC status. Together, they contribute to France's reputation as the country that produces the greatest variety of wine in the world.

The lesser known wine regions are:

Jura.
Jurançon.
Savoie.
Provence.
Midi.
Cahors.

Jura

Lying east of Burgundy and west of the Swiss border, Jura is not a large wine area. Yet, it produces red, white, and rosé wines, still and sparkling wines, vins jaunes or yellow wines, and vins de paille or straw-colored wines. The most outstanding of Jura's wines come from the areas of Château-Chalon, l'Etoile, and Arbois.

Vin jaune, of which the most famous is Château Chalon, is made in a rather unusual way. After fermentation, the wine is aged for at least six years in small barrels that are not completely filled, thus exposing the wine to air. The resulting oxidation causes a yeast film to form, similar to that produced in certain sherries by a similar exposure. Château-Chalon (which is the name of a village, not a vineyard) is a most curious white wine; although not fortified, it is similar to dry sherry. Vin jaune is one of the longest-lived wines in France, easily capable of reaching 50 years or more.

Vin de paille derives its name from the old process of laying the grapes on beds of straw to dry and almost become raisins before pressing. The resulting wine is, of course, sweet, golden, and usually quite high in alcohol.

L'Etoile is the name of the village where still and sparkling white wine is made. Arbois is the name of the village where red and rosé wines are produced from the Poulsard, Trousseau, and Pinot Noir grapes, dry white wines come from the Savagnin (Traminer), and Chardonnay.

Jurançon

Located on the Pyrenees foothills south and west of Pau in southwestern France, the region produces a rather sweet, golden wine. It is made from grape varieties unknown in other districts—the Petit Manseng, the Gros Manseng, and the Courbu. It has a special, spicy bouquet and flavor that some locals have compared to the scent of carnations and the taste of cinnamon or cloves.

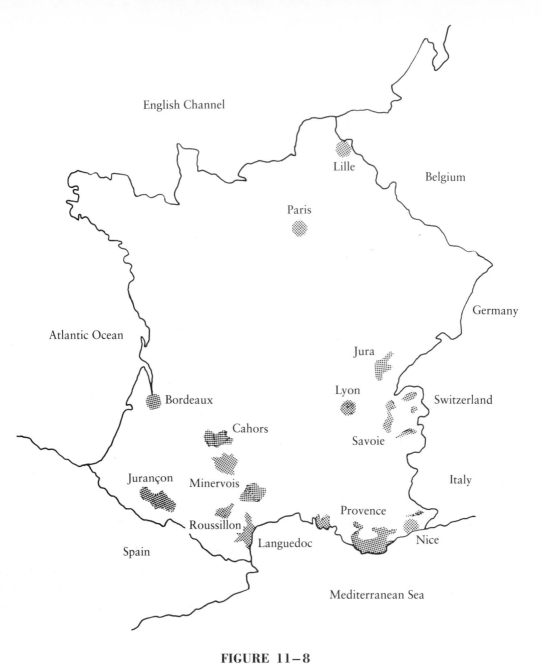

FIGURE 11-8

• • •

Map of other wine regions of France

Savoie

Located in the foothills of the French Alps, it is the most mountainous wine region of France, south of Lake Geneva and bounded on the east by Italy. From this land of fresh alpine air come delightful white and sparkling wines. Of the still whites, the best known are Crépy and Seyssel. Crépy is a light dry wine made primarily from the Chasselas (or Fendant) grape. Seyssel white wine is pale, fresh, light, very dry, produced round, and located near the headwaters of the Rhône River. Seyssel is made of the Roussette grape. This same wine is also used to make one of the very best sparkling wines of France, surpassed perhaps only by Champagne.

Provence

This region extends along the Mediterranean coast for over 120 miles from Marseille to just east of Nice. Wine makers grow a wide variety of grapes for red, white, and rosé wines. Of them, the rosés are the best known and most plentiful. Rosé wines are produced from a variety of grapes. They tend to be dry, fresh, and fruity, and are at their best in their youth. Some of the best rosés come from the little fishing village of Cassis some 20 miles east of Marseille. The wines in this area are strong, robust, and full-flavored. Bandol, a few miles east of Cassis, and the areas near Aix-en-Provence and above Nice, also produce good rosé.

The best white wine of Provence comes from Cassis. Its dry white wine is made principally from the Ugni Blanc grape, traditionally the wine to drink with Bouillabaisse. Bandol Pleasant red wines are mostly from the Mourvèdre grape, plus Grenache and Cinsault.

Midi

A vin du Midi is commonly understood to mean an ordinary table wine produced along the Mediterranean coast of France between Nimes, Carcassonne, and the Spanish border. The best known, perhaps, are Corbières, Minervois, Picpoul de Pinet, and Costières du Gard.

Cahors

Cahors produces an interesting, excellent, almost legendary red wine grown near the old city of this name situated north of Toulouse. It is made principally from the Malbec grape, the most deeply colored of French red wine grapes—dark crimson tinged, one might almost say "with black." Slow-maturing, remarkably long-lived, firm but not harsh, it has unmistakable distinction and a special cachet of its own. Those interested in wine discoveries will do well to seek it out.

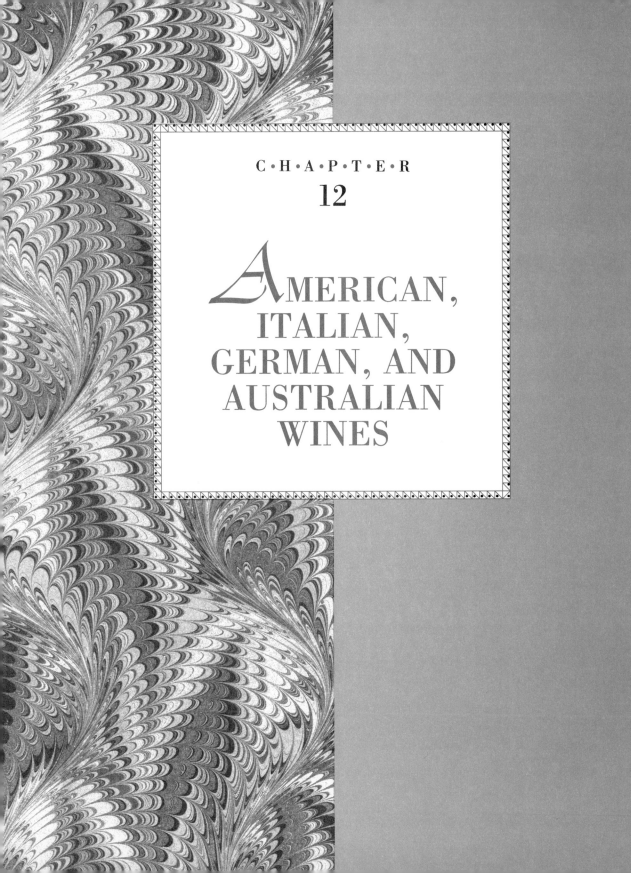

AMERICAN, ITALIAN, GERMAN, AND AUSTRALIAN WINES

CALIFORNIA

· · · · ·

California is the leading wine-producing region in the United States (see Figure 12–1). Its major centers include the Napa Valley, Sonoma and Mendocino counties, the central valley, and the central coast (south of the San Francisco Bay).

Napa Valley

The Napa Valley is the center of American wine growing. It was not the first of America's wine-growing regions, nor is it the largest, but it has always been the best known. Napa's climate is unquestionably ideally suited to grape growing, and its long and distinguished history of grape growing is thoroughly documented. Many areas can boast sublime climate and lengthy genealogy, but nowhere else in this country is there the concentration of grape growing and wine making that exists in the Napa Valley.

It is actually becoming difficult to keep up with the rapidly increasing number of new wineries in Napa county. Three-quarters of the bonded wineries are new since 1966, when Robert Mondavi built his winery in Oakville, the first new winery of any size in the valley since repeal. It seems entirely likely that Napa will have 200 wineries in the next decade.

Krug was the pioneer wine grower in the Napa Valley. He used the first mechanical press and built the first commercial winery of any size in the county. Krug has been associated with every venture for the promotion of the industry throughout the state, from its inception to the present, giving a lifetime and a fortune to the work.

Krug's spirit has outlived him. You do not have to look far today to find wineries that serve as virtual graduate schools of oenology. It is no accident that all of these are among the highest rank of wine producers.

It is Mondavi who most neatly fits the Krug mold, challenging his comrades to reach for higher levels of wine making, constantly experimenting, and always providing inspiration and encouragement to the hesitant and unsure. It is no coincidence that Robert Mondavi spent most of his early years at the Krug Winery.

It was Napa's enticing climate that caused the valley's early inhabitants to consider grape culture. Rainfall averages 25 to 35 inches per year, and summer temperatures are routinely in the 80s and 90s. The growing season is well over 200 days, long enough to mature the most stubborn of Cabernet Sauvignon grapes.

Weather watchers divide the county into four climatic zones. The region south of Napa falls into the maritime classification. The San Pablo Bay narrows the range between day and night temperature. It also lessens seasonal changes. Summer fogs are common and the growing season shorter. The Carneros district is thus the coolest of the Napa microclimates and is best suited for the earliest ripening varieties.

The second climatic zone is the coastal zone. It is delineated as running from north of Napa to about Lodi Lane (just north of St. Helena). As with the valley as a whole, this region is progressively warmer the farther north of the bay one travels. Fog usually stops at Yountville, and this region is considered suitable for both early and late ripening varieties. There is little question that some of the world's finest Cabernet grapes are grown in and around Rutherford.

North of Lodi Lane and on into Calistoga, the climate is classified as transitional. Distinctively warmer than its opposite Carneros, the Calistoga area shows off Petit Sirah and Zinfandel grapes, though many other varieties are grown there as well.

Major wine-producing regions

A. Napa Valley

B. Sonoma-Mendocino

C. Central Coast

D. Central Valley

FIGURE 12–1

• • •

Map of California wine-producing regions

Pope Valley and Chiles Valley represent the interior zone because their weather patterns are dominated by the continental air mass. Of all the county's climate zones, this is the least influenced by the bay or the Pacific Ocean. As in Calistoga, Petit Syrah and Zinfandel grapes do quite well, but there is generally less tolerance for other varieties. Thermograph readings have shown that some areas of Pope Valley are not nearly as hot as has commonly been accepted, so growers there are trying some Chardonnay and Sémillon varieties. The learning never ceases.

As important as climate is, there are many other factors that have to be considered, including exposure, drainage, elevation, and soil. Soils are vitally important. Most Napa Valley soils are ideal for the support of the culture of the grape. They are generally high in mineral content and well drained. The latter is essential, as grapevines do not like wet feet.

Much of the upper valley shows the area's volcanic history in its soils. Rhyolite, basalt, and other volcanic rocks are omnipresent, the result of the eruptions of Mt. St. Helena and other volcanic cones millions of years ago. Volcanic materials are also rich in calcium and sodium, which are beneficial to grapevines.

The lower valley, from the entry of Conn Creek south, shows increasing amounts of sedimentary acidic and igneous materials, also beneficial for grape growing. Much of the valley floor is covered with the deep sediment and gravel deposited by the Napa River and its tributaries. The alluvial soil is rich in minerals and provides excellent drainage.

As it has taken centuries for European growers to discover which varieties fit best, so it has taken decades to determine the proper varieties for each region within the Napa Valley. As the wine industry matures, it is learning to take advantage of local conditions to produce distinctive wines by planting precisely the right grape in the right place. At present, this is still in the experimental stage. Only a few individual sites have established reputations for growing particular grapes outstandingly well. The vineyards with the highest quality potential are those with upland soil and low frost risk (which usually go together), planted with the grapes indicated for that temperature zone.

Some grape varieties suitable for the three temperature zones of the Napa Valley are:

Warm	Moderately Warm	Cool
Petit Syrah	Cabernet Sauvignon	Chardonnay
Zinfandel	Zinfandel	Sylvaner
Cabernet Sauvignon	Sémillon	Johannisberg Riesling
Sauvignon Blanc	Merlot	Gewürztraminer
Barbera	Chenin Blanc	Pinot Blanc
Grenache	Grey Riesling	Pinot Noir
Gamay	Gamay	
Carignan		

The Napa Valley's best wines are Cabernet Sauvignon among reds and Johannisberg Riesling and Chardonnay among whites.

ESTATE 1983 BOTTLED

Inglenook.
V I N E Y A R D S

Sauvignon Blanc
NAPA VALLEY

PRODUCED AND BOTTLED BY INGLENOOK VINEYARDS
RUTHERFORD, CALIFORNIA · USA
750 ML ALCOHOL 12.5% BY VOLUME

VINTAGE SELECTION

1974

Charles Krug
NAPA VALLEY
CABERNET SAUVIGNON

PRODUCED AND BOTTLED BY
Charles Krug Winery
ST. HELENA · CALIFORNIA
ALCOHOL 12% BY VOLUME

Beringer
Napa Valley
Chardonnay

PRODUCED AND BOTTLED BY
BERINGER VINEYARDS, ST. HELENA, NAPA VALLEY, CALIFORNIA
ALCOHOL 13.0% BY VOLUME

Beaulieu Vineyard
BV
ESTATE BOTTLED
NAPA VALLEY
GAMAY BEAUJOLAIS

PRODUCED AND BOTTLED BY BEAULIEU VINEYARD
AT RUTHERFORD, NAPA COUNTY, CALIFORNIA
ALCOHOL 12.5% BY VOLUME

LA CREMA

PRODUCED & BOTTLED BY   LA CREMA, PETALUMA, CA, U.S.A.

ALC. 12.5% BY VOL. 750 ML.   CONTAINS SULFITES

CALIFORNIA

CHARDONNAY

1986

STERLING VINEYARDS.

ESTATE BOTTLED

1987

Cabernet Sauvignon

NAPA VALLEY

GROWN, PRODUCED AND BOTTLED BY
STERLING VINEYARDS
CALISTOGA, NAPA VALLEY, CA
ALC. 12.8% BY VOL. · BW CA 4533

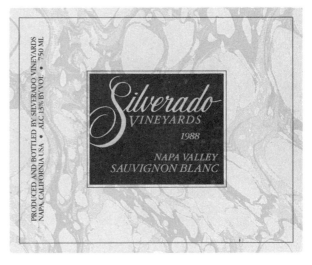

PRODUCED AND BOTTLED BY SILVERADO VINEYARDS   ALC. 13% BY VOL. · 750 ML
NAPA, CALIFORNIA USA

Silverado
VINEYARDS
1988

NAPA VALLEY
SAUVIGNON BLANC

CHATEAU MONTELENA

ESTABLISHED 1882

CALIFORNIA
Zinfandel

PRODUCED AND BOTTLED BY CHATEAU MONTELENA
WINERY • CALISTOGA, NAPA VALLEY, CALIFORNIA
ALCOHOL 14.3% BY VOLUME

Heitz Cellar

NAPA VALLEY
CHARDONNAY
ALCOHOL 13% BY VOLUME
PRODUCED AND BOTTLED IN OUR CELLAR BY
HEITZ WINE CELLARS
ST. HELENA, CALIFORNIA

GUSTAVE
NIEBAUM.
COLLECTION

REFERENCE

1989

CHARDONNAY

NAPA VALLEY

PRODUCED & BOTTLED BY GUSTAVE NIEBAUM COLLECTION, RUTHERFORD, CA, USA

Coastal NAPA RIDGE

NORTH COAST
CHARDONNAY

1989

CELLARED & BOTTLED BY NAPA RIDGE WINERY
ST. HELENA, CALIFORNIA, ALC. 13% BY VOLUME

SIMI

Sauvignon Blanc

MENDOCINO COUNTY 18.5%
SONOMA COUNTY 70%
NAPA COUNTY 11.5%

1990

750 ml.

ALC. 13.7%
BY VOL.

ALEXANDER VALLEY

CHATEAU SOUVERAIN

1 9 8 8

CABERNET SAUVIGNON

Alexander Valley

TABLE WINE

PRODUCED & BOTTLED BY CHATEAU SOUVERAIN, GEYSERVILLE, CALIFORNIA

ESTATE BOTTLED

Sierra Vista

EL DORADO
ZINFANDEL
1988

ALC. 13.5% BY VOL.

PAUL MASSON

MONTEREY COUNTY
FUMÉ BLANC
(SAUVIGNON BLANC)

ESTATE
BOTTLED

PRODUCED AND BOTTLED BY THE PAUL MASSON VINEYARDS
SARATOGA, CALIFORNIA, U.S.A. · ALCOHOL 13.0% BY VOLUME   750ml

WENTE BROS.

MONTEREY
PINOT NOIR

PRODUCED AND BOTTLED BY WENTE BROS.
LIVERMORE. CALIFORNIA. U.S.A.
ALCOHOL 12½% BY VOLUME

Sonoma County

Like many California counties, Sonoma is almost a little world in itself and has an astonishingly wide diversity of climates and soils. The interior, from San Francisco Bay and the town of Sonoma northward to Santa Rosa and Guerneville, is as cool as Burgundy in France. In the Russian River Valley, from Healdsburg to Asti and beyond, there are thousands of acres of rolling hills and vineyards as productive and as warm as those in central Italy.

One of the colorful personalities to settle in the Sonoma area was Colonel Agoston Haraszthy de Moskea. Colonel Haraszthy contributed to the development and knowledge of the wine industry in California by importing grapes from Europe and making very high-quality wines. His experimental work in the vineyard and in the cellar in Sonoma proved that California was capable of producing some of the best grapes and wines in the world.

Mendocino County

Mendocino county is north of Sonoma and its principal city, Ukiah, is 120 miles from San Francisco. Mendocino county established a reputation in the late 60s and early 70s, when new premium varietal cuttings were introduced by the firm Parducci and Fetzer.

Winery and vineyard development in the last decade have made this county one of the top premium growing districts in the state, certainly destined to become increasingly important in the fine wine production of California. Some of the major wineries in Mendocino county include Fetzer Vineyards, in Redwood Valley, and Cresta Blanca Winery and Parducci Wine Cellars, in Ukiah.

Central Valley: San Joaquin

The central valley produces four out of every five bottles of California wine. Conditions are totally different from those among the coastal hills. The soil is rich in river deposits, fertile and flat for 400 miles north to south and up to 100 miles across. The climate is reliably stable and often hot.

There are a number of gigantic wineries situated in the valley. E. J. Gallo, located in Modesto, is the biggest winery in the world; it accounts for one out of every four bottles of wine sold in the United States. The winery, founded in 1933 by Ernest and Julio Gallo, markets a complete range of generic and varietal table wines. Gallo's most popular table wines are Hearty Burgundy and Chablis Blanc.

United Vintners, owned by Heublein, Inc., is the second largest wine producer in the United States. Its brands, most of which are bottled at Madera, include Italian Swiss Colony, Inglenook, Petri, and Lejon.

Another large California wine company is Guild, a cooperative of a thousand grape growers. Most wines are bottled at Lodi. Guild markets such brands as Roma, Cresta Blanca, and Cribari. Other central valley wineries are Franzia Brothers, East-Side JFJ Bronco, Gibson Gillmarra, and California Growers Winery.

In addition to these large companies, there are also a few wineries in the central valley producing distinctive wines in comparatively small quantities. Angelo Papagni, a grape grower with more than 2,000 acres of vineyards, built a winery near Madera (California) and began to make varietal wines in 1973, including one from Muscat called Muscato d'Angelo. Ficklin, also located near Madera, has been making limited amounts of Tinta Port since 1948, and in 1977 Andrew Quady built a winery in Madera to produce vintage dated port from Zinfandel grapes.

Central Coast

The area just south and east of San Francisco Bay is wine country as old as the Napa Valley. Its wineries are fewer, but several of them are among California's most famous names.

The University of California at Davis enologists found that Soledad in the Salinas Valley has the best conditions suited to the best wine grape varieties of all California. Chalone, 2,000 feet up in the hills just east of Soledad, is where a limestone slope and a cool climate produce Chardonnay and Pinot Noir that are as good as any in California.

Other Wine Regions of California

San Benito County

San Benito county lies directly east or inland from Monterey Bay, and the vineyards are in the high country south of the town of Hollister and of San Juan Baustista, which was one of the original Spanish missions, just over a hundred miles due south of San Francisco. Almaden has planted more than 4,000 acres and uses San Benito as an appellation for some of its wines.

San Luis Obispo

There are few wineries in San Luis Obispo, which is north of Santa Barbara, but Hoffman Mountain Ranch has already become known for its Chardonnay and Pinot Noir. Estrella Vineyards produced its first wines in 1978.

Santa Barbara County

The Santa Barbara county vineyard acreage jumped from virtually none in the 1960s to more than 6,000 today. Halfway between the cities of Santa Maria and Santa Barbara is the Firestone Vineyard. Firestone made its first wines in 1975 and has won a following for Johannisberg Riesling. Other wineries in this region are the Valley Winery, Santa Ynez, Benedict, and Zaca Mesa.

OREGON
· · · · ·

Similar in climate to Burgundy, in France, it is no wonder that the state of Oregon has had great success in producing high-quality Pinot Noir wines rivaling and even bettering their French counterparts. With generally dry summers, the air is cool and the sky cloudy; however, some days can be as hot and sunny as California. Though Pinot Noir is Oregon's claim to fame, the state also produces very high-quality Chardonnay, Chenin Blanc, Gewürztraminer, Sauvignon Blanc, and Rieslings.

Williamette Valley

The Williamette Valley runs north to south parallel to the coast for about 175 miles from Portland down the state (see Figure 12–2). It is on the west side of the Cascade mountains and protected from coastal weather by another range. The landscape is quite hilly with slopes facing

FIGURE 12–2

• • •

Map of the wine-producing regions of Oregon and Washington

1981

Siskiyou Vineyards

Oregon Wine
GEWÜRZTRAMINER
ALCOHOL 11% BY VOLUME

Produced and Bottled by Siskiyou Vineyards
Cave Junction Oregon BW-OR-72

SB
Sokol Blosser
1979

Yamhill County
Pinot Noir

HYLAND VINEYARDS
*A smooth, medium-bodied wine blended from selected barrels of
Pinot Noir grapes grown by Hyland Vineyards.*

PRODUCED AND BOTTLED BY
SOKOL BLOSSER WINERY, DUNDEE, OREGON (BW-OR-66)
Alcohol 12.5% by Volume

The Eyrie Vineyards
WILLAMETTE VALLEY
DRY TABLE WINE

Oregon Chardonnay

south, allowing them to take advantage of the sunshine. The rest of the valley is located in the Dundee Hills in the red soil that produces the most successful grapes.

Priding itself in its top-rated wines, Oregon has banned the use of generic labeling such as Chablis. Unlike California, Oregon makes no jug wine and insists that varietal wines be made from 90 percent of the grape named on the label, with the exception of Cabernet Sauvignon at 75 percent. All labels must also bear the name of the geographic area of the grapes—valley or county—and all the grapes used must come only from these places.

Because of these strict regulations, one can easily see why Oregon has continued to produce world-quality wines, especially Pinot Noir, since the 1970s. Some of its best wineries include the Eyrie Vineyards, Knudson-Erath, Sokol Blosser, and Tualatin Vineyards.

WASHINGTON STATE
· · · · ·

Second only to California, Washington's production of wine has continued to increase on a yearly basis since the mid-1960s. This is astonishing when one considers that any wine is made at all in such an unlikely climate. In fact, the state is subject to many microclimates, ranging from the very cold and damp areas in the west, to the desertlike conditions in the east. One can safely say that the state has similar conditions to some of the most famous wine-making regions of France.

Wine-Producing Regions

The Cascade mountain range conveniently divides the state of Washington into two wine-producing areas: eastern, desertlike lands that require large-scale irrigation; and the western area, which is very cool and damp (see Figure 12–2). The east is represented by two distinct regions; the Walla Walla Valley and Yakima Valley. Both are located in the southernmost part of the state, with the Walla Walla Valley actually running into Oregon.

Washington produces many varietal wines such as White Riesling, Sauvignon Blanc, Chardonnay, Pinot Noir, and Cabernet Sauvignon. The most famous producers include Chateau Ste. Michelle and Columbia Crest (a subsidiary), Preston, and Salishan.

PRESTON
WINE CELLARS

WASHINGTON STATE

PINOT NOIR BLANC

1981

PRODUCED AND BOTTLED BY PRESTON WINE CELLARS
PASCO, WASHINGTON   ALCOHOL 11.4% BY VOLUME

1979
Salishan
Vineyards

Washington
Pinot Noir

PRODUCED & BOTTLED BY PONZI VINEYARDS
BEAVERTON, OREGON BW-OR-56
ALCOHOL BY VOLUME 12%

1979 Salishan Vineyards
Pinot Noir

Salishan Vineyards is located
in La Center, Washington,
30 miles from the volcanic
Mount St. Helens. The vineyard
is on the west side of the
Cascade Mountains, where
as in France, the moderate
maritime climate produces that
combination of rainfall,
cloudiness, sunshine and heat
that produces fine wine grapes.

The Pinot Noir grape especially
flourishes in this part of the
Northwest, producing a wine
with intense fruit flavor.

This particular wine has been
aged in French Oak barrels
to further develop its character.
It goes well with all red meats
and game.

VINTAGE 1978

Chateau
Ste. Michelle®

Washington State

CABERNET SAUVIGNON

Produced and Bottled by Ste. Michelle Vineyards
Woodinville, Wash. Alcohol 12½ % by Volume

NEW YORK STATE

· · · · ·

New York state is the most important wine-growing area in the eastern United States (see Figure 12–3).

Finger Lakes

Probably the two most significant facts that have constrained wine making in upstate New York are climate and prohibition. The types of grapes grown are influenced by both. *Vitis vinifera* vines do not grow well in the colder climate, as do their counterparts, *Vitis labrusca* and the

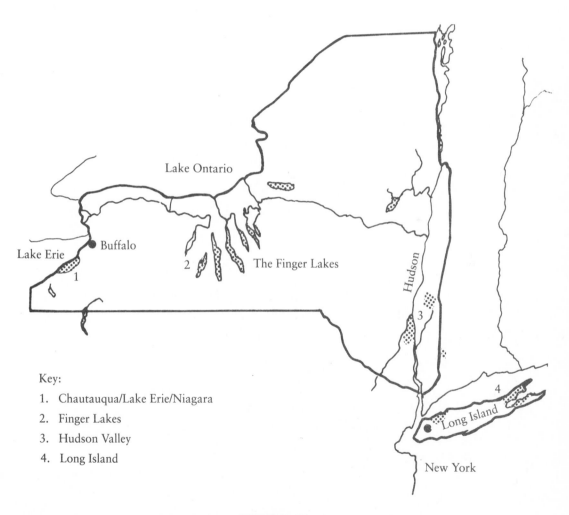

Key:

1. Chautauqua/Lake Erie/Niagara
2. Finger Lakes
3. Hudson Valley
4. Long Island

FIGURE 12–3

· · ·

Map of New York state wine-producing regions

hybrids. Therefore, wine makers contented themselves with growing and producing from the latter two types.

Prohibition, on the other hand, caused grape growers to opt for such grapes as the Concord, which was used in jam and jelly production when wine making was outlawed in 1919. However, in the early 1950s, Dr. Konstantin Frank, a pioneer in wine-making technology, succeeded in grafting *Vitis vinifera* vines onto hardy rootstocks from Quebec, Canada. Since then, New York state has been able to make wines from *Vitis vinifera* grape varieties.

Since *Vitis labrusca* grapes produce good-quality sparkling wines, New York has become renown for these. Hybrid grapes have also contributed to the large-scale production of such wines as Aurora, Baco Noir, de Chaunac, Marechal Foch, Seyval Blanc, and others. *Vitis labrusca* varieties include the ever-famous Concord, as well as the Catawba, the Delaware, the Duchesse, and Niagara.

The Finger Lakes, the largest of which are Canandaigua, Keuka, Seneca, and Cayuga, serve to warm the cool winter days, reducing damage from possible frost. The soil is stony and well-drained, much like that of the Rhine Valley in Germany. The most famous wineries include Bully Hill, Heron Hill, the Taylor Wine Company, and Widmer Wine Cellars.

Hudson Valley

The Hudson Valley is located approximately 60 miles south of Albany and runs between New York City and Poughkeepsie. The soil for grape growing is not very high quality; many soil varieties from loam to flint to gravel and stones are present. The climate here is similar to that of the Finger Lakes region and most of the same grapes are grown. The most noted wineries include Benmarl, Brotherhood, and Windsor.

Erie-Chautauqua Region

Located some 125 miles west of Lake Keuka to the southeast side of Lake Erie, this area also includes the southwestern edge of New York state up to Lake Ontario. The climate here is similar to that of the Finger Lakes, the air being warmed by the effects of the large bodies of water. The soil conditions here are also similar to the Finger Lakes region: stones, gravel, and adequate drainage.

Long Island

Warmed by the effects of the air off the sea, Long Island produces wines from two delimited areas: the North Fork and the Hamptons. Because of the weather conditions, grapes of the *Vitis Vinifera* varieties—Chardonnay, Gewürztraminer, Sauvignon Blanc, Cabernet Sauvignon, and Merlot—have been grown with great success. Wineries include Pindar Vineyards, Hargrave Vineyards, and the Long Island Vineyard.

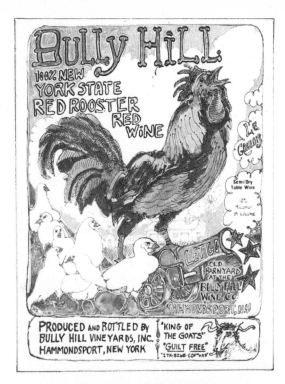

WIDMER

SINCE 1888

SELECT AMERICAN
RHINE WINE

A delicate light semi-dry white table wine with a fragrant bouquet and fruit-like taste. Enjoy it chilled with seafood, chicken and other light meals or by itself.

MADE AND BOTTLED BY WIDMER'S WINE CELLARS, INC.
NAPLES, N.Y. • ALCOHOL 11% BY VOLUME.

WIDMER

Since 1888

NAPLES VALLEY
BRAND
PREMIUM AMERICAN
ROSÉ

A soft, fragrant, fruit-like wine with a touch of sweetness. Adaptable to any wine or enjoy it before dinner or anytime, serve chilled.

MADE AND BOTTLED BY WIDMER'S WINE CELLARS, INC.
NAPLES, N.Y. • ALCOHOL 11% BY VOLUME.

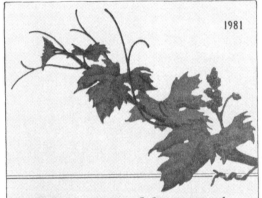

1981

Hargrave Vineyard
North Fork
Long Island   New York

Sauvignon Blanc

Estate Grown, Produced & Bottled By Hargrave Vineyard
Cutchogue, N.Y.   13.0% Alcohol By Volume

ITALY

• • • • •

Italy is a vessel full of wines. Stretching from the Alps to almost within sight of Africa, Italy boasts of a wide range of climates and soils (see Figure 12–4). The grape varieties are distinctly Italian, as are the traditions of wine making.

FIGURE 12–4

• • •

Map of Italian wine-producing regions

Italian wines differ markedly not only from those of other countries but also among themselves. While some Italian wines are produced from single grape varieties, many are made from mixtures of several grapes and are therefore unique wines impossible to duplicate elsewhere. Most of Italy is mountainous and most of the grapes used to produce Italian wines are hill-grown.

All wines leaving Italy for consumption in the United States are subject to special laboratory checks to ascertain their quality and purity. Only wines that pass these tests are granted the Marchio-Nazionale, the mandatory red seal inscribed with the letters INE, which appear on the neck band of all Italian wines sold in the United States.

Denominazione di Origine Controllata (DOC)

Italy established the Denominazione di Origine Controllata (DOC) for wine in 1963, setting up a system of rules for the protection of wine names. This law controls or protects the denomination or name of wine origins. This means that a wine cannot be made or sold under any of the 200 plus names of origin thus far approved unless that wine has been produced in precisely defined areas from the right grapes and aged and bottled according to precise rules to achieve a particular quality.

The DOC is difficult to obtain, and some wines have been turned down. In practical terms, if a bottle carries the DOC label, you can be sure that the wine is from the area named, produced from the prescribed proportions of specific grapes by the traditional methods, and has been properly aged. Also, the vineyards have been surveyed and their maximum grape production and wine does not exceed the yield allowed. All wine sales have to be recorded in ledgers that are subject to inspection.

Denominazione di Origine Controllata e Garantita (DOCG) are simply DOC wines with a higher quality standard, not easily obtainable in the United States.

Red Wines

Piedmont

Piedmont means at the foot of the mountains. The two best red wines of Piedmont are Barolo and Barbaresco, which take their names from villages. They are made from the Nebbiolo grape. Barolo produced around the town of that name southwest of Alba is full-bodied, long-lived, and needs several years to develop its qualities. Barolo must have a minimum alcoholic strength of 13 percent. The village of Barbaresco, northeast of Barolo, gives its name to another famous red wine made entirely from the Nebbiolo. Barbaresco only differs from Barolo in coming from another area.

There is another famous Nebbiolo wine of the Piedmont that comes from vineyards around Gattinara. Barolo, Barbaresco, and Gattinara require considerable aging and are among Italy's greatest reds.

Five other villages in the vicinity of Gattinara produce red wines made primarily from Nebbiolo that have as much as 50 percent other varieties. The best of these wines come from the villages of Ghemme, Boca, Fara, Sizzano, and Lessono.

Piedmont is also famous for red wine made from the Barbera-Grignolino-Dolcetto-Freisa grapes. All of these wines are likely to have a geographical district name from a limited and theoretically superior area following the grape name.

Valle d'Aosta

Valle d'Aosta is Italy's smallest region. Grapes are grown high on hillsides in the Aosta Valley. The Valle d'Aosta's best known wine produced from the Nebbiolo grape is Donnaz. It is a smooth, full-bodied red wine that takes its name from a local town.

Lombardy

Among the Alps of the Valtellina 2,500 feet above sea level are the red wines coming from a narrow strip of vineyard that hugs the north bank of the River Adda. They go by the names of Inferno, Grumello, and Sassella. Their grape is the Nebbiolo. The Nebbiolo grape is grown to produce a hardier red wine than in Piedmont, but one that achieves real delicacy with aging.

Veneto

Veneto is one of Italy's largest producing regions. It is best known for the wines of Verona. One of the two best red wines of Veneto is Bardolino, which is produced around the village of the same name and is an excellent red wine, fruity and charming. Bardolino is made mostly from Corvino, Negrara, and Molinara grapes. The other is Valpolicella, which is produced northwest of Verona. There are five townships in the delimited zone. Four grape varieties are grown: Corvino, Molinara, Negrara, and Rondinella.

Trentino-Alto Adige

Parts of the Adige Valley from below Trento to Bolzano are almost carpeted with vines. In the Trentino or lower valley, the Teroldego grape gives its name to a quality wine, a big red, full-flavored with a bitter, nutty aftertaste. Other Trentino area wines include those sold as Marzemino d'Isera, Sorni, Rosato d'Avio, Valdadige, and Vallagarina.

Friuli-Venezia Giulia

The province of Friuli-Venezia Giulia has a full range of variety wines from Cabernet to Merlot. None of them has distinguished itself so far. These wines come from six main areas of production.

Liguria

Liguria, the narrow coastal strip of the Italian Riviera, produces relatively little wine, but one area is famous for its elegant dry red wine, sometimes called Rossese.

Emilia Romagna

Emilia Romagna produces two reds of importance. Lambrusco, a unique, semidry, semi-sparkling red, comes from the grape of the same name grown in the vicinity of Modena. Sangiovese is used in the Romagna hills to make a full-bodied, well-balanced red wine, whose bouquet is intensified by age.

Tuscany

Tuscany is the home of Italy's most famous wine, Chianti. This wine is produced from a mixture of the Sangiovese and Canaiolo grapes plus a small amount of Trebbiano and Malvasia grapes. Chianti is made in two styles. The first is for drinking young and fresh and is traditionally placed into the familiar straw-covered flask (fiasco). The second style of Chianti is left to mature three or more years in oak casks, thereby acquiring great power and delicacy known as Riserva. A good Riserva will be full-bodied and can reach the distinction and sometimes the longevity to match wines anywhere in the world.

From Montepulciano comes a red wine called Vino Nobile di Montepulciano made primarily from the Sangiovese grape and similar in style to Chianti. The small hill town of Montalcino produces a truly great red, Brunello di Montalcino, made from a variety of the Sangiovese grape. Brunello di Montalcino is even bigger and more fragrant than Chianti Riserva and needs many years to mature.

Marches

In this Adriatic coastal region, the Montepulciano and Sangiovese grapes produce two good reds, Rosso Conero, a dry, robust red wine that ages nicely, and Rosso Piceno, a soft wine of ruby-red color.

Umbria

In the heart of Umbria near Assisi is the tiny Torgiano area, which produces a red wine. Once of purely local fame, this wine has been developed by an able family firm into a wine of national renown. Torgiano red has a pleasant scent and a pronounced flavor and ages beautifully.

Latium

In the Aprilia district between the Alban hills and the sea, Sangiovese and Merlot red grapes produce good-quality wines usually under the grape name. Merlot di Aprilia is a dry, medium-bodied red.

Abruzzo and Molise

Grapes are grown mainly in the narrow coastal plain of these regions on the Adriatic side of central Italy. The Montepulciano grape from the picturesque old town of this name in Tuscany is widely cultivated in this Adriatic coastal region. The Montepulciano d'Abruzzo is a pale pleasant red wine.

Campania

This Italian region in southern Italy near Naples is famous for its red wines, of which Taurasi is the majestic chief. It is as broad, dark, and deep as a southern wine should be. Its grape, the Aglianico, ages very nicely. Other important red wines of Campania are Hirpinia and Lacrima Christi, which are made red, white, and rosé.

Apulia

Apulia, a producer of good-quality table wine, was once known mainly for its strong wines used for blending. To date, recent prosperity has resulted in the purchase of more wine-making plants and in better care of the vines. One of the best areas is Castel del Monte, inland between Bari and Foggia, where very enjoyable reds are produced. From the north of the region comes San Severo red from the Montepulciano grape.

Basilicata

Inland in this region is the extinct volcano Vulture on whose slopes grows the unusual Aglianico grape. A dry red, Aglianico del Vulture, after a few years in the bottle, can be one of the best wines of southern Italy. There are also several local wines made from this grape.

Calabria

Here in the peninsula, Calabria has one strong red of reputation, Ciro. The wines of Ciro claim descent from those of the ancient Greek settlers. The red is a big, robust wine. Calabria produces three additional wines made from a combination of red and white grapes.

Sardinia

This large island off the west coast of Italy produces many attractive wines. Monica di Sardegna is a red wine produced principally from the Monica grape.

Sicily

This island has moved rapidly toward the production of quality table wine. The slopes of Mount Etna, in strictly delimited areas, provide Etna, a dry, robust, and ruby-colored red wine. Corvo di Salaparuta wines from near Palermo have been known outside the island for 150 years. The red Corvo is a velvety wine with an interesting aroma. Segesta red table wine, named after the ancient Greek city of Segesta, is well balanced and has a generous taste.

White Wines

Italian white wines are golden, greenish, and amber. They are dry, crisp, fruity, and sweet. The white wines of Italy are truly unique among the wines of the world.

Piedmont

Piedmont is a region where white wines are not very common. However, Piedmont is the home of Asti Spumante, the sweet, flavorful sparkling wine.

The region's most important white and sparkling wines are Cortese di Gavi from the Cortese grape; fresh-crisp Erbaluce di Caluso from the Erbaluce grape; dry-fresh Cortese del Alto Monferrato-Cortese; and delicate-dry Caluso Pasito from the Erbaluce grape. This dessert wine made from dried grapes is delicate and sweet and gold to amber in color. Also, Asti Spumante, from the Moscato di Canelli grape, is delicately sweet, and Moscato d'Asti, from the Moscato Bianco grape, is still and sweet.

Lombardy

Capriano del Colle Trebbiano, from the grape Trebbiano, is dry and tart. Franciacorta Pinot is from the grape Pinot Bianco.

Trentino Alto Adige

Alto Adige   This collective controls the production of eight white varietals. Each wine must be made from at least 95 percent of the named grape. Alto Adige is an official bilingual area, where both Italian and German are spoken. For this reason, some of the labels are written in German. The grapes of this region are Moscato Giallo, Pinot Bianco, Sylvaner, Traminer Aromatico, Sauvignon, Riesling Renano, Pinot Grigio, and Riesling Italico.

Friuli-Venezia Giulia

Aquileia   This cooperative controls the production of seven white wines. Each must be made from at least 90 percent of the named grape, which includes Pinot Bianco, Pinot Grigio, Riesling Renano, Sauvignon, Tocai, Traminer Aromatico, and Verduzzo.

Collio Goriziano   This cooperative controls the production of six white wines. Each must be made from 100 percent of the named grape: Picolit, Pinot Bianco, Pinot Grigio, Ribolla, Tocai, Verduzzo, and Riesling Renano.

Grave del Friulo   This cooperative controls the production of four white wines. Each must be made from at least 90 percent of the named grape: Pinot Bianco, Tocai, Pinot Grigio, and Verduzzo.

Veneto

Montello Colli Asolani Prosecco   Dry and fruity from the Prosecco grape.

Prosecco di Conegliano Valdobbiadene   From the Prosecco grape.

Recioto di Gambellara   From 80 to 95 percent Garganega and 5 to 20 percent Trebbiano.

Recioto di Soave   From 70 to 90 percent Garganega and 10 to 30 percent Trebbiano.

Soave   Light body, fresh, fruity white wine made from 70 to 90 percent Garganega and 10 to 30 percent Trebbiano.

Tocai di Lison   Dry and fruity wine made from the Tocai grape.

Venegazzu Bianco   Unique brand name wine made from Prosecco Malvasi and Pinot Bianco.

Emilia Romagna

Albana di Romagna   This is a straw-yellow, typical Albana grape wine.

Bianco Colli Bolognesi   Delicate, light, slightly tannic white wine made from 60 to 80 percent Albana and 20 to 40 percent Trebbiano.

Monterosso Val d'Arda   This light white wine is made from 30 to 50 percent Malvasia, 10 to 30 percent Moscato, and 20 to 35 percent Trebbiano and Ortrugo.

Trebbiano Val Trebbia   This light-bodied, slightly dry white wine is made from 30 to 50 percent Ortrugo, 10 to 30 percent Malvasia, 15 to 30 percent Trebbiano and Moscato Bianco, and 15 percent Sauvignon.

Trebbiano de Romagna   This medium-bodied, dry white wine is made from the Trebbiano grape.

Liguria

Sciacchetra   This is a golden, full, rich white wine made from dried grapes, 60 percent Bosco and 40 percent Albarolo or Vermentino.

Cinqueterre   This is a delicate dry wine made from 60 percent Bosco and 40 percent Albarolo or Vermentino.

Tuscany

Bianco della Valdinievole   This is a dry, light white wine made from 70 percent Trebbiano and 30 percent Malvasia, Vermentino, and Canaiolo Bianco.

Elba Bianco   This dry white wine is made from at least 90 percent Trebbiano.

Galestro   This dry white wine is made from 60 percent Trebbiano with some Malvasia, Chardonnay, and Riesling.

Montecarlo   This smooth fruity white wine is made from 60 to 70 percent Trebbiano, 30 to 40 percent Pinot Grigio or Bianco, and Sémillon, Vermontino, and Sauvignon.

Montescudaio Bianco   This dry, pleasant white wine is made from 80 to 85 percent Trebbiano and 15 to 20 percent Malvasia or Vermentino.

Parrina Bianco   This dry, flowery white wine is made from 80 percent Trebbiano and 20 percent Ansonica and/or Malvasia.

Vernaccia di San Gimignano   This is one of few Italian whites that can take moderate aging. This wine is made from 100 percent Vernaccia de San Gimignano grape.

Umbria

Colli del Trasimeno   This fresh, dry, slightly tart white wine is made from 60 to 80 percent Trebbiano, and some Grechetto, Malvasia, Verdello, and Verdicchio.

Orvieto   This white wine is made both dry and semisweet, Abboccato. The Abboccato is the area's pride. Light and delicate, the dry Orvieto is well balanced with a flowery bouquet. Both wines are made with the Trebbiano, Verdello, Grechetto, Drupeggio, and Malvasia grapes.

Torgiano Bianco   This white wine is crisp and slightly tart. Made from 50 to 70 percent Trebbiano, 15 to 35 percent Grechetto, and 15 percent Malvasia and Verdello.

Marche

Bianchello de Metauro   This light, spicy, clean-tasting white wine is made from at least 95 percent Bianchello and some Malvasia.

Bianco dei Colli Maceratesi   This pale, dry white wine is made from 50 percent Trebbiano, 30–50 percent Maceratino, and 15–20 percent Malvasia and/or Verdicchio.

Galerio dei Colli Ascolani   This dry, slightly tart white wine is made from 80 percent Trebbiano, Passerina, Verdicchio, Pinot Bianco, and/or Pecorino, and a maximum of 7 percent Malvasia.

Latium

Est! Est! Est di Montefiascone   From the slopes around Lake Bolsena. The name derives from the steward of a 12th-century German Bishop, traveling to Rome, who was sent ahead by his master to mark the inns where good wine could be found by chalking EST (this is it) on the door. At Montefiascone, he was so enthusiastic that he chalked Est! Est! Est!! This wine is clear and dry and made from 65 percent Trebbiano, 20 percent Malvasia, and 15 percent Rossetto.

Frascati   From the region of Rome, white Frascati is known internationally. The wine is strong with a flavor of golden grape skins. It is made dry and semisweet. This white wine is made from Malvasia, Greco, and Trebbiano. These grapes are grown on volcanic soil and matured in deep cellars.

Bianco Capena   This light, dry wine is made from 55 percent Malvasia, 25 percent Trebbiano, and 20 percent Bellone.

Cerveteri Bianco   This light white wine is made from 50 percent Trebbiano, 35 percent Malvasia, and 15 percent Verdicchio.

Colli Albani   This light, fresh wine must be drunk as young as possible. It is made from 60 percent Malvasia, 25–50 percent Trebbiano, and 10 percent Bonvino and Cacchione.

Colli Lanuvini   This soft and dry white wine is made from 70 percent Malvasia and 30 percent Trebbiano and Bonvino.

Cori Bianco   This delicate white wine is made from Malvasia, Bellone, and Trebbiano.

Marino   This light, dry white wine is made from Malvasia, Trebbiano, Bonvino, and Cacchione.

Other Latium white wines   Other white wines of the region are Montecompatri Colonna, Trebbiano di Aprilia, Velletri Bianco, and Zagarolo.

Abruzzo

Trebbiano d'Abruzzo   A dry, velvety white wine with fresh bouquet made from the Trebbiano grape with 15 percent Malvasia, Coccocciola, and Passerina.

Apulia

Castel del Monte Bianco   This dry white wine is made from 65 percent Pampanino and 35 percent Trebbiano, Bombino Bianco, and Palumbo.

Leverano   This dry white wine is made from Malvasia, Bombino, and Trebbiano.

Locorotondo   A dry white wine made from 50 to 65 percent Verdesa, 35 to 50 percent Bianco d'Alessano, and 5 percent Bombino.

Martina Franca   A dry white wine made from 50 to 65 percent Verdeca and 35 to 50 percent Bianco d'Alessano.

Moscato di Trani   A sweet wine whose grapes are dried slightly on mats. Made from 85 percent Moscato Bianco and 15 other aromatic grapes.

Ostuni   This dry white wine is made from 50 to 85 percent Impigno, 15 to 50 percent Francavilla, and 10 percent Bianco d'Alessano and/or Verdeca.

Malvasia delle Lipari   From the Lipari Island, this sweet aromatic white wine is made from 95 percent Malvasia and 5 percent Corinto Nero.

Moscato di Noto   Made in three styles from Moscato Bianco.

Moscato di Pantelleria   Delicate, sweet white wine made from the Moscatellona.

Moscato di Siracosa   Velvety, sweet white wine made from 100 percent Moscato Bianco.

Regaleali Bianco   This unique brand name wine is made from the Cararratto and Sauvignon.

San Severo   A dry white wine made from 40 to 60 percent Bombino, 40 to 60 percent Trebbiano, and 20 percent Malvasia and Verdeca.

Campania

Capri Bianco   A dry, light, refreshing white wine from the Island of Capri; made from 50 percent Greco Falanghina and Biancolella.

Fiano de Avellino   A dry white wine improved with three to four years bottle aging; made from Fiano and 15 percent Greco.

Greco di Tufo   Full of character white wine made from 85 percent Greco de Tufo and 15 percent Coda di Volpe.

Solopaca Bianco   A dry, velvety white wine made from 50 to 70 percent Trebbiano, 20 to 40 percent Malvasia, and 10 percent Coda di Volpe.

Calabria

Ciro Bianco   Dry and fruity white wine made from Trebbiano and Greco Bianco.

Greco di Bianco   This white wine is made from dried Greco grapes and has a deep golden color.

Melissa   A white wine made from 80 to 95 percent dried Greco Bianco and 5 to 20 percent Trebbiano and/or Malvasia Bianca.

Sardinia

Malvasia di Cagliari   White wine produced from the Malvasia grape and made in varieties from dry to sweet.

Moscato di Cagliari Sweet or dry white wine made from the Moscato grape.

Moscato di Sorso Made from the Moscato grape, the wine is sweet golden yellow.

Nasco di Cagliari Made from the Nasco grape, it slightly bitter; made dry or sweet.

Nurragus di Cagliari Pale, dry white wine made from 85 to 95 percent Nuragus and 5 to 15 percent Trebbiano, Vermentino, Clairette, and/or Semidano.

Sicily

Alcamo Dry, fresh, and fruity white wine made from 80 percent Cataratto Lucido and some Damaschino and Trebbiano.

Etna Bianco Dry, fresh white wine made from 60 percent Carricante and 40 percent Lucido.

PRINCIPESSA

VINTAGE 1983

GAVI

DENOMINAZIONE DI ORIGINE CONTROLLATA
DRY WHITE WINE
Produced in Gavi, Italy on the estate of Principessa Gavia
Bottled by: V.B. Cellars-Strevi
750 ml.   VILLA BANFI U.S.A.- OLD BROOKVILLE,N.Y. IMPORTER   Alc.11% vol.

Naturally   Sparkling
Red   Wine

BRACHETTO d'ACQUI

Denominazione di Origine Controllata

VILLA BANFI U.S.A.
OLD BROOKVILLE, N.Y.
IMPORTERS

750 ml.- Produced in Italy-Bottled by Villa Banfi Cellars, Strevi-R.I.504/Al-Alc.7.5% by Vol.

1978

CHIANTI
CLASSICO

DENOMINAZIONE DI ORIGINE CONTROLLATA

Riserva

VINTAGE RED WINE

BOTTLED BY

VILLA BANFI

MONTALCINO (ITALIA)

ALC. 12.5% BY VOL. 750 ML. PRODUCE OF ITALY

Brunello di Montalcino

DENOMINAZIONE DI ORIGINE CONTROLLATA

ESTATE BOTTLED BY
VILLA BANFI VINEYARDS
MONTALCINO-ITALIA

1979

RED VINTAGE WINE
ALC. 13% BY VOL. 750 ML. PRODUCT OF ITALY

158

PRINCIPESSA

VINTAGE 1989

GAVI

DENOMINAZIONE DI ORIGINE CONTROLLATA
DRY WHITE WINE
Produced in Gavi, Italy on the estate of Principessa Gavia
Estate bottled by Banfi Cellars Strevi

750 ml. Alc.11.5%/vol.

ORVIETO
CLASSICO

DENOMINAZIONE DI ORIGINE CONTROLLATA

1990

RUFFINO

BOTTLED BY RUFFINO S.p.A. - NELLE CANTINE DI PONTASSIEVE - ITALIA - 326/FI

750 ml e   Alc. 11,5 % by vol

Banfi
ASTI SPUMANTE

Naturally Sparkling White Wine

COL-DI-SASSO

RED TABLE WINE
OF TUSGANY

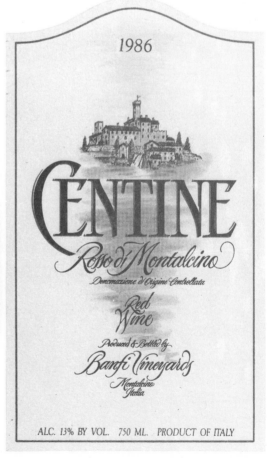

1986

CENTINE

Rosso di Montalcino

Denominazione d'Origine Controllata

Red
Wine

Produced & Bottled by

Banfi Vineyards
Montalcino
Italia

ALC. 13% BY VOL.   750 ML.   PRODUCT OF ITALY

159

GERMANY

· · · · ·

The vineyards of Germany are located in the southwestern corner of the country (see Figure 12–5). Most are on the land's very high and steep slopes, usually facing to the south. At a latitude parallel to that of Labrador, growing seasons can be cut short by an early autumn.

Most vineyards are close to rivers, which moderate the local temperatures. Also, moisture, in the way of mist and fog, protects the grapes from unseasonable frosts. These rivers also serve to reflect warm sunlight onto the vines, allowing them to reach the desired degree of ripeness.

Just as important is the soil in which the vines grow. Minerals and other natural elements affect how the wine will taste. The longer the required time for grapes to mature, the more evident those elements will appear in the bouquet and taste.

Germany has a variety of soils ranging from sand to chalk to limestone to slate. Yet other areas contain loam, clay, and volcanic deposits. Over the centuries, the Germans have done much in the way of experimentation, matching different grapes with different soils in each region. Obviously, those varieties that grow and mature with the most success have been chosen for planting.

Again, as elsewhere, the three most important influences of the final product are the land, each microclimate, and especially the grapes themselves.

Grapes

Kerner

Kerner is a crossbred grape of Riesling and Trollinger; it successfully ripens early and abundantly. Known for its lively flavor and light bouquet, it accounts for about 6 percent of Germany's total output.

Müller-Thurgau

By far the most used grape in Germany, the Müller-Thurgau is a cross between the Riesling and Sylvaner grapes. Representing over 26 percent of all plantings, it also matures early. Because of its relation to Riesling, it shares much of the same acidic content and bouquet highlights.

Riesling

The finest and best known of all German grapes is the Riesling, which accounts for 20 percent of total production. It has a concentrated degree of sweetness and natural acidity because it ripens slowly. A grape of world quality, it produces wines that are quite fruity and age well.

Sylvaner

Another early ripening grape, the Sylvaner is Germany's third most popular grape, accounting for 9 percent of the country's total output. It has a bouquet and flavor that is less pronounced than others.

FIGURE 12–5

• • •

Map of German wine-producing regions

Other Grapes

Other white grapes, which account for the remainder of Germany's output, include the Gewürztraminer, Morio-Muscat, Ruländer, and the Scheurbe. Red grape varieties include the Spätburgunder or Pinot Noir, the Portugieser, and the Trollinger.

German Wine Laws

German wines, unlike French wines, are classified according to their ripeness at harvest time. As stated, certain grapes grown in the various parts of the country ripen at different rates. In the more northern regions, the cooler climate dictates a longer growing season; the southern part benefits from more intense sunshine, and grapes ripen at a faster rate. A longer developing time usually guarantees that grapes will be very intense in bouquet and flavor. It is also necessary for the grapes to achieve an acceptable level of natural sugar and acid.

Under German wine law, two categories exist for rating all wines according to their ripeness and therefore their sweetness: Tafelwein and Qualitätswein.

Tafelwein

Tafelwein includes all those wines of fine quality that are created for everyday use; hence, the name, which means table wine. Tafelwein can come from any of four large areas. There is a subcategory, German Landwein, which can come from any one of 15 specific regions. Each region is known for its own characteristics.

Qualitätswein (Qualitätswein Bestimmter Anbaugebiete QbA)

Qualitätswein can only include superior wines that have reached 7.5 percent alcohol content. This is determined by the amount of sugar in the grape's juice at the time of picking. If the required sugar is not reached naturally, nongrape sugar is then added legally so that the potential alcohol level in the wine will be between 9 and 11 percent. QbA wines can be produced in 11 specific regions and only from approved varieties of grapes.

Qualitätswein mit Prädikat

This means wine with special attributes; these are the finest wines that Germany can produce. These special attributes will be listed on the label in order of quality, based on the ripeness or sugar level at harvest time. They are as follows, in ascending order:

Kabinett   The lightest and driest. An excellent accompaniment with all types of food; also, the most enjoyable on its own.

Spätlese   Literally, late harvest, the grapes being picked about one full week after the harvest begins officially. Fuller in body than Kabinett, the flavor is much more pronounced—rich, but not necessarily sweet. Under the proper conditions, the longer the grapes remain on the vine, the higher the level of sugar in the fruit.

Auslese   Late harvest *selected,* the grapes are very sweet, which will produce wines of intense flavors. They will, however, also be on the sweet side.

Beerenauslese   Late harvest, hand-selected, overripe grapes that are starting to shrivel on the vines. They may have been affected by noble rot, a fungus that actually enhances the flavor of some berries. Since Beerenauslese are picked very late in the harvest, fewer and fewer grapes will be left. Therefore, this type of wine is produced in small quantities. These wines are extremely rich and flavorful, sometimes compared to the great Sauternes of France, and favored by many as dessert wines.

Trockenbeerenauslese   These are individually picked grapes, selected when dried up into raisins. They have been affected by noble rot and the wine is full, rich, and luscious. It is described by many as nectar or even honey.

Eiswein   Made from grapes that have been frozen on the vine. Literally *ice wine,* an immense concentration of sweetness results since, when frozen, the water is actually separated from the juice. These wines are also rich in flavor, with a high content of acidity and sweetness.

Wine-Producing Regions

Germany has been divided into 11 wine regions, or anbaugebeite, each producing its own style of wine resulting from the grapes that are grown in each area, the soil found there, and the microclimate of each area. Each of these regions is further divided into two or more bereiche or districts. Each bereich is composed of grosslagen, collective vineyards, and many einzellagen or single vineyards. The smaller the area of origin, the more individual will be the bouquet and taste of that specific wine. The 11 wine regions of Germany are:

- Mosel.
- Ahr.
- Mittelrhein.
- Nahe.
- Rheingau.
- Rheinhessen.
- Rheinpfalz.
- Franken.
- Hessische-Bergstrasse.
- Württemberg.
- Baden.

SWITZERLAND
· · · · ·

Because of the nature of the terrain in Switzerland, it is surprising that the total acreage of Swiss vineyards has been on a steady increase over the past decade or so. Likewise, the yearly yields of grapes have grown consistently. By far the most important wine-growing region is the Valais, located in a valley of the Rhône (see Figure 12–6). Here, Burgundy's Pinot Noir and Gamay grapes are mixed to produce a wine called Dole, a light red. Another less-known wine is the Goron, also a red.

The white Chasselas grape, here called Fendant, accounts for two-thirds of all wine produced in the area. Other grapes, all white, such as the Muscat, Pinot Gris (Malvoisie), Johannesberg (Sylvaner), and Riesling are also grown.

To the northwest of the Valais is the canton of the Vaud, which produces Dorin, another name for Chasselas. Around the Geneva area, this same grape is known as Perlan. To the north, the area around Neuchâtel also produces Chasselas as well as Pinot Noir. In other areas near the Austrian and Italian borders, red wines such as Blauburgunder and Merlot complete the list of Swiss wines.

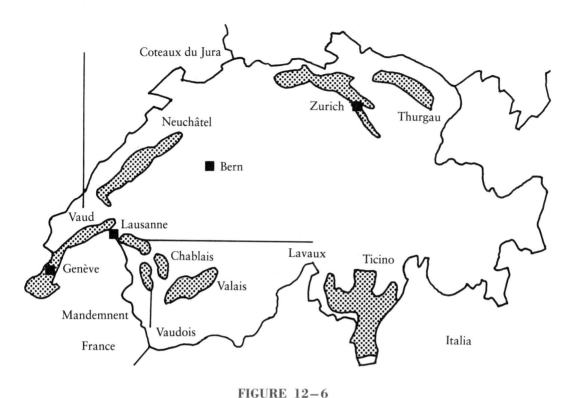

FIGURE 12–6
• • •
Map of Swiss wine-producing regions

AUSTRALIA
• • • • •

Australian wine makers have risen since the 1960s to take their rightful place beside the world-famous names of Europe and California. Known for their freewheeling enthusiasm for experimentation and innovative skills, they have gained notoriety worldwide. Australian wines possess characteristics that are somewhat unique. As the years go by, wine makers from down under are becoming more and more famous. Modern technology, travel, and communication have made it possible for Australia to improve the quality of its wine to the highest level. Today, despite different soils and varied climates, wine is made in all five Australian states (see Figure 12–7).

New South Wales (the Southeast)

Located approximately 125 miles north of Sydney is the Hunter Valley, which produces a unique style of robust red wines that are very strong and mouth filling. Although conditions are not conducive to grape growing, modern methods, including large-scale irrigation, have made it possible to produce some of the finest red wines in the world.

FIGURE 12-7

• • •

Map of Australian wine-producing regions

Over 50 varieties of grapes are grown here, the most famous being the Syrah, often called either Shiraz or Hermitage. Also on the rise is Cabernet Sauvignon, which likewise comes across as very big and peppery. White wines are made from Chardonnay and Sémillon and are just as powerful and full-bodied as the reds.

Since many wines are not called by their grape variety but by their vat numbers, an explanation of bottle contents is found on the labels. The most famous wineries include Tyrrells', Lakes' Folly, and Rothbury Estate.

Victoria (South)

Located just north of Melbourne on the south coast, this area produces a variety of wines that can all be described as quite unique. Very strong and fragrant, the Cabernet Sauvignon grapes produce the unmistakable Australian style of red wines that overwhelm the palate. Some have described these wines using such adjectives as "dirty animal," "sweaty," and "barnyard."

White wines such as Riesling can be equally potent, while Chardonnay and Sémillon can be very smooth and soft. Other specialty wines are the sweet Tokay and Muscat.

St. Huberts, Brown Brothers, and Taltarni are some of the better known wine makers in the area.

South Australia

To the west of Melbourne and north of Adelaide, South Australia is the largest wine producer in the country. Well-irrigated valleys provide the ideal soil conditions for grape growing. The Barossa and Clare valleys, as well as Coonawarra, are synonymous with the highest quality when it comes to naming Australian wines. The famous red earth of the Terra Rosa landstrip grows grapes for the finest wines anywhere.

Shiraz and Cabernet Sauvignon are produced in large quantity. Some have been compared to some of the more famous French reds. Once again, in their own inimitable style, they are extremely powerful and flavorful.

Chardonnay and Riesling grapes, as well as some Sémillon, produce the white wines of the area. Noteworthy wineries include Hardy's Wolf Blass and Penfolds.

Western Australia

In this remote area north of Perth are a wide variety of wines that are considered by many easterners to be of lesser quality than their own. Others feel that many of these wines are indeed very good. Chardonnay and Rhine Riesling represent the whites, while Cabernet Sauvignon, Zinfandel, and Shiraz make up the reds.

Tasmania

Because of its isolated location, Tasmania's wines are relatively unknown, or at least unappreciated. However, because it is further south than other wine-producing areas, it is capable of successfully growing grapes in a somewhat cooler environment. Also, its red basalt soil is ideal for grape growing. Here, red Cabernet Sauvignon, and white Chardonnay are produced.

CHILE

· · · · ·

In recent years, the Maipo Valley in Chile, which is near Santiago (see Figure 12–8), has been gaining in reputation as a producer of inexpensive, high-quality wines. In this area, vines have very long lives of up to 100 years and are not subject to problems such as root louse infestation, mold, or mildew; therefore, grafting vines and root stocks is not necessary. The soil and climate provide ideal conditions for vine growing. Warm air off the ocean and cool mountain temperatures allow for a suitable region. Wineries such as Concha y Toro, Miguel Torres, and Santa Rita produce fine Cabernet Sauvignon, Sémillon, Riesling, and Gewürztraminer.

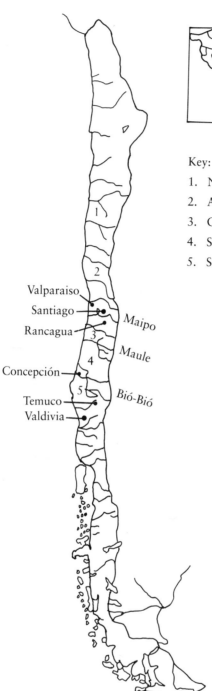

Key:

1. North Centre Region
2. Aconcagua Valley
3. Central Region
4. South Central Region
5. Southern Region

Valparaiso

Santiago

Rancagua

Maipo

Maule

Concepción

Bió-Bió

Temuco

Valdivia

FIGURE 12–8

• • •

Map of Chilean wine-producing regions

WALNUT CREST

1990

100%

CHARDONNAY

MAIPO WHITE WINE

CONT. 750 ML. • ALC. 11.5% BY VOL.

120

Santa Rita

SAUVIGNON-SEMILLON 1987

MAIPO VALLEY · CHILE

Alc. by volume 12%   Export wine produced and bottled
by Viña Santa Rita Ltda.   Net. Cont. 750 ml.

PRODUCT OF CHILE

CONCHA y TORO

ESTATE   BOTTLED

MAIPO 100%

CHARDONNAY

1988

CONT. 750 ML   DRY WHITE WINE   ALC. 12.5% BY VOL.

Undurraga®

Estate Bottled

MAIPO VALLEY SANTA ANA

Cabernet Sauvignon

CHILEAN RED WINE

PRODUCED BY VIÑA UNDURRAGA S.A.

ALC. 12% BY VOL., CONT. 750 ML.

PRODUCT OF CHILE 1985 RED WINE

CHEESE

Cheese is one of the oldest and best-loved foods in the world. Cheese dates back to when animals were first domesticated. The first cheese probably came into being by accident, when milk soured and solidified. Whatever its beginnings, cheese has been an essential part of every culture or civilization that has kept milk-giving animals.

About 10 centuries ago, Europe began to create complex cheeses such as hard-pressed and blue-veined cheeses. The monasteries of the Middle Ages introduced the soft-ripening cheeses. Every region produces a cheese that represents its own climate, soil, grasses, milk-producing animals, and cheese-making traditions.

The famous Camembert is made in Poitou along the Loire Valley in Normandy. South in the Pyrenees, the Basques produce their own varieties. In the small village of Roquefort, cheeses ripen in limestone caves. In the Alpine regions of Franche-Comte and Savoie, huge wheels of Gruyère ripen in mountainside caves. In Alsace, monks in the Middle Ages created a cheese called the Münster. Traveling from Alsace to Paris, one finds the most famous cheese of all, Brie, the king of soft-ripened cheeses.

HOW CHEESE IS MADE
· · · · ·

All cheese begins as milk. Most often, the milk is from a cow, although it can also come from a goat or sheep, or, for that matter, from any mammal be it camel, yak, or reindeer. Cheese also can be made from a blend of milk from more than one animal. The source of milk gives a cheese its fundamental character, but there are other factors that also determine the finished product. The quality of the milk, the fields in which the animals grazed, the kind of feed they ate, the season in which they ate it, and the care they received all contribute to the final product. Of great importance, of course, is what happens to the milk on its way to becoming cheese.

First, the milk must be made to coagulate; that is, to separate into curds—white, custardlike solids, and whey—a cloudy, sweet liquid. To do this, rennet is added to the milk. Rennet is obtained from the lining of the stomach of an unweaned calf.

After the curds are formed, they are cut or broken to free the curd from the whey. At this stage, the curds of most cheeses are heated so that still more of the whey will be removed. Each cheese is raised to a temperature considered right to set the moisture level for that kind of cheese. The curd is then separated from the whey by one of various methods. The whey may be drained out through a sieve in the bottom of the vat, the curds removed and put in perforated molds, or lifted up in a cloth attached to a hoop so that the whey can drain through the cloth.

Most cheeses are salted to reduce moisture, enrich flavor, and kill harmful bacteria. The curds are pressed to mold the cheese, to give it its traditional shape, and for some cheeses, to remove still more moisture. Flowery rind cheeses are sprayed with white mold. Monastery cheeses are washed. Both kinds are affected by the molds or bacteria to their surfaces. They are surface-ripened cheeses, aging slowly from the outside into the center. Curd destined to become blue cheese is inoculated with blue mold. Some hard cheeses are formed so that carbon dioxide, a natural by-product of curing cheese, cannot escape and consequently will develop the holes or eyes characteristic of their interiors.

Now the curing or aging process begins. Some cheese is aged in warm, humid atmospheres; some are placed in cool, dry places; others are placed in the natural limestone caves of their regions. Some are aged on straw mats whose texture becomes embossed into their surface. During this aging process, the cheeses may be brushed, turned, washed, scrubbed, oiled, wrapped, or left as they are. Rinds may form to protect the cheese and allow its interior to ripen properly. Some rinds develop naturally; other rinds develop because of the surface molds that have been added. Some rinds grow thick and tough; others remain thin and fragile. Some cheeses are cured for days; some are cured for months; some require years to reach perfection.

It takes only one variation—the temperature at which the cheese is made, the way it is cured, or the way it is stored—to create a distinctly different product.

Soft-Ripened Cheese

Soft, shiny, buttery smooth and rich, these cheeses have an interior that, when perfectly ripe, runs like thick honey. They have a bouquet that is fragrant and full and a taste that leaves a fruity, lingering tang.

Soft-ripened cheeses receive their remarkable elegance from the way in which they are made and ripened. Soon after the cheese has been separated from its whey, and before it is put to cure, its surface is sprayed with a white mold related to penicillin. The cheese is then placed in a cool drying room for a week during which it becomes firm and the downy white rind begins to appear on its surface. At the end of the week, it is removed and placed in a cave for about 10 days. From there, it is ready for market.

The most celebrated of the soft-ripened cheeses are Camembert and Brie. The village of Camembert in the northern province of Normandy gave its name to the cheese. All Camembert cheeses are packaged in the traditional round, light wooden box invented in the late 19th century specifically for the cheese. The finest Bries are named after the town or village in which they originated. Examples are Brie de Melun and Brie de Meaux.

Coulommiers, another soft-ripened cheese, is a cousin of Brie. Made as a smaller, round-shaped pie, it shares Brie's suppleness, smell, and bouquet. Carre de l'Est is made as a small 4-inch square. Its flavor is reminiscent of a mild Brie. Chaource, from the Champagne region, is creamy and plump. Cylindrical in shape, it has an edible white crust and a subtle mushroom aroma.

There is another group of soft-ripened cheeses that share common family traits—the washed rind types. They are usually thicker than those with flowery rinds and tend to have stronger aromas. These cheeses are made as their flowery rind relatives are in the initial stages of production. However, their curing time is two to three times longer, and during their final curing period in the cave, they are washed with salt water about twice a week in order to thicken the crust and to maintain the cheese's moisture.

Pont-l'Evêque is an old Norman cheese. It is a small, plump cheese with a smooth golden rind marked by the straw on which it was placed during its six weeks of curing. The interior is soft and yellow. The taste carries a pronounced tang, and the aroma is savory and approaches pungency. Epoisses, a centuries-old cheese of Burgundy, is a supple, flat disk with a smooth, shiny rind. Its taste is tangy and its smell, especially as it matures, grows increasingly penetrating.

Münster, from the Province of Alsace, originated in a monastery during the Middle Ages and was named for the city of Münster, contraction of the word for monastery. It is a fine cheese, made as a flat disk that can vary from a few ounces to a few pounds, and is highly aromatic. Despite its intense aroma, the cheese has a much more delicate taste, reminding one of mushrooms and leaving a lingering flavor.

Maroilles was first made in the 10th century at the monastery in Maroilles. Long known as Vieux Puant, or hold stench, Maroilles does its best to live up to the name. It is a square, supple slab weighing just under 2 pounds, and its interior is creamy. Both its smell and taste grow more vigorous with age.

Strong cheese really comes into its own, however, with Livarot. Livarot is an ancient product of Normandy, named after a tiny town near Caen. Finer in texture and feel than many strong cheeses, it is nevertheless among the tangiest in taste. Its aromas, stinging, and redolent, are second to none among France's strong entries in the cheese world.

Semisoft Cheese

Semisoft cheeses are creamy and rich, with velvety textures and aromas that range from mild to strong. All of them have washed rinds, which means they were coated with a solution during their formation stage; thus, they ripen from the outside in.

These cheeses are made by draining the whey from the curd through a cloth and then pressing the new cheese. The length of time that the cheese is drained and pressed varies according to the amount of moisture the cheese maker wants to be retained in the finished product. Some of these semisoft cheeses have a natural rind; others are covered with a wax coating for protection. They mature with a thin, somewhat shiny rind that can vary in color from yellow to brownish orange and red depending on the kind of cheese, the solution in which it was washed, and the number of times it was washed.

Creamy Cheese

This is the simplest country cheese. It is fresh, uncured, and only one step removed from milk, because it is made only by draining the curd. Still very moist, it is ready to eat. Creamy cheeses are so delicate that few of them leave their native farmland. Among the exceptions that can be found in the United States are Petit-Suisse and Fountainebleau.

Many fresh, unripened cheeses are crèmes. They get their special creamy lightness from being blended with whipped cream during production.

Semihard and Hard Cheese

Semihard and hard cheeses carry their most prominent family resemblance not so much in a common taste or aroma, or because they are derived from the milk of the same animal (although in fact, they are all made of cow's milk), but rather in their textured, firm, supple, and sometimes buttery bodies. Most of these firm-textured cheeses are formed into large wheels, some having holes or eyes. Many are cooked cheeses, and all are pressed.

Cantal

Cantal is France's oldest cheese, as well as being one of the oldest in the world. Made into a tall, thick cylinder that can weigh 100 pounds or more, Cantal takes three to six months to cure. The finished cheese has a tough, gray inedible rind; a smooth, firm, yellow interior; a mild, nutty flavor; and an individualistic taste.

Emmenthal Français

Emmenthal Français is an enormous cheese weighing as much as 220 pounds. It has a light, fruity aroma, and a nutty taste, and large, widely spaced eyes. The eyes of these firm, Gruyère-type cheeses occur because the cheese is formed in a way that does not allow the carbon dioxide, a natural by-product of curing cheese, to escape. Thus, the holes, or eyes, develop.

Beaufort

Beaufort is firm and supple, with a mild, fruity taste and scent. However, it has smaller eyes than Emmenthal.

Comte

Weighing about 75 pounds, it is the smallest of the French Gruyère cheeses. Its aroma is mild, and its taste is flavorful and lightly salty. Its eyes are relatively small, ranging in size from that of a small nut to that of a cherry. Comte has been made in the Jura Mountains since the 13th century.

Gruyère

Gruyère became a generic name in France. Emmenthal, Beaufort, and Comte are the best known.

Processed Cheese

Processed cheeses are sometimes presented in their simple, unadorned style, sometimes herbed, spiced, enhanced by fruits or nuts, and otherwise flavored in the process. Some are soft, others hard, sliceable, and spreadable.

Some processed cheeses are coated with marc, which are grape seeds left after the grapes have been pressed for wine. The seeds, which are inedible, impart a grape flavor to the cheese. Others may be flavored with walnuts, onions, pimientos, caraway, black peppers, raisins, green peppers, or kirsch.

Processed cheeses or fromage fondus are almost all blends made with Gruyère as the base. These blends mix one or more varieties of cheese with an emulsifying agent, heating the combination to give a homogeneous quality to the finished product. Cream, butter, milk, or whey is sometimes added. Processed cheeses are raised to high temperatures during their production. They do not tend to ripen much after being cooled and packaged.

Blue-Veined Cheese

Blue-veined cheese, with its distinctive marbling and tangy flavor, is one of the aristocrats of the cheese world. These cheeses vary from semifirm to creamy to crumbly, but they share one major characteristic—their blue-green veining, which distinguishes them from all other cheeses. Blue-veined cheese comes by its veins either naturally through the fermentation process, or by inoculation with a strain of penicillin to help start or hasten the process. Unlike soft-ripened cheeses, which develop from the outside in, fermentation in blue cheeses begins at the center and works its way toward the outer edges. As the cheese develops and the blue veins spread, they begin to resemble a sprig of parsley; hence, the veining is often called persille, or parsleyed.

In a good blue cheese, the veins must be well distributed and extend from the core to the outer reaches of the cheese. The cheese must show signs that it has been properly aged, and will offer the special piquancy found only in blue cheeses.

If blue cheese is one of the blue bloods of the cheese world, Roquefort is the bluest blood of all. It is also one of the world's oldest cheeses, dating back to the days of the Romans. It is a singular cheese, made of sheep milk and ripened in the natural limestone caves of Combalou in south-central France. The region is harsh and barren, water is scarce, and the climate is extreme. On the causse, or plateau, the sheep of Roquefort graze, possibly the only animals that could live on this desolate, stony terrain. Sheep, however, are notoriously small milk givers, averaging barely 2 quarts a day, a 10th of what a cow is capable of giving. It is milk unequalled in quality—creamy, rich, almost buttery, so thick, in fact, that to drink it, one must first dilute it with water.

After the cheese is made, inoculated, washed, and salted, it is placed in the region's famous limestone caves. Cool, damp, and drafty, it is these caves that more than anything give Roquefort its special quality. The cheeses spend 60 to 90 days in the caves. When they emerge, they are moist and creamy cylinders weighing about 5 pounds and offering that indefinable flavor and texture unique to Roquefort. No other cheese, including other blues, is quite like it. That is why only this cheese, made of sheep milk and cured in the caves of Combalou, can bear the Roquefort appellation of origin on the package foil (a red oval mark with a sheep in the middle).

Other blue-veined cheeses are made of cow's milk and are produced in many areas of France. Bleu des Causses is made in the same region as Roquefort and is cured in humid cellars similar to the caves used for Roquefort. It is a firm, savory, cow's milk cheese, shaped as a flat cylinder of about 5½ pounds with well-distributed veins and a pungent blue-cheese aroma. Bleu d'Auvergne is a firm, slightly oily cheese with an assertive aroma and taste. Fourme d'Ambert, a product of the mountainous area of Auvergne, is named after its shape, a 9-inch-tall cylinder. It is a firm cheese with a pleasantly light aroma and a pronounced savory taste.

Chèvres (Goat) Cheese

The goat is a sturdy, agile, erratic animal that can graze where cows fear to tread, whose milk produces a deliciously tart and tangy cheese. It is an uncommon cheese made from the milk of an animal that does not give much of it. While cows may give 10 to 20 quarts of milk each day, goats rarely give more than 2. While a cow is receptive to a bull any time of the year, assuring the world a continuing supply of milk, the female goat will accept the male goat only in the autumn. It is no surprise that goat or chèvre cheese constitutes only about 4 percent of total cheese production.

But it is not simply the scant supply that makes chèvre a coveted luxury. It is the cheese itself—its distinctive flavor, the hint of sharpness and acidity in even the freshest young cheese, its slight, almost pepperish sting, and its earthy, nutty character.

Chèvre cheeses come in classic shapes; little cylinders, cones, pyramids, logs, ovals, shallow disks, and buttons. Dozens of these pungent little cheeses abound in Burgundy, the Alps, in the Loire Valley, and in Provence. Some chèvres are wrapped in leaves to keep them moist, while some are rolled in herbs. Most come unadorned, as pure and white as fresh cream cheese. Chèvre cheese varies in texture from soft to firm, and in taste from the tangy innocence of a young cheese to the startling acidity of an old cheese.

Pyramide, from the Loire region, is named after its shape—a truncated pyramid barely 3 inches high. It comes downy white and dusted with ashes. A traditional chèvre with its small size and big flavor, it has the forward taste and the lightly moldy aroma of goat. It is also known as Yalencay.

Also from the Loire region is Saint-Maure, a creamy cylinder about 6 inches long with a rather pronounced goat flavor. Selles-sur-Cher, on the other hand, is a truncated cone about 1-inch thick with a light goat smell and a mild flavor. Banon, a goat cheese of Provence, is a 3-inch disk wrapped in chestnut leaves that have been cured in brandy and tied with rafia. Rocamadour is a small, thin disk, averaging only 1 ounce in weight. It has a concentrated goat flavor. Still, it is not nearly as intense as Crottin de Chavignol, a hard, sometimes brittle little cheese. Dry and with a dark exterior, Crottin de Chavignol surpasses most other goat cheese in its strong smell and sharp taste.

Saint-Marcellin is a popular cheese that is made from both goat's and cow's milk. Despite the combination, it is the distinctive flavor and the white paste of the goat that predominates. It is tangy, mouth filling, and slightly acid, as all good chèvres are.

Goat cheese is a unique cheese with a singular flavor and taste that can be found in no other cheese.

HOW TO SERVE CHEESE
· · · · ·

Cheese tastes best and shows its finest flavor at room temperature. Semifirm and firm cheeses need at least an hour to warm to room temperature. Soft and semisoft cheeses usually need a half-hour or more. Very large pieces of cheese require more time than smaller ones.

Cheese should be cut according to its shape (see Figure 13–1), so that the rind is evenly distributed. Serve cheeses on wooden cheese boards, trays, and straw mats. Arrange the cheeses with enough room between them to make cutting easy. Have a cheese cutter or knife for each cheese.

Round and square cheese (Camembert)

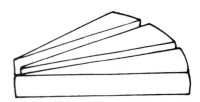

Brie — Cut from center out
in pie-shaped wedges.

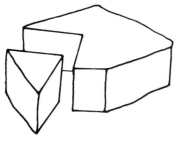

Cone or pyramid shapes cut
in small triangular wedges.

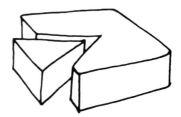

Pont l'Évêque

Large blue-veined cheese cut
in triangular wedges.

Small patty-shaped cheese
such as Chèvres cut in half.

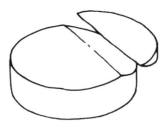

Cylinder types cut in
thin slices from the top.

FIGURE 13—1

• • •

Cutting cheese

TABLESIDE PREPARATION

INTRODUCTION TO TABLESIDE
COOKING AND FLAMING
· · · · ·

Throughout the years in the development of restaurant service, many dishes have evolved that have lent themselves to being prepared tableside. Basic principles must be emphasized in considering dishes suitable for tableside cooking. Following these principles, cooking can be accomplished within a reasonably short period of time.

The most important tableside prepared items are:

1. Salads that mostly involve simple assembly of prepared ingredients.
2. Pastas that demand merely the finishing touches of saucing and garnishing.
3. Meat, poultry, and fish dishes.
4. Hot and/or cold desserts either prepared or flamed tableside.

Liqueurs and Spirits for Flaming

Higher proof spirits are the most suitable for flaming dishes. The most desirable choices are usually Cognac, Armagnac, or Calvados, rum, or whiskey, although other spirits such as vodka may be used.

To flambé, the hot pan containing a food item is removed from the guèridon to prevent the possibility of premature ignition, and the liquor is added to the pan. When the pan is returned to the flame, it will often ignite. If the alcohol does not flame immediately, the chef de rang will swirl and tilt the pan slightly, causing fumes from the alcohol to rise, make contact with the flame, and ignite.

When using wine and spirits in cooking, it is important that most of the alcohol evaporates, or burns off, since the culinary intention in adding wine and spirits is most often to give flavor, character, and flair, not alcohol. Taste is important; therefore, one should select the flavored wines and liqueurs best suited for the dish being prepared.

The following are the names of liqueurs and spirits that can be used for flambé.

Liqueur

Name	Predominant Flavor
Crème de Banana	Banana
Benedictine	Aromatic herb compound
Crème de Cacao	Chocolate or cocoa and vanilla
Crème de Cassis	Black currant
Cherry brandy	Cherries
Cointreau	Orange
Curaçao	Orange

Crème de Fraises	Strawberries
Crème de Framboise	Raspberries
Grand Marnier	Orange
Maraschino	Cherries
Crème de Peche	Peaches

Distilled Spirits

Name	Predominant Flavor
Armagnac/Cognac	Brandy
Calvados	Brandy—apple
Kirsch	Brandy—cherries
Mirabelle	Brandy—plum
Irish whiskey	Grain "barley"

Fortified Wines

Fortified wines are useful in tableside cooking because they generally require less reduction to communicate their flavor and bouquet. For cooking tableside, the principal fortified wines merit particular attention.

The following are the tableside fortified wines most often used for cooking.

Name	Place of Origin
Marsala	Italy
Port	Portugal
Sherry	Spain
Madeira	Portuguese Islands of Madeira
Vermouth	Italy, France

Shrimp Sauté with Garlic

Yield: 2 servings

Ingredients:

Mise en Place by Chefs in the Kitchen:

Shrimp, 16/20, butterfly	8	
Butter, clarified	2 oz.	
Lemon juice	½ lemon	
Garlic, crushed	1 tsp.	
Fortified wine	1 oz.	
Salt and cayenne pepper	To taste	
Fresh parsley	1 tbsp.	Chop

Method of Preparation:

Tableside Cooking by Chef de Rang:

1. Heat pan, add butter, and heat.
2. Add shrimp and sauté both sides.
3. Remove pan from heat, pour wine on shrimp, return to heat.
4. Add garlic, lemon juice, and seasonings. Mix well; simmer 2 minutes.
5. Place four shrimp per portion on preheated dinner plate. Garnish.

Veal Scallops in Wine Sauce

Yield: 2 servings

Ingredients:

Mise en Place by Chefs in the Kitchen:

Veal scallops, approx. 1½ oz. each	6 slices
Butter	1 oz.
Oil	1 oz.
Flour, seasoned	1 oz.
Mushrooms	2 oz.
Marsala wine	1½ oz
Demi-glace, veal	2 oz.
Salt and white pepper	To taste
Parsley, chopped	As needed
Croutons	2

Method of Preparation:

Tableside Cooking by Chef de Rang:

1. Heat pan, add butter and oil, and heat.
2. Coat veal slices in seasoned flour; shake off excess flour.
3. Place veal slices in pan and brown both sides on high flame.
4. Add mushrooms and sauté.
5. Add Marsala wine and simmer 2 minutes.
6. Add demi-glace, bring to boil, and season.
7. Place croûtons on preheated dinner plate, place veal slices on croûtons, and napper with sauce.
8. Garnish with chopped parsley.

Veal Piccata

Yield: 2 servings

Ingredients:

Mise en Place by Chefs in the Kitchen:

Olive oil	1 oz.
Butter	1 oz.
Flour	As needed
Veal scaloppine, 2 oz. each	6
Salt and black pepper	To taste
Lemon juice	½ lemon
White wine, dry	3 oz.
Lemons, pinwheel slices (without rind)	4

Method of Preparation:

Tableside Cooking by Chef de Rang:

1. In a heated sauté pan, add olive oil first, then butter.
2. Lightly coat the scaloppine with flour.
3. Sauté the scaloppine; season with salt and pepper.
4. After turning scaloppine, squeeze lemon juice on top.
5. Add white wine and simmer.
6. Remove the scaloppine to preheated dinner plate, layer three per plate, and napper with sauce.
7. Garnish with four lemon pinwheels on side of plate.

Variations:

A. Supplement with capers to create grenobloise.
B. "à la Française": Flour and egg wash scaloppine.

Fettuccine Alfredo

Yield: 2 servings

Ingredients:

Mise en Place by Chefs in the Kitchen:

Butter	1 oz.
Cream, heavy	½ cup
Egg yolks	1
Fettuccine (cooked)	8 oz.
Grated cheese	2 tbsp.
Salt	To taste
Black pepper, freshly ground	1 dash

Method of Preparation:

Tableside Cooking by Chef de Rang:

1. Add butter to pan and melt.
2. Add cream and mix with whisk.
3. While whipping, add egg yolks slowly; be careful not to touch sides of pan with yolk so yolks will not cook separately from sauce.
4. Add fettuccine and keep mixture moving, shaking pan until pasta is thoroughly heated.
5. Sprinkle cheese, add salt and pepper to mixture, and mix well.
6. Portion on preheated dinner plates.

Variation:

Substitute hollandaise sauce for egg yolk for easier blending and richer taste.

Flaming Steak with Peppercorns

Yield: 2 servings

Ingredients:

Mise en Place by Chefs in the Kitchen:

Butter, fortified with 1 tsp. oil	1 oz.
Sirloin steaks, coated with crushed black peppercorns (5 oz. each)	2
Cognac	2 oz.
Demi-glace	4 oz.
Salt	To taste

Method of Preparation:

Tableside Cooking by Chef de Rang:

1. Heat Suzette pan until very hot, then add butter and oil.
2. When butter is melted, add steaks.
3. Cook to desired doneness.
4. Remove pan from heat; pour Cognac, return to heat, and flame.
5. When flame subsides, remove steaks and place on preheated dinner plates.
6. Add demi-glace to pan and mix with Cognac. Add salt, then mix well.
7. Spoon sauce alongside steak.

Variations:

A. Dijon mustard may be lightly brushed on steak before coating with peppercorns, or add mustard to sauce in pan.
B. Medallions of tenderloin may be substituted for sirloin.
C. Green peppercorns may also be used.
D. Supplement with light cream.

Steak Tartare

Yield: 2 servings

Ingredients:

Mise en Place by Chefs in the Kitchen:

Anchovies	4	
Dijon mustard	1 tsp.	
Olive oil	1½ tsp.	
Wine vinegar	½ tsp.	
Lemon juice, fresh	¼ lemon	Strain
Cognac	1 oz.	
Onions	2 tsp.	Chop fine
Capers	1 tsp.	
Parsley	1 tsp.	Chop fine
Egg yolks, raw	2	
Tenderloin, raw	10 oz.	Chop
Rye bread	6 slices	Slice, toast, cut into points

Method of Preparation:

Tableside by Chef de Rang:

1. In a chilled salad bowl, mash anchovies with fork.
2. Add mustard and blend in oil.
3. Add vinegar, lemon juice, Cognac, onions, capers, parsley, and egg yolks. Mix all ingredients together.
4. Add meat and mix thoroughly.
5. Reconstitute mixture into original shape on two cold dinner plates.
6. Arrange toast points around Steak Tartare.

Variations:

A. Substitute shallots for onions.
B. Supplement with Worcestershire Sauce, soy sauce, tabasco, or a combination.
C. Supplement with Hungarian paprika.
D. Supplement with horseradish.
E. Pumpernickel or toasted French bread may be substituted for rye bread.
F. Egg yolk and parsley may be omitted from dressing, and used as a garnish.

Notes:

(a) Chopped tenderloin is the leanest beef available. Even the leanest sirloin would have at least a 12 percent fat content. The leanest possible meat should be used to make it easily digestible.

(b) State and local health departments caution against the use of raw eggs due to the risk of salmonella poisoning.

Émincé of Chicken with Fines Herbes

Yield: 2 servings

Ingredients:

Mise en Place by Chefs in the Kitchen:

Chicken fingers	12 oz.	
Butter	2 oz.	
Flour, seasoned	2 oz.	
Lemon juice	½ lemon	
Fortified wine	2 oz.	
Shallots	1 tsp.	Chop
Tarragon	1 tsp.	Chop
Parsley	2 tsp.	Chop
Salt and white pepper	To taste	

Method of Preparation:

Tableside Cooking by Chef de Rang:

1. Place 1 oz. of butter in pan and heat.
2. Coat chicken fingers in flour; shake off excess flour.
3. Place chicken fingers in hot butter and brown.
4. Remove pan from heat, add fortified wine, return to heat.
5. Set aside chicken fingers in pan.
6. Place second ounce of butter in pan.
7. Add all herbs and lemon juice; allow to simmer.
8. Combine all ingredients with chicken fingers; season.
9. Portion into servings on preheated dinner plates.

Pommes Normande

Yield: 2 servings

Ingredients:

Mise en Place by Chefs in the Kitchen:

Sugar, granulated	3 tsp.	
Butter	1 oz.	
Apples, ripe	2	Peel, core, slice ¼-inch
Calvados or Applejack	2 oz.	
Heavy cream	2 oz.	
Cinnamon sugar mixture	½ tsp.	

Method of Preparation:

Tableside Cooking by Chef de Rang:

1. Place sugar and butter in crêpe pan; allow to lightly caramelize.
2. Add apples; allow to simmer.
3. Remove pan from heat, pour Calvados, return to heat, and flame.
4. Sprinkle cinnamon sugar over flame.
5. When flame subsides, remove apples to preheated dessert dishes. Add cream to finish sauce; bring to a boil and blend well.
6. Spoon sauce over apples.

Variations:

A. Substitute brown sugar for granulated sugar.
B. Substitute nutmeg for cinnamon.

Banana Flambé

Yield: 2 servings

Ingredients:

Mise en Place by Chefs in the Kitchen:

Sugar, granulated	2 tbsp.	
Butter	1 oz.	
Bananas	2	Cut ½ by width and ½ by length
Rum, dark (Myers's)	1½ oz.	
Banana liqueur	1½ oz.	
Cinnamon sugar mixture	½ tsp.	
Vanilla ice cream (4-oz. scoop)	2	

Method of Preparation:

Tableside Cooking by Chef de Rang:

1. Add sugar and butter to hot Suzette pan; lightly caramelize.
2. Add bananas and coat with caramel.
3. Remove pan from heat, pour rum, return pan to heat and flame.
4. While still flaming, sprinkle cinnamon sugar over pan.
5. Lower flame and remove pan from heat. Add banana liqueur and return pan to réchaud.
6. Allow to reduce, then place four quarters of banana and napper sauce over scoops of ice cream, which previously had been served into coupe.

Variations:

A. Replace granulated sugar with brown sugar or honey.
B. Supplement with lime or lemon juice.
C. Stir with lemon half.

Cherries Jubilee

Yield: 2 servings

Ingredients:

Mise en Place by Chefs in the Kitchen:

Sugar, granulated	2 tbsp.
Cherries, dark, sweet, pitted	10
Kirschwasser	1½ oz.
Peter Heering	1½ oz.
Lemon	½
Cherry juice	3 oz.
Vanilla ice cream	2 scoops

Method of Preparation:

Tableside Cooking by Chef de Rang:

1. Heat Suzette pan; sprinkle sugar over pan. When sugar is totally caramelized, or inverted, add cherries.
2. Place ½ lemon on fork, stir to speed up the reinversion of hardened sugar.
3. When inverted, remove pan from heat, pour both liqueurs, return to heat, and flame.
4. Add cherry juice. Move cherries to the side of the pan to prevent them from being overcooked.
5. Bring sauce to a froth.
6. Spoon cherries over ice cream and napper with sauce.

Variations:

A. Sprinkle a mixture of cinnamon and sugar over cherries while the liquor is still ignited.
B. Replace Peter Heering with Crème de Cocoa, or use Vandermint.
C. Replace Kirschwasser with brandy.

Note:

To reduce preparation time, cornstarch may be premixed with cherry juice. In this case, the inversion of the sugar can be bypassed.

Crêpes Suzette

Yield: 2 servings

Ingredients:

Mise en Place by Chefs in the Kitchen:

Sugar, granulated	2	tbsp.
Butter	1	oz.
Orange	1	
Lemon	1	
Orange juice	4	oz.
Grand Marnier	2	oz.
Crêpes	4	
Cognac	1	oz.

Method of Preparation:

Tableside Cooking by Chef de Rang:

1. Heat Suzette pan; sprinkle sugar over pan. Add butter and mix until all sugar is dissolved.
2. While sugar is dissolving, zest the peel of orange and lemon over pan.
3. Add orange juice. (If sugar caramelizes too quickly, add juice to pan while zesting.)
4. Remove pan from heat, pour Grand Marnier, but do *not* flambé.
5. Return pan to heat, and then dip crêpes in sauce, one at a time. Fold into quarters. Move crêpes to the side of the pan.
6. When all crepes are folded, remove pan from heat, pour Cognac, return to heat, and flame.
7. Bring sauce to a froth and serve. Napper sauce over crêpes.
8. Garnish with orange zest.

Variation:

For a more syrupy sauce, caramelize sugar first, then add butter.

Zabaglione

Yield: 2 servings

Ingredients:

Mise en Place by Chefs in the Kitchen:

Egg yolks	2
Sugar, granulated	2 tsp.
Marsala	3 oz.

Method of Preparation:

Tableside Cooking by Chef de Rang:

1. Beat egg yolks and sugar in cold zabaglione pan.
2. When some volume is reached, add Marsala and beat a little more.
3. Apply to low heat, keeping sides of pan clean so as not to leave beaten yolk mixture on sides that might become mixed with final product.
4. When mixture has reached a ribbonlike texture (determined by testing on the back of a spoon), pour into champagne glasses.

Variations:

A. Lady fingers may accompany this dish.
B. Zabaglione may be poured over fruit.
C. Grand Marnier or Kirschwasser may be poured in champagne glasses ahead of time.
D. Marsala may be replaced with a sweet, white wine.

Café Diable

Yield: 2 servings

Ingredients:

Mise en Place by Chefs in the Kitchen:

Sugar	1 tsp.
Cinnamon stick	1
Horse's neck*	1
Cognac	1 oz.
Grand Marnier	1 oz.
Espresso	5 oz.

Method of Preparation:

Tableside Cooking by Chef de Rang:

1. In a diable réchaud, add sugar, cinnamon stick, horse's neck, Cognac, and Grand Marnier.
2. When liqueurs start to steam, pierce one end of horse's neck with a long-handled fork. With the other hand, use a ladle and remove a small amount of liquor from bottom of réchaud and expose it to the flame until it ignites.
3. Raise horse's neck about 12 inches above pan and pour liqueur down rind. Continue until cloves glow bright red. Extinguish flame in réchaud by pouring in espresso.

Notes:

Diavolo in Italian; *Diablo* in Spanish.
*Horse's neck: The skin of an orange that has been removed by carefully peeling from top to bottom while rotating orange in hand. Stud with cloves approximately 1 inch apart.

```
• • • • • • • • • • • • • • • • • • • • • • • • • • • • • • • • • • • • • • • • • • • • • • •
```

Irish Coffee

Yield: 2 servings

Ingredients:

Mise en Place by Chefs in the Kitchen:

Lemon, wedge	2
Sugar, granulated	2 tbsp.
Irish whiskey	2 oz.
Coffee	10 oz.
Heavy cream, whipped	2 oz.

Method of Preparation:

Tableside Cooking by Chef de Rang:

1. Rim footed glass with lemon and dip it in sugar.
2. Heat over flame slightly, rotating glass.
3. Remove from heat, pour whiskey, return to heat, and flame. Swirl glass so flame rises. Flame for approximately 1 minute.
4. Add coffee and fill to about ½ inch below rim.
5. Add whipped cream.

Variations:

Use liqueurs from any country to create different international coffees:
A. Jamaica: Jamaica Rum and Tia Maria.
B. Mexico: Kahlua.
C. Amaretto: Lover's Coffee.

Note:

Coffee with two liqueurs is prepared by the same method, except that the second liqueur, usually a cordial, is floated on the whipped cream or heated in a ladle and then poured over the whipped cream. The first liquor is usually of high alcohol content; for example, brandy or whiskey.

```
• • • • • • • • • • • • • • • • • • • • • • • • • • • • • • • • • • • • • • • • • • • • • • •
```

TABLESIDE CARVING

• • • • •

In the following section, you will be shown the correct procedures for carving many different food items within the dining room. It is important to note that these methods were chosen from a number of ways to perform the same task. When working in the field, you will find many other examples of how these carvings are executed. With field experience you will develop methods for carving that are most suitable and convenient for you.

Carving in the dining room inevitably differs from carving in the kitchen for the following reasons:

1. Emphasis within the dining room is not only on making an effective presentation, but the presentation should be accomplished with dexterity and some degree of flair.

2. Some food items will be cooling while the carving is being performed, meaning speed should be of utmost importance.

3. Scrupulous attention must be paid to the appearance of all the implements and equipment used.

4. Proper portioning will vary in importance according to what items are being carved. It is harder to gauge portions of jointed items such as roast ribs of beef or saddle of lamb than those of chateaubriand or entrecôte double.

Carving remains an area of activity that underscores the skills of the chef de rang and reveals the work for which training and flair are required.

Carving Tools

One of the principles of carving in the dining room is that one should use the specially sharpened boning knife and the longer and thinner bladed carving knife plus a carving fork for carving fowl and meat items (see Figure 14–1).

Serrated slicing knife, ideal for slicing items presented in puff pastry or brioche dough.

Flexible, narrow-bladed slicing knife, ideal for slicing salmon and roast ribs of beef.

Slicing knife with pointed tip, used primarily for slicing and carving red meat items and fowl.

Light 8-inch or 10-inch French knife and 4-inch to 6-inch boning knife. Both knives can be used for boning chicken, duck, or squab. The small French knife is usually used for the larger items and the smaller boning knife for the smaller items.

Paring knife used for peeling fruits and vegetables.

Styles of meat forks

Apple
corer

Pineapple
corer

Zester used for zesting fruit peelings into tableside items

FIGURE 14–1

• • •

Tools used by the carver

Carving Fowl (Chicken, Duck, Pheasant, and Goose)

Present the item to be carved with the breast of the bird facing the guest. To transfer the bird from the platter to the carving board, insert the fork into the neck cavity while inserting the carving knife into the large stomach cavity (see Figure 14–2).

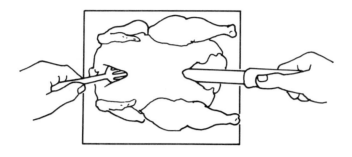

FIGURE 14–2

• • •

Transferring the whole bird

Insert the fork under the neck cavity and through the spine or on the top of the bird. Slice through the skin around the leg joint with the carving knife, cutting away any fat and connective tissue near the thigh joint (see Figure 14–3).

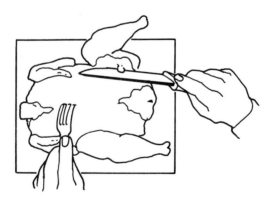

FIGURE 14–3

• • •

Cutting away fat and connective tissue

With the tip of the knife, find the joint and separate it. This will disconnect the leg from the body (see Figure 14–4).

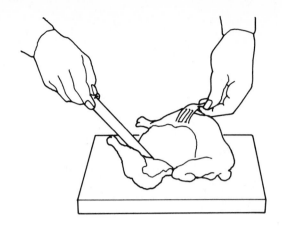

FIGURE 14–4

• • •

Carving the thigh joint

Hold down the leg with the fork and slice through the knee joint to separate the thigh from the drumstick (Figure 14–5).

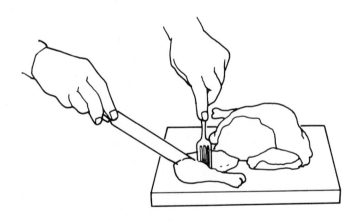

FIGURE 14–5

• • •

Carving the knee joint

Repeat the procedure to remove the other leg and return the legs to the platter.

Figure 14–6 shows how to carve the breast while it is still attached.

To remove breast, insert the fork under the wing and through the spine. With the tip of the carving knife, make a cut along the wishbone and along the breastbone. Slice down between the breast meat and breastbone using the entire blade of the knife.

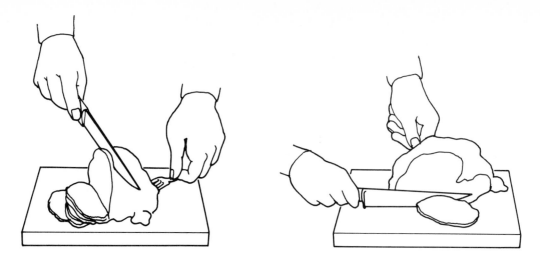

FIGURE 14—6
• • •
Carving the breast

Follow the contour of the rib bones down to the carving board and slice through the wing joint. This will remove one half the breast with the wing attached (Figure 14—7).

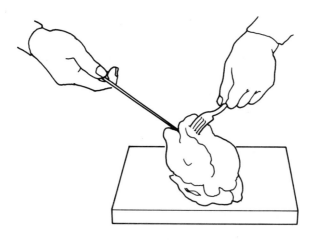

FIGURE 14—7
• • •
Removing the breast with the wing attached

Repeat the procedure to remove the opposite side of the breast.

The wing may be removed from the breast meat at this time if so desired and returned to the platter. The breasts, wings, thighs, and drumsticks are illustrated in Figure 14—8.

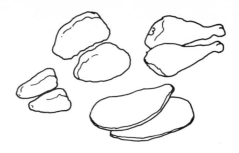

FIGURE 14–8

• • •

Breasts, wings, thighs, and drumsticks

Carving Chateaubriand

Present platter to guest. Transfer Chateaubriand to the carving board using a large serving spoon and fork. Hold the meat steady with the serving fork and slice half-inch portions using the entire length of the carving knife. Slice from one end to the other end, being sure not to pierce the meat with the tines of the fork (Figure 14–9).

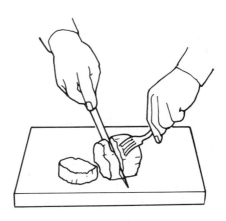

FIGURE 14–9

• • •

Chateaubriand

Carve all slices *across the grain* of the meat to ensure a more tender product. Transfer slices back to the platter, have the assistant waiter remove the carving board, arrange plates, and portion slices equally.

Carving Rack of Lamb

Present platter to guest. Transfer rack to the carving board using a large carving fork and slicing knife. This is done by lightly piercing the fork between the rib bones and the meat (Figure 14–10).

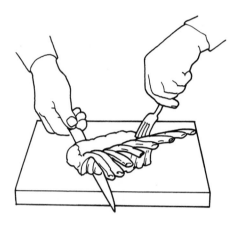

FIGURE 14–10

• • •

Transferring rack of lamb

Slice down between each rib bone separating the chops as carving proceeds. Continue until all ribs have been separated. Transfer to platter, have your assistant remove the carving board, arrange plates, and portion four chops on each plate (Figure 14–11).

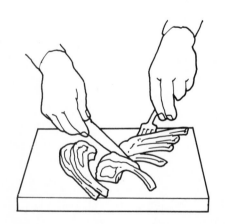

FIGURE 14–11

• • •

Slicing between each rib and arranging the platter

Boning Fish

Sole

Hold the sole steady using a fish fork or serving fork. Press and scrape away the outer edges of the fins using a fish knife, palette knife, or serving spoon (Figure 14–12). These fins are more like cartilage than hard bone.

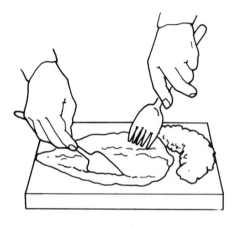

FIGURE 14–12

• • •

Cutting away the outer edges of the backbone

Now draw the knife or spoon down the center line of the fish from head to tail (Figure 14–13).

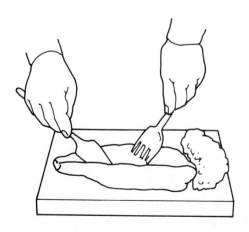

FIGURE 14–13

• • •

Cutting the center line

Place the fork into the slit just made to hold the fish steady. Gently push the top fillets away from the skeleton using the knife or spoon (Figure 14–14).

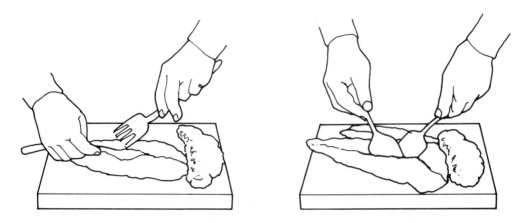

FIGURE 14–14

• • •

Gently separating the fillets

Wedge the backbone between the first two tines of the fork and lift it away from the bottom fillets while holding down the fillets with the spoon or knife (Figure 14–15).

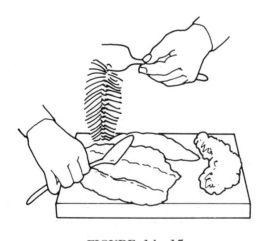

FIGURE 14–15

• • •

Removing the backbone

The sole is now ready to be plated (Figure 14–16).

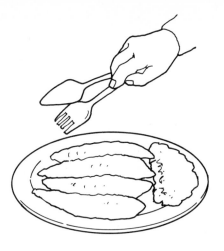

FIGURE 14–16
• • •
Plating the sole

Trout

Present platter to guest. Remove all the fins by pulling them away from the fish using a fish fork and fish knife or palette knife. Place fins to the outer edge of the platter (Figure 14–17).

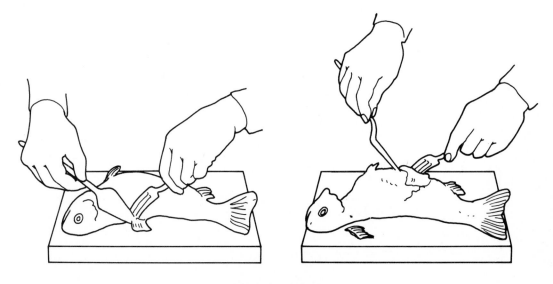

FIGURE 14–17
• • •
Cutting away the fins

Slide the knife under the skin and peel the skin away from the flesh with the help of the fork (Figure 14−18).

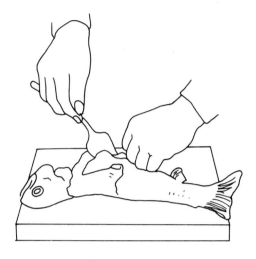

FIGURE 14−18

• • •

Gently separating the skin

Draw the knife along the center line from the head to the tail. Place the fork into the slit just made to hold the fish steady. Gently push the top fillets away from the skeleton using the knife (Figure 14−19).

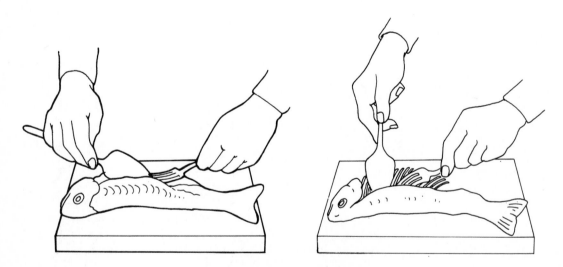

FIGURE 14−19

• • •

Gently separating the fillets

Insert the first two tines of the fork into the backbone just behind the head (Figure 14–20).

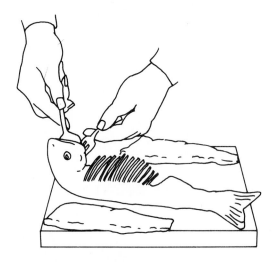

FIGURE 14–20
• • •
Locating the backbone

Lift the head with the fork while pushing the bottom fillets away from the skeleton with the knife (Figure 14–21).

FIGURE 14–21
• • •
Removing the backbone

Usually, the head and tail will remain attached, but it is not uncommon for the head to fall off during boning. Do not be concerned if it does—just remove it. Plate the trout fillets in an attractive manner (Figure 14–22).

FIGURE 14–22
• • •
Plating the trout fillets

Carving Fruit

Apple or Pear

When preparing an apple or pear tableside to be used in a hot dessert or simply served fresh and raw, it is customary to first peel the fruit. Place the fruit on its side and steady it using the curved side of a fork. Slice off the end with a small, sharp knife (Figure 14–23).

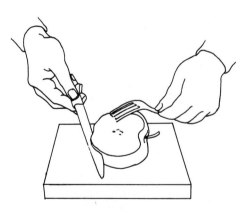

FIGURE 14–23
• • •
Slicing the end of the apple

Now place the cut end on the fork while bracing the end with the knife (Figure 14–24).

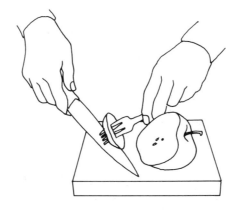

FIGURE 14–24
• • •
Placing cut end on fork

Insert the fork into the cut end of the apple and slice away the other end (Figure 14–25).

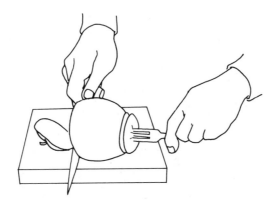

FIGURE 14–25
• • •
Slicing the other end of the apple

Now hold the fork up on one hand and peel the skin away while turning the apple (Figure 14–26). Be sure the fork is firmly inserted into the apple to avoid having it fall off the fork.

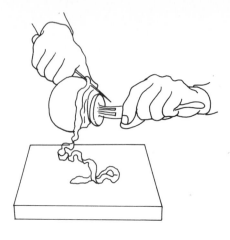

FIGURE 14–26
• • •
Peeling the skin away

Once peeled, remove the fork and lay the apple on one of the flat cut ends. Remove the core using a fruit corer (Figure 14–27).

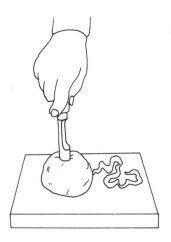

FIGURE 14–27
• • •
Removing the core

The fruit may now be sliced into rings or wedges as desired and served or used for a hot dessert such as Apples Normandy (Figure 14–28).

FIGURE 14−28
• • •
Slicing and plating the apple

Banana

Bananas may be carved on a china plate, silver platter, or carving board. Slice away the two ends far enough back to expose the flesh (Figure 14−29).

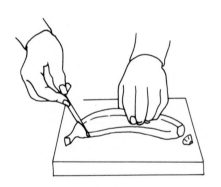

FIGURE 14−29
• • •
Slicing the ends

Now slice the banana in half lengthwise (Figure 14−30).

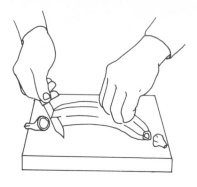

FIGURE 14–30

• • •

Slicing the banana in half lengthwise

With the two halves laying flat side down, remove the skin. This is done by piercing the skin with the first tine of a fork and peeling it away from the flesh (Figure 14–31).

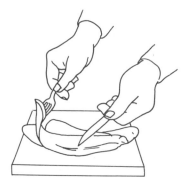

FIGURE 14–31

• • •

Peeling the banana

Use the knife to steady the banana as it is peeled.

Peach

Peeling a peach depends on the desire of the guest. Peach skin, although fuzzy, contains desirable flavors and many people like to eat it. If peeling is desired, the same procedure as for peeling an apple can be used. To carve, lay the peach on a plate or carving board and steady it with a fork. Slice wedges lengthwise and roll the peach as carving proceeds until all the flesh is removed from the stone. Be sure to slice down to the stone to ensure a clean separation of flesh from stone (Figure 14–32).

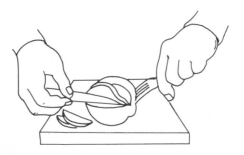

FIGURE 14–32

• • •

Separating the flesh from the stone

SALAD MAKING

• • • • •

Salad is a menu item that can be effectively merchandised in the dining room, resulting in greater guest satisfaction as well as higher check averages. The tableside preparation of salads and appropriate dressings allows the waiter to demonstrate an individual style and showmanship. Also, preparing salads tableside demonstrates to the guest the freshness and quality of the ingredients used.

Traditionally, wooden salad bowls, spoons, and forks are used for mixing. However, an exception can be made for glass salad bowls, because the merchandising effect is enhanced when a glass salad bowl is placed on a larger container filled with crushed ice and rotated while the salad and dressing are mixed.

Basic Ingredients for Dressing

Oils

The classic oil in salad dressing is olive oil of the first pressing. Other oils include corn oil, which is light and fresh tasting, and ground nut oil. The oil should be clean, clear, sparkling, and free from a strong odor.

Vinegar, Lemon, and Lime

The choice should usually be a wine vinegar or vinegar of fruit extracts; but excellent results may come from the use of lemon or lime juice.

Mustard

Mustard is a common ingredient in a wide range of dressings. French mustard should be the choice for vinaigrette-style dressings. By far the most commonly used mustard is a moutarde forte de Dijon. This is a strong yellow mustard by French standards, but if used with discretion, it normally gives the right degree of bite to a dressing or vinaigrette.

Herbs and Seasonings

Much can be done to vary the eye appeal and taste of the salad by addition of herbs and seasonings, either mixed within the dressing or added to the salad. Chopped chives, fennel, tarragon, shallots, chopped mint, and dill may be given a place in the dining room or guéridon mise en place. Horseradish, olives, grated cheese, tabasco, chili sauce, soy, and Worcestershire sauces may also be introduced into salad dressings. A selection of peppers, including white and black peppercorns in separate mills, can be offered. Cayenne and paprika are also important for salad preparation.

The chapon, a crust of bread rubbed with garlic, is not as widely used at the guéridon as it might be and certainly it imparts a delicious hint of garlic during dining room salad mixing. Garlic is a suitable item for using at the guéridon. Rubbing the mixing salad bowl with a clove of garlic is, in fact, an admirable way of imparting this flavor.

In blending dressings in the dining room, there is room for individuality, and there is certainly no reason why the dining room staff should not experiment, adapt, and blend, using personal imagination and flair.

Basic Green Salads

Chicory	Curly-leaved, slightly bitter.
Endive	A tight cluster, a tangy taste.
Dandelion greens	Wild and bitter.
Bib lettuce	Tender and nutlike.
Romaine	Stiff leaves, vigorous taste.
Escarole	Like chicory, but with broader leaves and a stronger flavor.
Watercress	Spicy green for accent.

Caesar Salad

Yield: 2 × 4-oz. servings

Ingredients:

Mise en Place by Chefs in the Kitchen:

Garlic, large clove	1	Peel
Salt	1 tsp.	
Anchovy, large	1	Drain
Dijon mustard	1 tsp.	
Olive oil	2 oz.	
Wine vinegar	½ tsp.	
Lemon juice, fresh	¼ lemon	Strain
Egg	1	Coddle
Pepper, black, freshly ground	4 turns	
Romaine	¼ head	Clean, dry, tear into bite-sized pieces
Croûtons	¼ cup	½-inch cut
Grated Parmesan cheese	1 tbsp.	

Method of Preparation:

Tableside Preparation by Chef de Rang:

1. Season the bowl with garlic clove, using salt as an abrasive.
2. Remove salt and garlic when the bowl is well seasoned.
3. Add anchovy and mash with a fork. Move the anchovy to one side of the bowl, and add mustard.
4. Blend oil into mustard, slowly and steadily.
5. Add wine vinegar, lemon juice, egg yolk (separate yolk and discard white), and pepper. Mix well.
6. Add romaine and roll lettuce. Roll all the above by rotating service spoon and fork from back to front of bowl until lettuce is fully coated.
7. Add croûtons and roll as in step 6.
8. Add cheese and roll. Serve immediately.

Variations:

A. Supplement with two dashes of Worcestershire sauce and one dash of tabasco sauce when adding lemon juice.
B. Supplement with two dashes of soy sauce when adding lemon juice.
C. Use dry mustard instead of Dijon. Blend oil and vinegar and emulsify. Then add dry mustard.
D. Raw egg yolk may be omitted due to the concern over salmonella poisoning.

Note:

When increasing Caesar salad to a larger amount, do not increase the amount of garlic, anchovies, and mustard proportionately; that is, if you double the recipe, use less than twice the amount of garlic, anchovies, and mustard.

Cold Spinach Salad

Yield: 2 4-oz. servings

Ingredients:

Mise en Place by Chefs in the Kitchen:

Garlic, large clove	1	Peel
Salt	1 tsp.	
Olive oil	3 tsp.	
Wine vinegar	1 tsp.	
Pepper, black, freshly ground	2 turns	
Spinach leaves, fresh	8 oz.	Clean, dry, tear into bite-sized pieces
Egg, hard-boiled	1	Chop fine
Mushrooms, large	2	¼-inch slices
Bacon	1 tbsp.	Fry, ½-inch pieces

Method of Preparation:

Tableside Preparation by Chef de Rang:

1. Season the bowl with garlic clove and use salt as an abrasive.
2. Remove garlic and most of salt. Leave some salt for seasoning.
3. Add oil and pour vinegar into it. Be sure to maintain 3:1 ratio.
4. Add pepper to finish seasoning of dressing.
5. Add spinach and roll greens from front to back, top to bottom, within bowl.
6. Add egg, mushrooms, and bacon; and roll (as performed in Caesar Salad).
7. Serve immediately.

Variations:

A. Supplement with lemon juice or Worcestershire sauce.
B. Supplement with white or brown sugar.
C. Supplement with honey.

Hot Spinach Salad

Yield: 2 4-oz. servings

Ingredients:

Mise en Place by Chefs in the Kitchen:

Bacon	3 tbsp.	1-inch cut
Sugar, granulated	2 tsp.	
Olive oil	1 tsp.	
Wine vinegar	1 tsp.	
Lemon juice, fresh	⅛ lemon	Strain
Salt	Dash	
Pepper, black freshly ground	2 turns	
Spinach leaves, fresh	8 oz.	Clean, dry, tear into bite-sized pieces

Method of Preparation:

Tableside Cooking by Chef de Rang:

1. In heated Suzette pan, add bacon.
2. When bacon is half-cooked, add sugar and invert (cook until liquified).
3. When bacon is fully cooked and sugar inverted, add oil, vinegar, lemon juice, salt, and pepper.
4. Mix well, and pour over spinach leaves.
5. Serve immediately.

Variations:

A. Supplement spinach with ripe olives, onions, cooked eggs, or sliced mushrooms, finely chopped or julienne.
B. Supplement with Worcestershire sauce or garlic.
C. Supplement with brandy, flambé, and pour flaming over spinach.
D. Substitute brown sugar for white.

Napkin FOLDING AND TABLE DRAPING FOR BUFFETS

NAPKIN FOLDING

· · · · ·

The napkin folds illustrated in Figures 15–1 through 15–16 are but a few of the many decorative presentations of napkins. The actual determination of which fold to use in a dining room is a matter of personal taste of the *owner* or chef de service. The less the napkin is folded, the better it is for the guest. The napkin will hold folds better if it is starched, but overstarched napkins are not comfortable for wiping mouth or hands. The material used for napkins should be absorbent.

1. Fold the napkin into four equal parts.

2. Fold A into center line as shown.

3. Now fold B to match A.

4. Fold the front corners of A and B diagonally.

5. Lift folds A and B and support on the turned back corners to create the wings. Place on table with points facing the diner.

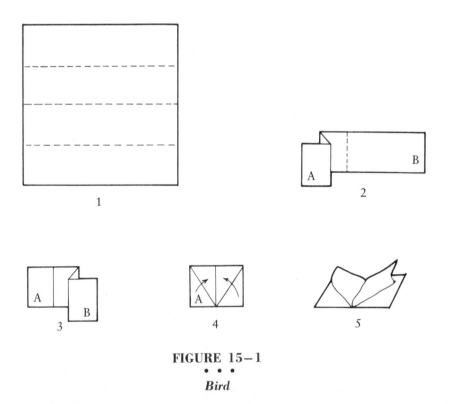

FIGURE 15–1

· · ·

Bird

1. Fold the napkin in half.
2. Fold corners A to B and C to D.
3. Fold top back at the dotted line.
4. Turning the points to the top, bring the left-hand corner around and tuck behind the front flap.
5. Napkin after step 4.
6. Turn the napkin around and repeat step 4.
7. Finished fold.

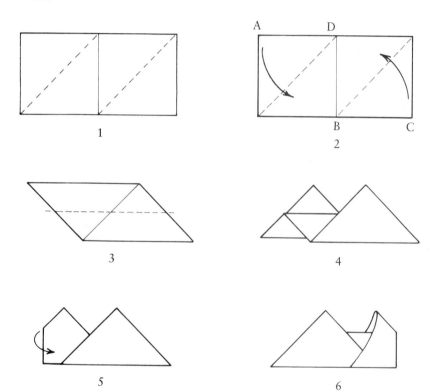

FIGURE 15-2

• • •

Bishop's hat

1. Lay the napkin flat and fold along dotted lines bringing points A to point B.
2. Fold A to B. This will give a W effect if viewed from the end of the napkin.
3. Pleat the napkin, making 2-inch pleats.
4. Hold the napkin at the bottom bringing points A and B together.
5. Open the pleats and pull down one side.
6. Turn the napkin around and repeat step 5.
7. Open the napkin into a fan shape and stand on the place setting.

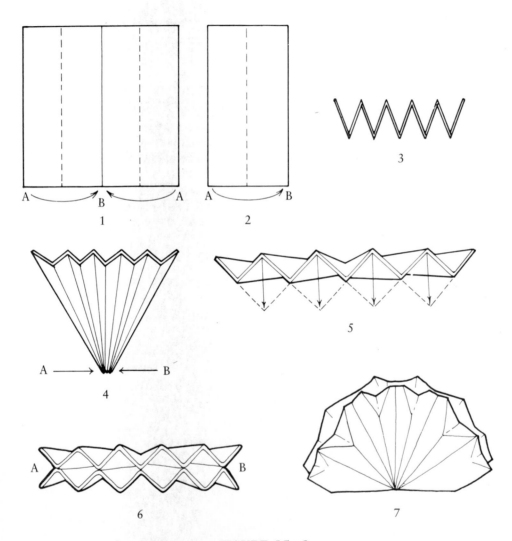

FIGURE 15—3

• • •

Chinese fan

1. Fold in fourths as indicated by dotted lines.
2. Fold diagonally.
3. Turn napkin so that points are away from you. Fold sides B along dotted line to meet at center A.
4. Turn the points of B under.
5. Fold along the center line A and stand the napkin with fold uppermost.
6. Pull up the four pleats and arrange to produce the finished fold.

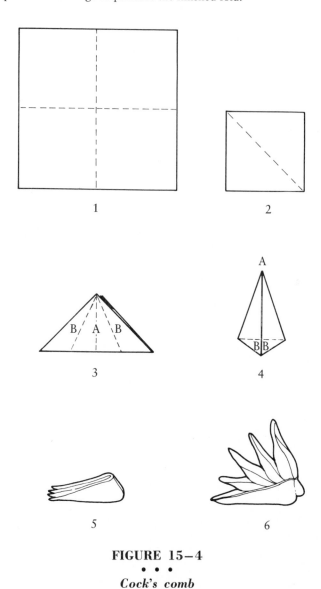

FIGURE 15—4

• • •

Cock's comb

1. Fold the napkin into thirds.
2. Fold corners A and B upward to center line.
3. Fold corner C to D and E to F.
4. Place fingers of left hand inside fold and turn down point GH at the dotted line to form a cuff.
5. Mold the napkin into a cone and set on the table with the points of the cuff facing the diner.

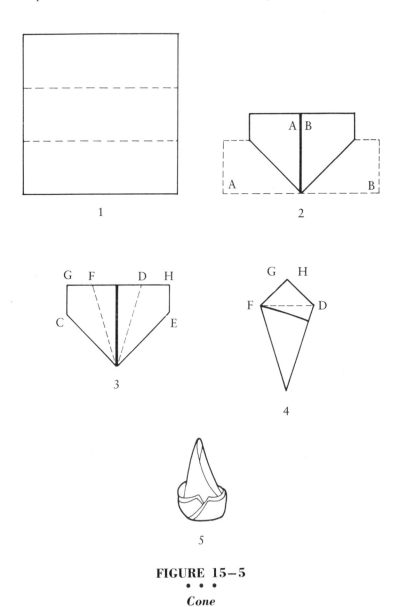

FIGURE 15–5
• • •
Cone

226

1. Fold the napkin into thirds as shown.
2. Fold at line B leaving about 6 inches at end A.
3. Pleat from C to B.
4. Fold in half as shown.
5. Fold triangle A over along the dotted line; this will form a support for the finished fold.
6. Open out the pleats and arrange as shown.

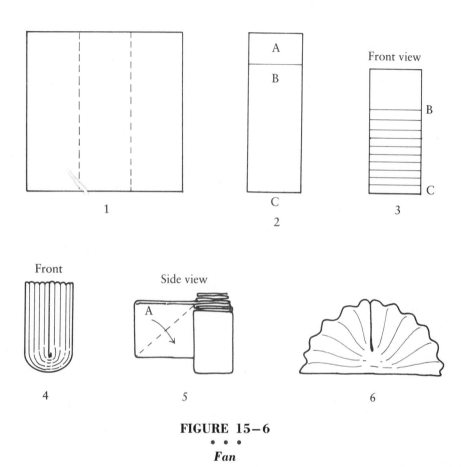

FIGURE 15−6
• • •
Fan

1. Fold the napkin in thirds along the dotted lines to form a rectangle. Turn the napkin so that the narrow side is toward you.

2. Fold ends A and B over 1/4 of napkin along the dotted lines.

3. Fold B over once more to center.

4. Turn edge A over so that it meets the edge of the top fold B.

5. Turn edge C under so that A is now the top. Position on plate.

Note: The name card or menu may be placed in between the steps of this fold.

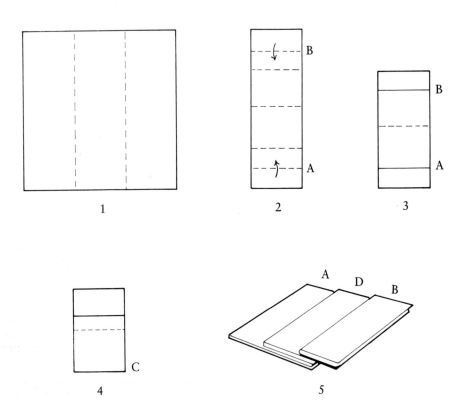

FIGURE 15–7

• • •

French pleat

1. Fold the napkin into thirds as shown.

2. Fold edges A to center line B.

3. Fold corners C to center line.

4. Napkin after step 3.

5. Take the napkin in both hands and turn it over with the points toward you and the plain side uppermost; roll to form a cone.

6. Tuck corner A into corner B.

7. Place on the table with the opening down and the points toward the diner.

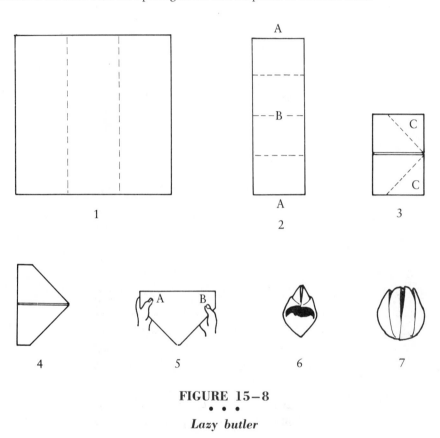

FIGURE 15–8

• • •

Lazy butler

1. Fold the napkin at the dotted line.
2. Fold corners A up at the dotted lines.
3. Fold B up at the dotted line.
4. Fold B down at the dotted line.
5. Napkin after step 4.
6. Turn the napkin so that side C to D is away from you. Fold corner C as shown. Fold corner D up at the dotted line and tuck into the pleat at C.
7. Stand the napkin on the table with point E up.
8. Pull down the pleats to produce the finished fold.

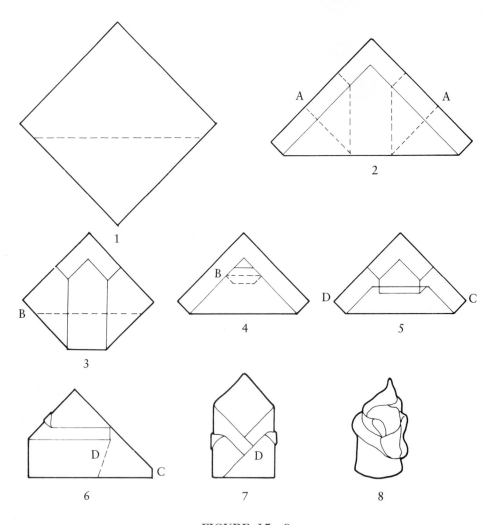

FIGURE 15–9

• • •

Lily

1. Lay napkin flat and fold along the dotted lines.
2. Turn through 45° and fold along the dotted lines.
3. Turn again and fold along the dotted lines.
4. Turn napkin over and fold along the dotted lines.
5. Napkin after step 4.
6. Place a tumbler over the points in the center.
7. Pull each of the 12 points gently away from underneath, taking opposing corners in turn.
8. Finished fold.

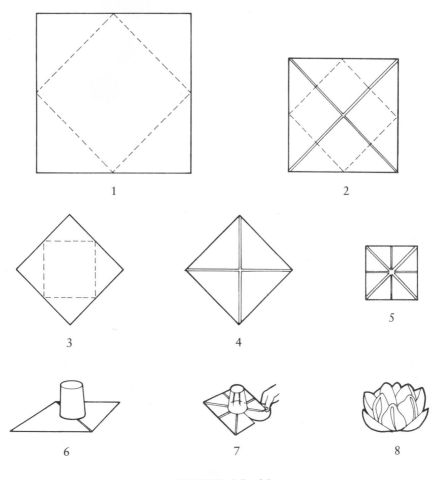

FIGURE 15−10

• • •

Lotus

231

1. Fold the napkin into thirds.

2. Fold at lines A to bring sides B to the center.

3. Napkin after step 2.

4. Turn the point to the right, folding along the center line.

5. Turn the napkin over and fold the portion BB up and away from you at the dotted line shown in previous diagram.

6. Fold CC in half toward you; this will make the heel.

7. Fold CC around and tuck into pleat D.

8. To finish this fold, insert the fingers between the folds and curl this part around the slipper.

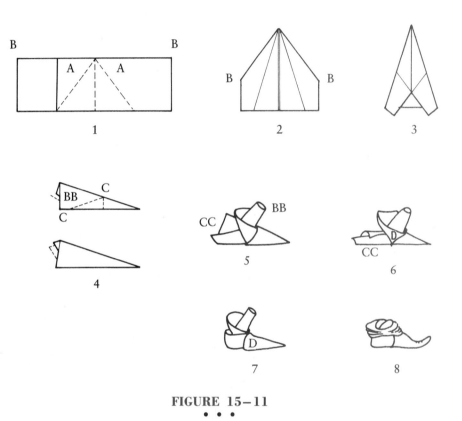

FIGURE 15–11

• • •

Pixie's slipper

1. Fold the napkin into four, ensuring that four loose edges are at A.
2. Fold down top flap as indicated.
3. Fold along dotted line.
4. Fold down second flap.
5. Fold second flap along dotted line.
6. Tuck second fold under first fold.
7. Fold napkin along dotted line, putting the fold underneath.
8. Fold napkin along dotted line.
9. Finished fold.

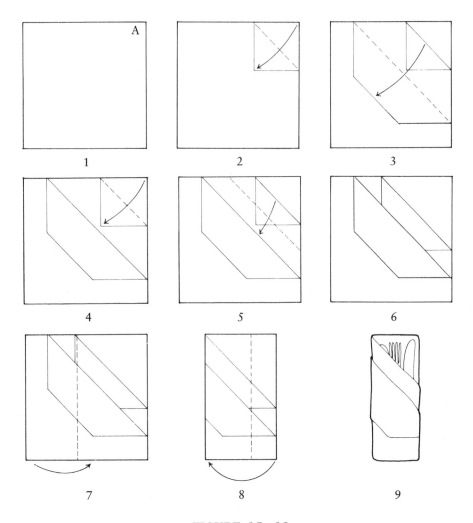

FIGURE 15–12
• • •
Pocket

1. Fold the napkin into fourths as shown.
2. Fold corners A and B along the dotted lines to center line C.
3. Turn the napkin over.
4. Roll corners A and B outward as shown.
5. Fold corners A and B to the top along the dotted lines.
6. Napkin after step 5.
7. Turn napkin over. Arrange on the table with the point toward the diner.

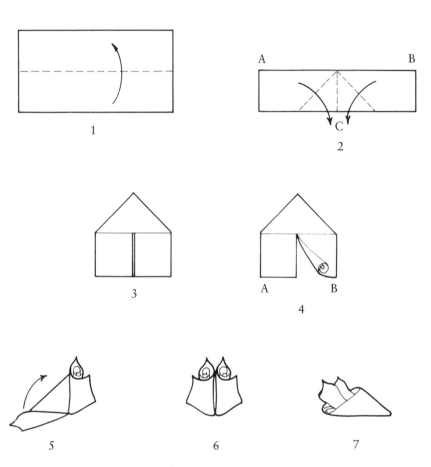

FIGURE 15–13
• • •
Rocket

1. Fold the napkin into thirds as shown.

2. Fold corners A diagonally to center line.

3. Fold back corners A.

4. Keeping the two sides flat on the table, press them toward the middle; this will make the center line stand up. Fold sections B under at the dotted line.

5. Open out the center fold and arrange on the table with the point away from the diner.

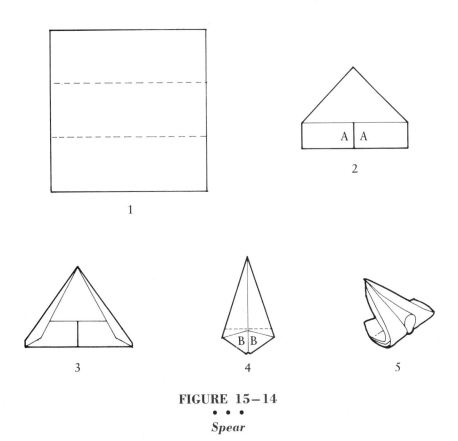

FIGURE 15—14

• • •

Spear

1. Fold the napkin into thirds along the dotted lines.

2. Lay both hands, palms up, on the napkin, taking corner A between the thumb and forefinger of the left hand and corner B with the right hand.

3. Turn the hands palm down, retaining hold of the corners.

4. Turn hands in toward body in a circular motion.

5. Complete the motion; this will trap hands.

6. Release hands and place the napkin into a glass or arrange it flat on showplate.

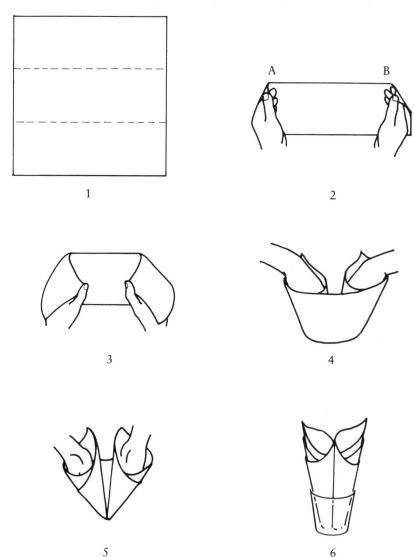

FIGURE 15—15

• • •

Twirl

1. Fold the napkin in half diagonally, then fold corners A to B.
2. Fold the two flaps marked A up to B.
3. Fold the two flaps marked A out to the dotted lines at B.
4. Fold A to B, ensuring that the fold falls along the bottom dotted line.
5. Fold bottom edge A along dotted line marked B, then tuck ends marked C around the back to make the napkin stand up.
6. Finished fold.

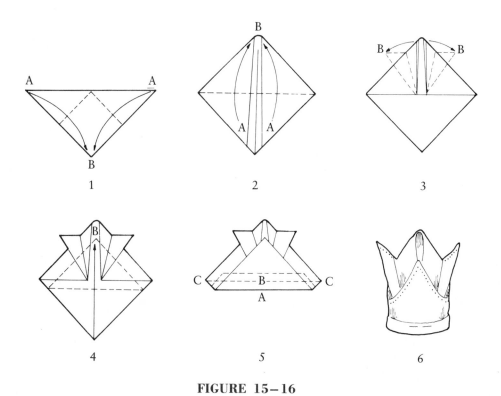

FIGURE 15–16

• • •

Viking hat

TABLE DRAPING FOR BUFFETS

· · · · ·

A properly draped table for a *buffet* adds a finished look to the dining room.

Straight Drape

After tables have been positioned, cover each with a silencer. Next, lay draping material over the *front* of the table, allowing it to hang down 1½–2 inches from the floor. Do not allow drape to touch floor, because it then becomes a safety hazard. Leave sufficient material to cover the side of the table. Pin or tape drape to silence cloth. Cover table with a cloth folded to the exact dimensions of the tabletop(s).

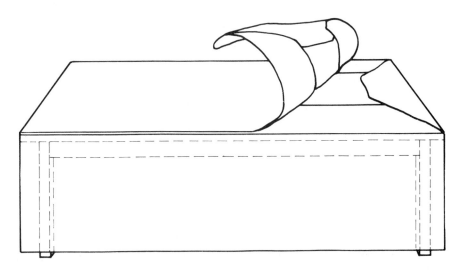

FIGURE 15–17

· · ·

Straight pleat

Pleated Drapes

If pleats are to be used, it is important to remember that three times the number of feet of material will be necessary to make pleats. Prepare the tables with silence cloths. Before pinning the draping cloth (recommended when pleating), make pleat by folding the material under, then measuring the desired pleat size. Repeat procedure until tables are draped. If using a closed pleat, always have pleats folded away from the guests' approach to the table. Always be sure to tuck enough material under the fold at the table to prevent the pleat from opening at the floor. When the table has been draped, finish covering top as in the directions for straight draping.

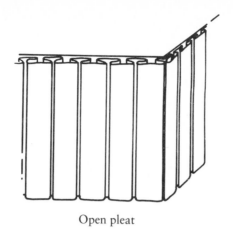

Open pleat

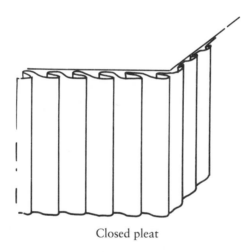

Closed pleat

FIGURE 15—18

• • •

Pleated drapes

C·H·A·P·T·E·R

16

DINING ROOM EQUIPMENT

THE FOOD TRAY (OVAL)

· · · · ·

A large oval food tray is used to allow servers to carry several dishes to the table at one time. It is usually lined with cork or rubber to prevent plate slippage and accidents.

General Guidelines for Handling a Tray

The server should handle the tray as follows:

- Place a service towel on the tray to help absorb spills, retard slippage, and keep the tray's surface clean. Soiled towels should be replaced as needed.
- Balance the contents of the tray evenly when serving or clearing before lifting.
- Avoid placing tall or top-heavy items at front, back, or outer edges to prevent their toppling and injuring guests. When possible, lay these items on their sides either at the center of the tray or inside, close to the server's shoulder.
- Stack like items on each other when completely cleared of food scraps.
- Remove cups from saucers, underliners from plates, and flatware from china to prevent slippage. Stack and place utensils flat in center of trays, between stacked china, or on shoulder side.
- Set the tray stand close to the table when serving, server facing guest, and farther away when clearing, server between guest and tray.
- Carry even an empty tray above shoulder level at all times.
- Signal a server in front of you by saying "Behind you" to prevent collisions.

Improper Tray Handling

The following practices may be dangerous to guests and servers or detract from the guests' dining experience. Do not:

- Leave unsightly soiled trays in the dining room for extended periods. If this cannot be avoided, cover stacked china and food refuse with a service towel.
- Combine soiled objects and food scraps on the tray when serving the next course of fresh food. Dispose of dirty items beforehand.
- Overload the tray or attempt to carry too much.
- Stack plates on other plates still containing food scraps or flatware. Scrape off scraps onto one plate and stack beneath.
- Stack odd-shaped items, such as oval plates, on round items, or vice versa.

Tray Stands

Tray stands have collapsible leg frames connected by two cloth or fiber support straps to hold the legs rigid when set up. Frames can be heavy plastic, wood, or metal. Some include a low-level shelf that can be used as a small side stand. When not in use, stands should be collapsed and placed out of busy traffic lanes to prevent accidents.

- Carry the stand in the folded (collapsed) position, at the server's side, while walking in the dining room.
- Extend right arm, which holds the stand, and flick wrist so that the support legs separate, bringing the stand to an upright position (legs should be parallel to the server's body position, support straps perpendicular).
- Turn to the right, bend the knee, and lower the tray to a perfectly horizontal position until it sits on the support frame. The server then pushes the level tray across the support straps onto the center of stand.
- When lifting the tray from the stand, the server reverses the procedure, standing with the left hip by the support straps.
- Bend the knee and place the left hand under the tray while supporting it with the right hand.
- Collapse the tray stand against the hip and remove it to an out-of-the-way area.
- Carry the tray on the palm or fingertips, depending on its weight.

Beverage Tray

- Carry the beverage tray at waist level in the left hand.
- Balance glassware evenly.
- Keep the tray away from the table when serving, in case of spills.
- Keep the tray surface clean and dry at all times.

COFFEE MACHINE
· · · · ·

At the beginning of the day or shift:

- Turn on the coffee machine ahead of the time it will be needed.
- Turn on hot plates. Set adjustable plate to the high position, enabling water to boil for tea service.

At the end of the day or shift:

- Shut off and/or unplug the machine.
- Remove the water spray fixture; clean and replace it.
- Remove the grounds basket; clean and replace it.

Glass and stainless steel coffee pots should be cleaned at the end of each shift. Use a commercial cleaner and brush, or a mixture of vinegar or lemon juice, salt, and ice cubes, which help to act as an abrasive. Pots should be kept fresh smelling, without any burnt coffee stains and odors. Remember: Never leave empty glass pots on hot plates.

ICE MACHINE SAFETY
· · · · ·

- Always use metal or plastic scoops, *never use glasses* (always ice your glass, never glass your ice).
- Do not leave scoops in the ice, as they will become buried as new ice cubes are produced. Always set scoop on top of machine or in provided holders.
- Never bury items to be chilled inside of the machine. If not readily visible, they can be broken by someone who unknowingly comes to get ice and hits the item with the scoop. Also, this practice violates health and safety codes.
- If glass is broken anywhere near an ice bin or machine, the machine must be emptied, wiped clean, and refilled. Never assume that all broken glass has been retrieved. Any remaining fragments might end up in someone's food or beverage, with serious injury or even death resulting. Make sure this doesn't happen by completely cleaning ice bin areas and machines.
- Always treat ice as food! Keep ice supply covered when not being used.

SODA MACHINE
· · · · ·

Each tank is connected to two plastic lines. One permits CO_2 gas to enter the tank, while the other allows the soda syrup mixture to pass to the dispensing unit.

A soda tank is completely empty when no syrup (color) is visible in the plastic line. In this case, only soda water will be dispensed. The tank will obviously weigh considerably less than it did when completely full.

When soda is dispensed and no bubbles appear, it is apparent that the line has gone flat and that the CO_2 tank is empty. This can be verified by checking the pressure gauge located on the tank housing. The indicator needle will be in the RED area on the gauge and the tank will feel very light.

Changing the Soda Tank

Remove each line by pressing down on each housing unit of each terminal. Pull up on metal collars and remove. To replace the tank, position each housing unit over the proper post. The post for the CO_2 line will be marked In on the soda tank. Press housing over the position. Pull up on the collar and push unit into place. Release the collar, which should now be secure on the post. Repeat for the syrup line.

Each CO_2 tank comes with a built-in wrench that allows for easy removal of the connector housing. First, turn off the gas. Then, unscrew the housing nut with the wrench. Position the new tank and screw in the housing nut, making sure that the nut is very tightly secured. Turn on the gas. The indicator needle should then jump to the full position. In some units, a rubber gasket is needed to prevent gas leakage. Make sure that the gasket is placed inside the housing unit before securing it to the gas tank.

BREAD WARMER

· · · · ·

The bread warmer should be turned on ahead of time (approximately 1 hour) so that it will be ready when needed. For soft breads, place a small cup containing a water-soaked sponge or napkin in each warmer drawer, as this will keep rolls moist and prevent them from becoming dry and hard. This is not necessary for hard, crusty breads.

At the end of each shift:

- Turn off the warmer.
- Remove water cups.
- Remove the drawer and empty it of any remaining product, then wipe it clean. Stale bread may be sent to the kitchen for use as crumbs.
- Replace the drawer.

TOASTER

· · · · ·

Some toasters use a timer-setting method to ensure proper toasting. Others use a rotisserie cycle span.

To clean the toaster:

- Shut off the toaster.
- Remove grills and crumb catch pans from unit.
- Clean crumbs and burnt product from each.
- Replace in toaster.

VARIOUS TYPES OF TABLEWARE

· · · · ·

Pottery

The term *pottery* properly applies to clay products of primitive people or decorated art products made of unrefined clays and by unsophisticated methods. As a generic name, pottery includes all fired clayware. As a specific name, pottery describes low-fired porous clayware, which is generally colored.

Ceramic products acquire strength through the application of heat. Along with the heat, the chemical composition of the materials used determines the strength, porosity, and vitrification of the fired product. Primitive pottery, often baked in the sun and composed of one or more unrefined clays, had little strength and was quite porous.

Earthenware

Earthenware is a porous type of ceramic product that, fired at comparatively low temperatures, produces an opaque body not as strong as stoneware or china and lacking the resonance of those products when struck. The product may be glazed or unglazed.

Stoneware

Stoneware is a nonporous ceramic product made of unprocessed clays, or clay and flux additives, fired at elevated temperatures. It is quite durable but lacks the translucence and whiteness of china. It is resistant to chipping and rings clearly when struck. It differs from porcelain in that it produces colors other than white. These result from the iron or other impurities in the clay.

Ironstoneware

Ironstoneware is the historic term for durable English stoneware. The composition and properties of this product are similar to porcelain except that the body is not translucent and is off-white. In more recent times, this term has been used to describe a number of other products.

Cookingware

Cookingware is a broad term applied to earthenware, stoneware, porcelain, and china designed for cooking or baking as well as serving. It has a smooth, glazed surface and is strong and resistant to thermal shock.

Fine China

Fine china is a term applied to a thin, translucent, vitrified product, generally fired at a relatively high temperature twice: first, to mature the purest of flint, clay, and flux materials; and second, to develop the high gloss of the beautiful glaze. It is the highest-quality tableware made for domestic or retail trade.

Porcelain

Porcelain is a term used frequently in Europe for china. European porcelain, like china, is fired twice. In this country, porcelain may be fired in a one- or two-fire process. Porcelain has a hard, nonabsorbent, strong body that is white and translucent. European porcelain is made primarily for the retail market.

Bone China

Bone china is a specific type of fine china manufactured primarily in England. The body contains a high proportion of bone ash to produce greater translucency, whiteness, and strength. Like fine china, it is made primarily for the retail trade.

Restaurant China

Restaurant china is a uniquely American blend of fine china and porcelain, designed and engineered specifically for use in commercial operations. The body was developed in the United States to give it great impact strength and durability, as well as extremely low absorption, which is required of china used in public eating places. Decorations are applied between the body and the glaze, thereby protecting the decoration during commercial use. Most of this tableware is subject to a high temperature during its first firing and a lower temperature during its second. However, some restaurant china is fired in a one-fire operation during which the body and glaze mature at the same time. Like fine china, American restaurant china is vitrified.

GLASSWARE
· · · · ·

Many styles of glassware exist today in the foodservice industry. Restaurateurs are faced with numerous patterns and varying levels of cost and quality. Each operator will select the glassware that best suits the particular needs of the operation. The glassware available to foodservice operators falls into two general categories: heat treated and lead crystal.

Heat Treated

Most glassware used in the foodservice industry is of the heat-treated type. The process involves heating the glass and then cooling it rapidly. This mild form of tempering gives strength to the glass, adding resistance to chipping and breakage. Heat-treated glassware is recommended for production-oriented restaurants where fast service is desired.

Lead Crystal

Often called 24 percent lead crystal, crystal is glassware that has lead oxide added during the formation of the glass. This creates a very hard glass and adds brilliance and clarity. Crystal rings like a tuning fork when struck with the finger, thus giving it an elegant feature.

Unfortunately, crystal chips easily and is not conducive to fast-service restaurants where excessive handling takes place. Most crystal glassware is found in fine dining establishments where the emphasis is on a formal, relaxed atmosphere rather than volume service.

For further descriptions of dining room equipment identification, see Appendix C.

MIXOLOGY

Mixology is the study of drink mixes. Those who study mixology—mixologists or bartenders—are required to master hundreds of beverage recipes. A bartender's career offers excellent opportunities to meet people while working in many types of establishments. Most bartenders work in restaurants and bars; however, there are job openings in hotels, private clubs, resorts, and cruise ship lines.

Although the atmosphere, decor, attitude, and policies may vary from house to house, basic procedures that the bartender should follow remain constant. This chapter will introduce a wide range of those procedures, as well as appropriate behavior for a bartender and drink recipes.

WHAT MAKES A GOOD MIXOLOGIST?
· · · · ·

First and foremost, a good bartender must have a genuine love for people and bartending that naturally results in keeping the best interests of the house and its guests in mind. Like the host or hostess of a party, he or she sets the tone of the evening and standards of decorum. A bartender must be adept at making guests feel at ease and seeing to their requests, while being alert to the many situations that can develop and handling them with the utmost *diplomacy*.

On the technical side, a good bartender must keep abreast of the changing tastes in beverages and be meticulous in preparing and presenting the mixes. Drinks must always be consistent, neither too strong nor too weak, and be made with only the best ingredients in the right proportions. This combination of technical expertise, warm hospitality, and good judgment makes a professional bartender the ultimate ambassador of charm and goodwill. A good bartender should:

1. Have obvious traits such as honesty, neatness, reliability, a sense of humor, speed, and accuracy.
2. Not smoke, eat, or drink behind the bar. These habits are not sanitary and may be prohibited by state and local law.
3. Be in control of any situation without the customer being aware of it.
4. Have pride in the knowledge and ability necessary to perform the job and in the service provided.
5. Be friendly and courteous, making guests feel welcome without being intrusive or overly chummy.
6. Be personable, which will usually produce a happy guest; a happy guest is the goal of every establishment.
7. Be efficient and even tempered in order to handle a full bar and drink orders from wait staff at the same time.
8. Be knowledgeable about current events and sports, around which most bar conversations revolve.
9. Have the responsibility that goes along with serving alcohol.
10. Generate and maintain guests in keeping with the values and image of the organization.

11. Be able to recall regulars' drinks, even if you don't remember their names. It makes individuals feel good if you remember their preferences; knowing their names as well makes them feel even better.

To sum it all up, a professional bartender should have:

1. Good hygiene.
2. Positive professional attitudes.
3. Mixology expertise.
4. Systematic (organized) techniques.
5. Knowledge of current events.

A good bartender must know the laws of alcohol service. House policy will guide you. Follow the laws to ensure responsible service.

RULES FOR A MIXOLOGIST
· · · · ·

1. Cultivate a good memory for faces and preferences of your regular customers. Greet them cordially.
2. Handle complaints with courtesy. If the customer complains about the drink, either fix it or mix another to maintain inventory control. Any other complaints or criticism should be referred to management. Always be cheerful; such behavior results in a good reputation.
3. After serving customers, step back or move away. Never give the appearance that you are listening to conversation. Do not join in unless asked!
4. Never hurry customers or be impatient if they are slow drinkers.
5. Be cooperative and pleasant with fellow employees. Customers can sense and detect tension.
6. Answer the telephone quietly. Never state that a particular person is present. Ask "Who is calling?" first, tell the caller you will check to see if that person is available, then let the customer decide whether or not to answer the call.
7. Keep ashtrays emptied and the bar dry and clean.
8. Use a fresh napkin with each drink.
9. Always use a fresh glass unless otherwise requested by the customer.
10. Use the appropriate glass and garnish.
11. Pick glasses up by the stem or base only, never by the rim or with fingers in the glass.
12. Never fill a glass to more than ¼ inch from rim.
13. When in doubt, use a measure for drinks. A little too much added to each drink is not much, but it adds up by the end of the day.
14. When pouring more than one drink of the same kind, fill the glasses ½ full, then come back and keep filling so that each glass is even. Never fill one glass at a time. Trying to even up already full glasses can be costly.

15. Use cubed ice or large pieces of ice. Fine ice melts too rapidly and dilutes the drink too fast.
16. Follow standard recipes or house recipes, but take into account the customer's tastes and preferences. Following recipes too rigidly may drive customers away, being too lax will increase bar costs.
17. Shake drinks in shaker rapidly. Too long a shake will dilute the drink.
18. Always place the glass on the bar/rail so that the customer can see what you are doing. Then proceed to use the shaker or mixer glass.
19. When finished with bottles, put them back in the proper place. This saves time.
20. Always ring drinks on the guest check and lay it face down in front of customer. Always fill in or write the order on the check.

BAR-OPENING PROCEDURE
· · · · ·

1. Open the bar on time. All mise en place should be complete and the bar fully stocked and ready.
2. Check cash register by first clearing it. Count bank cash and record. Count and check bar guest checks.
3. Place clean ashtrays on the bar with books of matches.
4. Fill three-compartment sink: (1) wash, (2) rinse, and (3) sanitize. Wash any glasses and leave on the drain board (see Figure 17–1).
5. Check the beer cooler and restock it according to need. Restock liquor issued for the day.
6. Check fruit garnish, fruit juice, cream, and other bar supplies. Wash containers and refill.
7. Prepare garnishes—sufficient for one shift. More can be prepared later for late shift.
8. Wash and polish the bar counter, wash sinks and ice bins, and wipe necks of bottles on the back bar.
9. Visit the restroom for self-inspection of uniform, hair, and so on. Keep the register key with you.

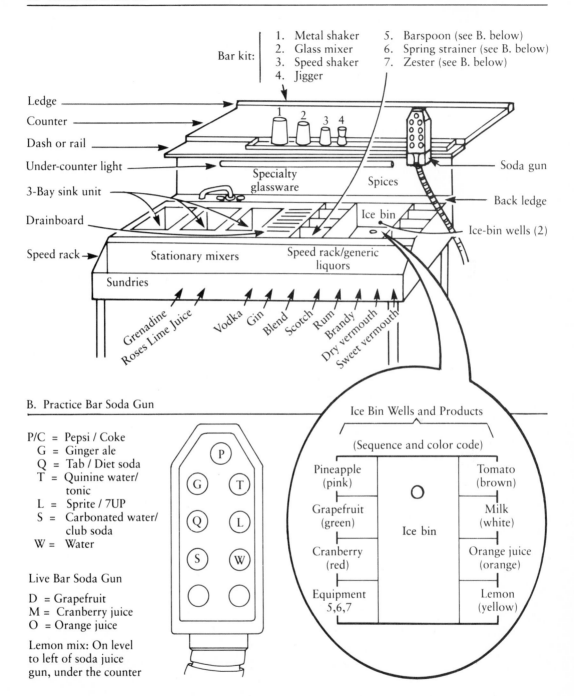

Bar kit:
1. Metal shaker
2. Glass mixer
3. Speed shaker
4. Jigger
5. Barspoon (see B. below)
6. Spring strainer (see B. below)
7. Zester (see B. below)

Ledge
Counter
Dash or rail
Under-counter light
3-Bay sink unit
Drainboard
Speed rack

Specialty glassware
Spices
Soda gun
Back ledge
Ice bin
Ice-bin wells (2)

Stationary mixers
Speed rack/generic liquors
Sundries

Grenadine
Roses Lime Juice
Vodka
Gin
Blend
Scotch
Rum
Brandy
Dry vermouth
Sweet vermouth

B. Practice Bar Soda Gun

P/C = Pepsi / Coke
 G = Ginger ale
 Q = Tab / Diet soda
 T = Quinine water/ tonic
 L = Sprite / 7UP
 S = Carbonated water/ club soda
 W = Water

Live Bar Soda Gun

D = Grapefruit
M = Cranberry juice
O = Orange juice

Lemon mix: On level to left of soda juice gun, under the counter

Ice Bin Wells and Products

(Sequence and color code)

Pineapple (pink)
Grapefruit (green)
Cranberry (red)
Equipment 5,6,7

Ice bin

Tomato (brown)
Milk (white)
Orange juice (orange)
Lemon (yellow)

FIGURE 17–1

• • •

Standard bar unit and setup

253

METHOD OF HANDWASHING GLASSES

• • • • •

1. *Wash* in first compartment with warm water at 110–120° F, using washing compound, brush, and *elbow grease.* Washing compound does not sanitize glasses.
2. *Rinse* glasses in second compartment by immersion in clean, warm water. Washing compound is rinsed off. Change the rinse water frequently. Do not rinse glasses in dirty water.
3. *Sanitize* glasses in third compartment by use of hot water or a chemical sanitizer. Making use of a long-handled wire basket, rinse glasses in clean hot water at a temperature of at least 170° F for no less than one-half minute. Auxiliary heat is necessary. An alternate method is to use a chemical sanitizing solution for at least one minute (see next section).
4. *Drain and air dry.* Do not towel—toweling recontaminates glasses. Store glasses, inverted, in a clean, dry place.

Using Chemicals

The sanitizing solution must contain one of the following:

1. At least 50 ppm of available chlorine at a temperature of not less than 75° F.
2. At least 200 ppm of a quaternary ammonium compound.
3. At least 12.5 ppm of available iodine in a solution with a pH not higher than 5.0 and a temperature not less than 75° F.

A suitable field test kit must be available that will effectively measure the chemical concentration at any time. These test kits should be made available by the distributor of the sanitizers or otherwise obtained from some other source.

BAR-CLOSING PROCEDURE

• • • • •

1. Wipe and clean speed rack well; wipe bottles and replace.
2. Wash and dry empty glass shelves to receive clean glasses.
3. Wash glassware—one type at a time—and replace on the shelf (wash cream drink glasses last).
4. Rinse and wash sinks, then dry to prevent rust or scale.
5. Wash and polish drainboard and other parts of sink.
6. Clean out ice bin, then wipe dry.
7. Sweep floor and remove garbage container.
8. Collect all used glassware and place on counter above sink area. Wash hands.
9. Wrap or cover all fruit garnish with lids or plastic wrap and refrigerate for next day.

10. Top all fruit juice containers, wash empties, and store.
11. Fill in day's requisition for liquor, beer, and so on.
12. Stock coolers for the next shift.
13. Count guest checks and check against issue register. Note the checks not used.
14. Close out cash register according to house policy. Return cash to the designated area or person.
15. Check security and lock up.

Note: Never sit at the bar when off duty. It is a bad habit and encourages familiarity with customers. It also gives employees a bad name and is unprofessional.

BACK BAR SETUP
· · · · ·

Row	Sequence
1	Proprietary brand distilled spirits in sequence of products: Scotches, Canadians, imported whites and Americans.
2	Generic liqueurs and flavored brandies—alphabetical A–T.
3	Rums, proprietary brand liqueurs—alphabetical and seldom used brands.

First Row
Chivas Regal
J&B
Dewars
Canadian Club
Seagram's VO
Seagram's 7
Smirnoff
Stolichnaya or Absolut
Beefeater
Tanqueray
Tequila
Old Grand Dad
Jack Daniels

Second Row
Crème de Almond or
Crème de Noyaux
Apricot-flavored brandy
Crème de Banana
Blue Curaçao
Dark Crème de Cacao
Light Crème de Cacao
Coffee-flavored brandy
White Crème de Menthe
Green Crème de Menthe
Orange Curaçao
Peachtree schnapps
Peppermint schnapps
Triple Sec

Third Row
Bacardi Light Rum
Mount Gay Gold Rum
Myers's Dark Rum
Amaretto di Saronno
Campari
Cognac
Cointreau
Drambuie
Frangelico
Galliano[1]
Kahlua
Midori
Peter Heering
Sambuca Romana
Southern Comfort

---
[1]Galliano bottle is to the left of the steps or shelf.

COCKTAILS AND MIXED DRINKS

• • • • •

Definition of a Cocktail

A cocktail is a fairly short drink made by mixing liquor and/or wine with fruit juices, eggs, and/or bitters, by either stirring or shaking in a bar glass (glass mixer). A mixed drink is liquor with a mixer, usually served in a tall glass over ice.

The object of a cocktail is to mix two or more ingredients so the result is a pleasant, palatable drink. Unless requested by the customer, no single ingredient should overshadow the rest. An unbalanced mixture produces an unsatisfying drink. Because cocktails are always mixed with ice, their strength varies with the length of time they remain in contact with the ice, which dilutes the liquor as it melts. Melting ice adds ½–¾ or more liquid to a cocktail if it is shaken for 10 seconds and proportionately more if shaken longer.

Differences between cocktails and mixed drinks include:

1. Glassware
   a. Cocktails—stem glass.
   b. Mixed drinks—base glass.
2. Procedure
   a. Cocktails—stirred or shaken.
   b. Mixed drinks—ice down-pour or speed shake.
3. Presentation
   a. Cocktails—up.
   b. Mixed drinks—tall with ice.

Note: The cocktails and mixed drinks presented in the following pages are only a sampling of a vast array of concoctions in mixology.

The following are definitions of procedures used in mixing or building cocktails or mixed drinks.

Cocktails served up

Stir   To gently agitate with ice; to chill and blend by stirring gently.

Shake   To violently agitate with ice; to disperse or incorporate heavy ingredients.

Mixed drinks and cocktails requested on the rocks

Ice down-pour   Ice, liquor, and mixer in service glass. Serve as is.

Speed shake   To agitate with ice; to disperse or incorporate heavier ingredients in service glass with ice.

These procedures are explained in greater detail later in this section.

Terms Used at the Bar

Float   Last ingredient added to a drink after usual procedure. Floats find their own space. *Do not incorporate.*

Hold/no garbage   No garnish.

Jigger   A legal measure of 1½ ounces.

Light   Short count on liquor. Same amount of mixer.

On the rocks	Served on ice, usually in RXS glass.	
Shot of	A measure of liquid, usually served straight up or neat. Volume determined by the house.	
Straight up or neat	Served without ice; never comes in contact with ice.	
Tall/long	Drink is served in 8–10-oz. glass, instead of 4–8-oz. RXS glass. Increase mixer, not liquor.	
Up	Prepared with ice to chill. Served without ice in a stem glass.	

Bases for Alcoholic Beverages

1. Vermouth.
2. Sours and Rose's lime juice.
3. Cream.
4. Polynesian or tropical.
5. Carbonated and juice-based highball.
6. Cordials.
7. Wines and punches.
8. Specialties: Frozen ice cream and spirited caffeines.

Note: The base ingredient or mixer never changes. Liquor changes according to the name of the drink.

Cocktails

	Procedure		Glass	
Category and Name of Drink	Served Up	Served on the Rocks	Served Up	Served on the Rocks
Vermouth Base				
Martini	Stir	Ice down-pour	Cocktail	Rocks
Manhattan	Stir	Ice down-pour	Cocktail	Rocks
Rob Roy	Stir	Ice down-pour	Cocktail	Rocks
Negroni	Stir	Ice down-pour	Cocktail	Rocks
Gibson	Stir	Ice down-pour	Cocktail	Rocks
Short Sours				
All sours	Shake	Speed shake	Sour cocktail	Rocks
Bacardi Cocktail	Shake	Speed shake	Sour cocktail	Rocks
Between the Sheets	Shake	Speed shake	Sour cocktail	Rocks
Side Car	Shake	Speed shake	Sour cocktail	Rocks
Daiquiri	Shake	Speed shake	Sour cocktail	Rocks

Category and Name of Drink	Procedure		Glass	
	Served Up	Served on the Rocks	Served Up	Served on the Rocks
Margarita	Shake	Speed shake	Champagne coupe cocktail	Rocks
Jack Rose Cocktail	Shake	Speed shake	Champagne coupe cocktail	Rocks
Kamakazi	Shake	Speed shake	Champagne soupe cocktail	Rocks
Gimlet	Shake	Speed shake	Champagne coupe cocktail	Rocks
Short Cream Base				
Brandy Alexander	Shake	Speed shake	Champagne coupe cocktail	Rocks
Grasshopper	Shake	Speed shake	Champagne coupe cocktail	Rocks
Golden Dream	Shake	Speed shake	Champagne coupe cocktail	Rocks
Pink Squirrel	Shake	Speed shake	Champagne coupe cocktail	Rocks

Mixed Drinks

	Procedure	Glass
Long Cream Base		
Orgasm	Speed shake	Highball
Toasted Almond Bar	Speed shake	Highball
Girl Scout Cookie	Speed shake	Highball
White Russian	Speed shake	Highball
Long Sours		
(Tom) Collins	Speed shake	Collins
Ward 8	Speed shake	Collins
Sloe Gin Fizz	Speed shake	Collins
Singapore Sling	Speed shake	Sling/Zombie
Long Island Ice Tea	Speed shake	Sling/Zombie
Tropical-Polynesian		
Mai Tai	Speed shake	Collins
Planter's Punch	Speed shake	Collins

	Procedure	Glass
Zombie	Speed shake	Sling/Zombie
Pina Colada	Speed shake	Sling/Zombie
Highball		
Soda Highball	Ice down-pour	Highball
Juice Highball*	Ice down-pour	Highball
All Cordials	Ice down-pour	Rocks

*Exception to the rule for juice bases speed shake juice-base highballs that have a liqueur with a juice mixer.

Cocktails

The cocktail is an American institution, and there are many versions of the name's origin. One version dates back to 1779 in a tavern near Yorktown, New York, owned by Betsy Flanagan. Betsy's Tavern was a meeting place for the American and French officers of Washington's Army, who drank a concoction called a bracer. Betsy arranged for the patrons of her tavern to have a chicken feast. After the feast, they moved to the bar to continue the celebration with bracers. To their amusement, they found each bottle of bracer decorated with a cock's tail. A toast was called for, and one of the Frenchmen exclaimed: "Vive le cock tail."

The primitive cocktail of the Manhattan pioneers consisted of cocks' tails, dipped in a concoction of pimientos, which tickled the throat to necessitate drinking. The French origin of the word *cocktail* is called *coquetel,* which dates back to the 18th century in Bordeaux.

The cocktail party is a phenomenon of the 20th century and is used for entertaining small or large gatherings. There are a great many cocktails that have been in vogue from time to time, but certain mixtures have stood the test of time and continue to win the approval of connoisseurs.

Stir Procedure—Vermouth Base

There is no standard recipe for Martinis on which all bartenders agree. Tastes change with time. The Martini has always been the most popular cocktail. It is a dry, sharp, appetite-whetting drink. Through the years the cocktail has become progressively drier. By the time it was referred to as a Martini, it had become a mixture of equal parts of gin and dry vermouth. Before World War I, the standard recipe was two parts gin to one part dry vermouth. For 20 years after repeal, the standard recipe was four to one. Today's recipe has returned to two parts gin, one part dry vermouth.

The Manhattan was named after Manhattan, New York. To cut the harshness of bootleg liquor, syrups and aromatic flavorings were used. The original Manhattan was made with bitters, sugar, and much more vermouth than we use today, in addition to whiskey or Bourbon. The basic recipe for a Manhattan is sweet vermouth and whiskey. If dry vermouth is used, then it becomes a Dry Manhattan. If both sweet and dry vermouth are used, it becomes a Perfect Manhattan.

A Rob Roy is a Scotch Manhattan. Scotch is used in place of the whiskey or Bourbon. The name Rob Roy comes from Scotland. One can make the same variations for a Rob Roy as for a regular Manhattan.

All vermouth-based cocktails are served up in a *cocktail glass*. The *stir* procedure is used, unless the customer requests the cocktail *on the rocks*. Then the procedure is *ice down-pour* and the drink is served *in a rock's glass*.

Martinis

Martini		*Extra Dry Martini*	
1½ oz.	Gin	2¼ oz.	Gin
¾ oz.	Dry vermouth	¼ oz.	Dry vermouth
	Olive or zest		Olive or zest
Dry Martini		*Smokey Martini or Silver Bullet*	
2 oz.	Gin	1½ oz.	Gin
½ oz.	Dry vermouth	¼ oz.	Dry vermouth
	Olive or zest	½ oz.	Scotch (float)
			Olive or zest
Vodka Martini		*Gibson*	
1½ oz.	Vodka	1½ oz.	Gin or vodka
¾ oz.	Dry vermouth	¾ oz.	Dry vermouth
	Olive or zest		Cocktail onions

Manhattans

Manhattan		*Southern Comfort or Deluxe Manhattan*	
1½ oz.	Bourbon or blend	1½ oz.	Southern Comfort
¾ oz.	Sweet vermouth	¾ oz.	Dry vermouth
	Cherry		Cherry or zest
Perfect Manhattan		*Dry Manhattan*	
1½ oz.	Bourbon or blend	1½ oz.	Bourbon or blend
¾ oz.	Dry vermouth and sweet vermouth combined	¾ oz.	Dry vermouth
	Zest or cherry		Zest

- A Martini is garnished with either a cocktail olive or lemon zest.
- A Manhattan or a Rob Roy uses a Maraschino cherry. When using dry vermouth rather than sweet, a lemon zest is used. When both sweet and dry are used, the garnish is optional—cherry or lemon zest.
- Negroni uses lemon zest due to the addition of Campari, which is an Italian apéritif.
- Gibson uses cocktail onions as its garnish, without them, it is a Martini.

Mechanics for Procedures

Stir   To stir is to gently agitate with ice; to chill and blend by stirring gently.

1. Chill stemmed glass by filling it with ice. Set aside. (Optional.)
2. Fill a mixing glass ¼ full with ice.
3. Pour base first, then liquor, into mixing glass.
4. Hold mixing glass with fingers closed at base and stir. Hold the barspoon by helix and roll it back and fourth between thumb and index finger for about 3 to 4 seconds. Gently remove barspoon.
5. Remove ice from chilled glass.
6. Using spring strainer over mouth of mixing glass, strain ingredients into glass.
7. Garnish.

Ice down-pour   Ice down-pour means that ice, liquor, and mixer are combined in the service glass. Serve as is; do not blend.

1. Fill a rocks glass with ice.
2. Pour liquor first, then base.
3. Garnish.
4. Add stirrer or sip-stix. (Customer will stir drink.)

The following recipes utilize the stir and ice down-pour procedures in their preparation.

Rob Roys

Rob Roy		*Dry Rob Roy*	
1½ oz.	Scotch	1½ oz.	Scotch
¾	Sweet vermouth	¾ oz.	Dry vermouth
	Cherry		Zest
Perfect Rob Roy			
1½ oz.	Scotch		
¾ oz.	Dry vermouth and sweet vermouth combined		
	Cherry or zest		

Negroni		Negronis	
1 oz.	Gin	¾ oz.	Gin
1 oz.	Sweet vermouth	¾ oz.	Sweet vermouth
1 oz.	Campari	¾ oz.	Campari
	Zest		RXS glass, ice down-pour
			Splash of club soda and zest (1 dash bitters, optional)

Shake Procedure—Sours and Rose's Lime Juice Base

Sours can be classified as short sours and long sours. Short sours are composed of liquor and/or liqueur with commercially prepared lemon mix or lime juice. Long sours have the same ingredients with the addition of a carbonated soda to cut the sour taste. Also, long sours are garnished with a cherry and an orange slice and served in a tall glass.

The Barcardi Cocktail was invented by the Barcardi Rum Company in 1936. The company filed suit in the Supreme Court of New York because a hotel was using another rum in its Bacardi Cocktails. It won the case and to this day it is still a legal misrepresentation to use a rum other than Bacardi rum in a Barcardi Cocktail.

The Daiquiri was named after the copper mines near Santiago, Cuba. An American engineer who was entertaining some visiting VIPs decided to treat them to a refreshing drink that he had concocted. He used fresh limes (that were growing by his house), added some sugar, and for the final zest, the local rum. The drink made such an impression on a guest that they later requested the drink they had by the daiquiri mines.

The Collins originated in England. It was named after a serviceperson, John Collin, who worked at the Limmer's Hotel.

The Singapore Sling was introduced in the early 1900s in Singapore.

All short sours are served up in a cocktail or sour glass. The only short sours that are garnished are sour-type cocktails, whiskey sour, Stone sour, and so on. The garnish is a cherry. The shake procedure is used, unless the customer requests the cocktail on the rocks. Then the procedure is speed shake in a rock's glass.

Mechanics for Procedures

Shaker   To shake is to agitate violently with ice; to disperse or incorporate heavier ingredients.

1. Fill a mixing glass ⅓ full with ice.
2. Add liquor and/or liqueur(s).
3. Add mixer and/or base ingredient(s).
4. Place metal cup or base over top of mixing glass (making sure metal cup is sitting on evenly, not at an angle).
5. Give top (bottom of metal shaker) a slight tap to create a vacuum.

6. Pick whole unit off the bar and flip it over, so that metal is to the floor and glass is to your shoulder.
7. In a quick, even movement, move unit back and forth in rapid succession.
8. At end of shake, position unit so that the metal shaker is still on the bottom. Hold unit in left hand, down low near base. Keep hands away from frost line area.
9. Look at metal cup for frost line. The next step is to look at the top of the mixing glass for the side of glass that is straight and not at an angle. Total unit should be to your right hand.
10. With the left hand holding the unit for balance, hold the right hand at an angle and hit the side of metal shaker at the frost line to break the vacuum.
11. Pull the mixing glass off and strain.
12. Garnish if required.

Speed shake Speed shake means to agitate with ice; to disperse or incorporate heavier ingredients in service glass with ice.

1. Fill a service glass with ice.
2. Add liquor and/or liqueur(s).
3. Add mixer and/or base ingredient(s).
4. Place speed shaker over the top of the glass.
5. Lift unit off rail or dash and invert the glass into speed shaker and shake.
    Note: When inverting glass, do not allow glass to shift, or an air pocket will form.
6. Pull the glass from the metal and transfer liquids back to the glass. (Do not pull the metal from the glass, as the foam will run down the sides.)
7. Add garnish and decoration if required.

The following recipes utilize the shake or speed shake procedures in their preparation.

Lemon mix and lime juice-based short sours

Whiskey Sour			*Daiquiri*	
1½ oz.	Whiskey		1½ oz.	Light rum
2 oz.	Lemon mix		2 oz.	Lemon mix
	Cherry			
Glass:	Sour			
Bacardi Cocktail			*Margarita*	
1½ oz.	Bacardi light rum		Rim Champagne coupe with salt. Set aside.	
2 oz.	Lemon mix			
½ oz.	Grenadine		1½ oz.	Tequila
			1 oz.	Lemon mix
			¾ oz.	Triple Sec
			Blend or shake	

Between the Sheets			**Jack Rose Cocktail**	
B - ½ oz.	Brandy		1½ oz.	Applejack
L - 1½ oz.	Lemon mix		½ oz.	Grenadine
T - ½ oz.	Triple Sec		1½ oz.	Lemon mix
Rye - ½ oz.	Rum			

Side Car			**Stone Sour**	
1 oz.	Brandy		1½ oz.	Apricot brandy
½ oz.	Triple Sec		1 oz.	Orange juice
1½ oz.	Lemon mix		1 oz.	Lemon mix
				Cherry
			Glass:	Sour

Kamakazi			**Gimlet**	
1½ oz.	Gin or vodka		1½ oz.	Gin or vodka
¼ oz.	Rose's lime juice		¾ oz.	Rose's lime juice
½ oz.	Triple Sec			Lime wedge (optional)
	Lime wedge (optional)			

Note: To rim or frost a glass, moisten the rim of the glass with a piece of citrus fruit, then dip in a dish of salt or sugar.

Long sours

Tom Collins

1½ oz.	Gin
2 oz.	Lemon mix

Speed shake—Collins

Fill with club soda and 7UP

Cherry and orange

Singapore Sling

1½ oz.	Gin
2 oz.	Lemon mix

Speed shake—Sling/Zombie

Fill with club soda and 7UP

½ oz. float—Cherry-flavored brandy or liqueur

Cherry and orange

Variations of Tom Collins

John Collins—made with whiskey

Joe Collins—made with Scotch

Ivan Collins—made with vodka

Variations of Singapore Sling

A fruit-flavored sling can be named from the flavoring; for example, Strawberry Sling. The float would be strawberry liqueur instead of cherry-flavored brandy or liqueur.

Sloe Gin Fizz		*Ward 8*	
1½ oz.	Sloe Gin	1½ oz.	Whiskey
2 oz.	Lemon mix	2 oz.	Lemon mix
Speed shake—Collins		½ oz.	Grenadine
Fill with club soda		Speed shake—Collins	
	Cherry and orange		Cherry and orange

Long Island Ice Tea

½ oz.	Vodka
½ oz.	Gin
½ oz.	Rum
½ oz.	Tequila
½ oz.	Triple Sec
¾ oz.	Lemon mix
Speed shake—Sling/Zombie	
½ oz. Coke—Float	
	Lemon wheel

Cream and Ice Cream Base

Cream drinks are very sweet, smooth, and pleasing to the palate. They are perfect after-dinner drinks, and many people like to order them instead of dessert. Cream drinks are ideal because they do not have a strong alcoholic taste.

There are two ways to prepare cream drinks: mix in a blender or use the shake procedure. A blender will thoroughly mix the ingredients and give the drink a creamier, frothy texture.

All cream-based drinks may use ice cream instead of cream. Usually vanilla ice cream is used, but any flavor that will mix with the flavor of the liqueur may be used; for example, coffee, strawberry, peach, or chocolate. Sherbets may also be used; then the name of the drink changes to "freeze." For example:

Summer Rum Freeze

1½ oz.	Bacardi Rum
2 scoops	Lime sherbet
3 oz.	Pineapple juice
¾ oz.	Cream or milk

Place all ingredients in the blender. Blend until creamy. Pour into a tall goblet. Garnish with pine-apple spear or lime wheel.

Procedure for Ice Cream—Blended Drinks

1. Place all ingredients in the blender. (Do not add ice, unless crushed ice is available.)
2. Blend until thick and creamy.
3. Pour into a tall goblet or tall pilsner glass. Place on an underliner or napkin.
4. Garnish with whipped cream, shaved chocolate, cherry, candied almonds, and so on. Be creative with garnishes. Eye appeal is important for presentation.

Short cream drinks are served up in a champagne coupe. The only cream base that has a garnish is the Alexander, which requires a sprinkle of nutmeg to complete the drink. Without it, it is rather bland. If blenders are not available, use the shake procedure. Long cream drinks are served in a highball glass, speed shake procedure, no garnish.

Note: White Russians are traditionally served in a rock's glass, but have been served in highball glasses, depending on house rules or customer's preference. Traditionally, a White Russian was a layered drink. Half and half cream set on top of the Black Russian.

Cream-based cocktails: *Short creams*

Brandy Alexander		Golden Dream	
1 oz.	Brandy	1 oz.	Galliano
1 oz.	Dark Cacao	½ oz.	Cointreau
1 oz.	Cream or milk	½ oz.	Orange juice
	Nutmeg	½ oz.	Cream or milk
Grasshopper		Pink Squirrel	
1 oz.	Light Cacao	1 oz.	Light Cacao
1 oz.	Green Menthe	1 oz.	Crème de Nouyaux or Crème de Almond
1 oz.	Cream or milk	1 oz.	Cream or milk

Long creams

Orgasm		White Russian	
1 oz.	Amaretto	1½ oz.	Vodka
½ oz.	Vodka	½ oz.	Kahlua
½ oz.	Kahlua	½ oz.	Cream or milk
Fill with milk or cream to a ¼ inch rim			
Girl Scout Cookie		Toasted Almond Bar	
1 oz.	Peppermint schnapps	¾ oz.	Amaretto
½ oz.	Dark Cacao	¾ oz.	Kahlua
Fill with milk or cream to a ¼-inch rim		Fill with milk or cream to a ¼-inch rim	

Cordials—Two-Liquor Drinks

Two-liquor drinks grew in popularity in the 1970s. Their overall flavor is sweet. Two-liquor drinks usually have a distilled spirit or brandy with a liqueur added. There should be more distilled spirit or brandy in the drink than the liqueur. Too much of the liqueur will ruin the drink by making it too sweet.

All two-liquor drinks are served on the rocks, in a rock's glass with the ice down-pour procedure. The exception to the rule for the following drinks is the Mud Slide, which takes speed shake, or if the customer requests otherwise.

Black Russian		*Stinger*	
1½ oz.	Vodka	1½ oz.	Brandy
¾ oz.	Kahlua	¾ oz.	White Menthe
Godfather		*Godmother*	
1½ oz.	Scotch	1½ oz.	Vodka
¾ oz.	Amaretto	¾ oz.	Amaretto
Sicilian Kiss		*Rusty Nail or Queen Anne*	
1½ oz.	Southern Comfort	1½ oz.	Scotch
¾ oz.	Amaretto	¾ oz.	Drambuie
Mud Slide		*B 52*	
¾ oz.	Vodka	⅓ oz.	Kahlua
¾ oz.	Kahlua	⅓ oz.	Bailey's Irish Cream
¾ oz.	Bailey's Irish Cream	⅓ oz.	Grand Marnier
Speed shake		Layered in order	
After 5			
⅓ oz.	Kahlua		
⅓ oz.	Bailey's Irish Cream		
⅓ oz.	Peppermint schnapps		
Layered in order			

Mixed Drinks—Highballs

A mixed drink contains a liquor and/or liqueurs with nonalcoholic mixers.

The gin and tonic originated in India during the late 1800s. British troops were required to take a daily dose of a medicine called *quinine* to guard against malaria. To offset the heavy bitterness of quinine, sugar and water were added. It was not too long before the troops started to add their favorite liquor, gin, to the medicine to make it even more palatable.

One of the first mixed drinks, the highball, became well known in the mid-1800s. *Highball* was a railroad term. Railroad men put a ball on a high pole to signal fast, oncoming trains that the track was clear and there was no need to slow down. When the men had time enough to stop for a fast drink of whiskey and ginger ale, they referred to it as a highball.

The Screwdriver supposedly received its name from American oil workers in Iran who had the habit of mixing vodka with orange juice and stirring it with their screwdrivers.

The basic concept behind adding a mix to a liquor is to cut the alcoholic bite of the drink. Highballs are served in a highball glass, sometimes spelled *hi-ball*. For carbonated mixers, water, and juices, the procedure is ice down-pour; if a juice mixer is used with a liqueur, speed shake.

Today's highball drink is made of many different combinations of liquors and flavored sodas. Water is also a base for a highball. No matter what the combination, the basic recipe is as follows:

1½ oz.   Liquor
4 oz.   Soda   Or to customer preference

1. Pour liquor over ice cubes in a highball glass.
2. Top with any flavored soda.
3. No garnish is usually provided, except for Cuba Libre, gin and tonic, or vodka and tonic, which have a lime wedge for a garnish. Scotch drinks will usually have a lemon twist or zest for garnish. All others are served as is.

Sometimes just a type of liquor is requested, and sometimes a specific brand. Some of the most popular highballs are:

Whiskey and ginger ale	Highball.
White wine and club soda	Spritzer.
Red wine and ginger ale	Wine cooler.
Dry gin and tonic water	Gin and tonic.
Vodka and tonic water	Vodka and tonic.
Scotch and club soda	Scotch and soda.
Seagram's 7 Crown and 7UP	7 and 7.
Scotch and water	Highball.
Whiskey, ginger ale, and club soda	Presbyterian.

Note: Drinks may also be ordered on the rocks with a splash of mix according to customer preference.

The following recipes utilize the ice down-pour procedure in their preparation.

Highballs: Juice base

Comfortable Screw		*Harvey Wallbanger*	
1½ oz.	Southern Comfort	1½ oz.	Vodka
4 oz.	Orange juice	4 oz.	Orange juice
Speed shake		½ oz.	Galliano (float)
Boccie Ball		*Tequila Sunrise*	
1½ oz.	Amaretto di Saronno	1½ oz.	Tequila
4 oz.	Orange juice	4 oz.	Orange juice
Float club soda		½ oz.	Grenadine (float)
Speed shake			

Cape Codder

1½ oz.	Vodka
4 oz.	Cranberry juice

Salty Dog

	Rim with salt
1½ oz.	Vodka
4 oz.	Grapefruit juice

Pearl Harbor

1 oz.	Midori
½ oz.	Vodka
4 oz.	Pineapple juice

Speed shake

Basic Bloody Mary Mix

1½ oz.	Liquor
4 oz.	Tomato juice
Dash	Salt and pepper
Dash	Lea & Perrins
Dash	Tabasco
Dash	Lemon mix
1 tsp.	Horseradish (optional)

Speed shake—goblet

	Celery stalk or lime wedge

Variations of Bloody Mary

Bloody Mary is made with vodka.

Bloody Maria is made with tequila.

Virgin Mary is a nonalcoholic Bloody Mary.

Red Snapper is a Bloody Mary mix with gin, also called a Bloody Jane.

Woo-Woo

1½ oz.	Peachtree schnapps
½ oz.	Vodka
	Cranberry juice to a ¼-inch rim

Speed shake

Madras

1½ oz.	Vodka
2 oz.	Cranberry juice
2 oz.	Orange juice

Sea Breeze

1½ oz.	Vodka
2 oz.	Grapefruit juice
2 oz.	Cranberry juice

Tootsie Roll

1½ oz.	Dark Cacao
4 oz.	Orange juice

Speed shake

Scarlet O'Hara

1½ oz.	Southern Comfort
4 oz.	Cranberry juice

Speed shake

Bloody Caesar

Rimmed goblet with salt and pepper

1½ oz.	Vodka
4 oz.	Clamato juice

Speed shake

Fuzzy Navel

1½ oz.	Peachtree schnapps
Speed shake	Orange juice to a ¼-inch rim

Alabama Slammer

½ oz.	Sloe Gin
½ oz.	Banana liqueur
	Orange juice to a ¼-inch rim
½ oz.	Southern Comfort (float)

"S" on the Beach

½ oz.	Peachtree schnapps
1 oz.	Vodka
2 oz.	Cranberry juice
2 oz.	Orange juice

Equal amounts to a ¼-inch rim

Speed shake

Watermelon

1 oz.	Southern Comfort
1 oz.	Crème de Nouyaux or Crème de Almond
	Pineapple juice to a ¼-inch rim

Polynesian-Tropical

Collins: Mai Tai and Planter's Punch

Sling: Pina Colada and Zombie

For all these drinks, garnish with two out of the three: Cherry, orange, or pineapple chunk. Use blender or speed shake procedure.

Mai Tai

S	½ oz.	Sugar or simple syrup
C	½ oz.	Orange Curaçao
R	1 oz.	Myers's rum (dark)
R	1 oz.	Mt. Gay rum (gold)
O	½ oz.	Crème de Nouyaux or Crème de Almond
L	1 oz.	Lemon mix

Pina Colada

C	1 oz.	Coco Lopez
P	3 oz.	Pineapple juice
R	2 oz.	Golden rum (Mt. Gay)

Planter's Punch

G	½ oz.	Grenadine
L	1 oz.	Lemon mix
O	1 oz.	Orange juice
M	1½ oz.	Myers's rum (dark)
S	½ oz.	Sugar or simple syrup

Zombie

G	½ oz.	Grenadine
2R	1 oz. {	Light rum (bar)
	1 oz. {	Myers's rum (dark)
L	2 oz.	Lemon mix
O	1½ oz.	Orange juice
C	1 oz.	Orange Curaçao

C·H·A·P·T·E·R

18

FEDERAL CONTROLS FOR ALCOHOLIC BEVERAGES

Liquor restrictions in the United States date back to colonial days. Regulations regarding liquor were mainly for revenue and later for the encouragement of sobriety.

HISTORY OF CONTROLS
· · · · ·

1. The Bureau of Alcohol, Tobacco and Firearms (BATF) was established in 1972. The original Federal Controls were organized in 1733 by the governor of Georgia, who prohibited the importation of hard liquors into the colony.
2. Both for revenue and as a deterrent, a tax was levied on the selling of distilled liquors in 1790. This led to the Whiskey Rebellion, an uprising that was put down by federal troops in 1794 in Pennsylvania.
3. In 1816, the first prohibitory law was the selling of liquor on Sundays.
4. By the end of 1833, more than 5,000 organized temperance groups totaled more than 1 million people.
5. In 1838, Massachusetts limited the amount of liquor one person could buy at one time. It was felt that drinking was a problem and should be controlled or stopped.
6. In 1846, Maine passed the first prohibition law.
7. On January 16, 1920, the National Prohibition Amendment (18th) became law. Prohibition cost the government about $1 billion per year, including loss in federal, state, county, and municipal revenues. Estimates are that Americans spent a total of $36 billion for bootleg and smuggled liquor during prohibition.
8. On December 5, 1933, the 21st Amendment was passed repealing prohibition, and the way was cleared for new controls. A system of federal regulation concerning trade practices and requiring permits was set up.

The Bureau of Alcohol, Tobacco and Firearms enforces the codes and laws established by the legislative and executive branches of the U.S. government. Distilled spirits in the possession of a retail dealer must be in bottles or similar containers that bear internal revenue tax stamps. A portion of the strip stamp must be kept affixed to each opened bottle. The penalty for unstamped liquors is a fine of not more than $10,000, imprisonment for not more than five years, or both.

The BATF exercises control over three broad areas:

1. Public protection.
2. Trade practices.
3. Revenue collection.

Retail dealers must obtain a federal tax stamp (F.T.S.) to determine the type of alcoholic beverage they may sell.

PROOF GALLON TAXES (DOMESTIC AND IMPORTED)

· · · · ·

All alcoholic beverages produced in the United States, as well as all imported beverages are subject to customs duties and internal revenue taxes. The tax rate is determined by the alcoholic content of the beverage. Each degree of proof is equal to ½ percent alcohol; therefore, a spirit of 90 proof contains 45 percent alcohol, 1 gallon proof contains 75 percent alcohol, and 1 gallon at 150 proof would equal 1.5 proof gallons. The trade term for a spirit of more than 100 proof is an *overproof* spirit.

A tax gallon is the gallonage on which duties and revenue taxes are paid. When the duties are determined, the tax gallons are equivalent to proof gallons at 100 proof or higher. If the spirits are less than 100 proof, the tax gallons are the actual wine gallons as measured quantitatively.

CUSTOMS DUTIES AND INTERNAL REVENUE TAXES

· · · · ·

Alcohol	Tax
Wine per Gallon	
0–14%	$ 1.07
14–21%	1.57
21–24%	3.15
Sparkling	3.40
Carbonated	3.30
Beer per 31 Gallons	
	$18.00
Distilled Spirits per Gallon	
	$13.50

The duties on imported alcoholic beverages are in addition to federal and state excise taxes that are also charged for alcoholic beverages. To determine the total tax on an imported beverage, add the federal tax, then add the state tax, and finally add the import duty. There may also be local sales taxes.

STATE CONTROL

· · · · ·

In addition to the federal government's control of the industry, individual states exercise a secondary control. Laws vary from state to state, but cannot conflict with federal laws and must meet all federal regulations. State regulations may be stricter than federal.

State control of the sale of alcoholic beverages falls into three types.

1. Open-license states, where private business makes both on-premise and off-premise sales of alcoholic beverages to all types of consumers. The operations vary in each state because of different taxes imposed on alcoholic beverages, and each state has different fees imposed on wholesalers and retailers. Furthermore, each state and/or municipality may have different hours for opening and closing, and different provisions with respect to the number of licenses permitted.
2. Control (monopoly) states control the sale of all alcoholic beverages distributed in their territories.
3. Control (monopoly) states only control the sale of distilled spirits and certain kinds of wines. Beer and some wines are sold by private businesses.

In the open-license states, trade is conducted as in other competitive businesses. Open states collect revenues from excise and sales taxes. In the control states, however, keep in mind that they themselves are in the liquor business and their function is also to make money. As a result, these states stock only those brands they believe will have the most sales, thereby limiting consumer choice.

DRAM SHOP LAWS
· · · · ·

Aside from federal and state liquor laws, there is a dram shop law that originated in 1873. Dram shop is also known as third-party liability.

In states that have dram shop, the innocent third party injured "in person, property, means of support or otherwise" by a drunken individual or minor can sue a restaurant, tavern, or liquor store owner and/or employees for having dispensed and sold the alcohol. Dram Shop applies to the sale of beer, wine, hard cider, or distilled beverages.

In states where dram shop liability is not imposed through alcohol beverage control (ABC) regulations, the courts apply common law, based on third-party liability case precedents. In those states, courts normally favor the victim over the seller, server, or employer on the grounds that state ABC laws were violated by dispensing liquor to an obviously inebriated patron or minor.

The remaining states provide neither means for recovering damages, choosing instead to follow the old common law rule: Only the drinker, not the seller or server, can be held responsible for his or her actions. Dram shop is the most critical issue affecting the nation's restaurants and bars since the repeal of prohibition.

Blood alcohol content (BAC), minimum drinking age, and first offense penalties under dram shop or common law vary from state to state. The basic rationale behind dram shop and common laws is that they will help deter drunk driving, thus decreasing the number of alcohol-related accidents, which claim thousands of lives each year.

ALCOHOL AND THE BODY

. . . . .

Alcohol is a food product that is classified as an intoxicating drug that depresses the brain and central nervous system. Alcohol contains what is described as "empty calories." One ounce of pure alcohol (100 percent) has 210 calories; 1 ounce of whiskey (43 percent alcohol—86 proof) has 75 calories; and a 12-ounce bottle of beer has 150 calories. These empty calories contain no vitamins, minerals, or other essential substances. Alcohol interferes with the body's ability to use other sources of energy.

Digestion

Alcohol requires no digestion and is absorbed through the bloodstream and transported to all parts of the body in a very short period of time. A small amount is immediately taken into the bloodstream by way of the capillaries in the mouth. The remaining portions travel to the stomach, where 20 percent is absorbed through the stomach lining. The amount of food in the stomach is an important factor when drinking. It will mix with the alcohol and slow down the absorption of the remaining 80 percent of alcohol as the stomach completes its digestion of the food.

The pylorus valve (the door between the stomach wall and small intestine) remains closed as long as there is food to be digested, and is sensitive to the presence of alcohol. When a person overindulges, the large concentration of alcohol tends to get "stuck" in the stomach because the pylorus valve remains in the closed position. When this pylorospasm happens, the alcohol trapped in the stomach may cause sufficient irritation and distress to cause a person to stop drinking (it's a self-protective mechanism that helps prevent overconsumption of alcohol). In the stomach, alcohol acts as an irritant. It causes the stomach lining to secrete excess amounts of hydrochloric acid, a digestive juice. A warm feeling is created in the stomach due to the irritation.

Absorption

Once in the small intestines, alcohol is absorbed into the bloodstream and passed into the body's transportation system. Alcohol is soluble in water and is able to pass through cell walls.

The percentage of alcohol, as well as the presence of carbonation, are important factors in the rate of absorption. The higher the percentage of alcohol, the quicker it is absorbed into the bloodstream. Beer has some food substances that will slow down the absorption rate. The rate of absorption into the bloodstream determines the level of intoxication. The faster the alcohol is absorbed, the more rapidly the blood alcohol level rises and the greater the impairment.

Absorption rate factors are:

1. Rate of consumption.
2. Height and weight.
3. Food in the stomach.
4. The amount of water in the body.
5. Medication (speeds up the effects of alcohol).

6. Strength of alcoholic beverage—the higher the percentage of alcohol, the faster it enters the bloodstream.

7. Type of alcoholic beverage. In order of speed in entering the bloodstream: carbonated drinks, straight distilled spirits, cream- or juice-based drinks, wine, beer (carbohydrates in wine and beer slow down absorption).

Blood Alcohol Concentration

The blood alcohol concentration represents the alcohol content of any body tissues composed of water. The alcohol content varies in proportion to the amount of water. It takes very little time for the tissues to absorb the alcohol circulating in the blood. Within two minutes, brain tissue reflects accurately the blood alcohol level. The higher the concentration of alcohol (up to 43 percent or 86 proof), the faster it is absorbed. Impairment is based on both the amount absorbed and the rate of absorption.

Alcohol will affect the brain and central nervous system more rapidly than other organs in the body. The concentration of alcohol causes the effect of intoxication and/or impairment. The table in the next section shows the rate at which alcohol will accumulate in the bloodstream, and common effects of alcohol on a 150–160 pound male. One drink equals 1 ounce distilled spirits, 3 ounces of Sherry, 5 ounces of wine, or 12 ounces of beer.

INTOXICATION
· · · · ·

Stage	Drinks per Hour	Blood Alcohol Content(BAC)	Rate to Metabolize and Effects Caused
1. Happy	1	0.02	Less than 1 hour; talkative, relaxed, some loss of judgment.
2. Excited	2½	0.05	2½ hours; loud, boisterous, fewer inhibitions, poor judgment.
3. Confused	5	0.10	5 hours; judgment impaired, slurred speech, staggering, mood swings, and double vision.
4. In a stupor	10	0.20	10 hours; after 6 hours, still legally drunk. Emotional, erratic behavior, unable to stand, loss of memory, barely conscious, and approaching paralysis.
5. Coma	1 to 1¼ pints	0.40–0.50	In a coma and dangerously close to death; brain centers are anesthetized.
		0.60–0.70	Death occurs.

· · ·
Five stages of intoxication

Different Effects on Men and Women

An average 120-pound female will get intoxicated faster than an average man of similar body weight due to a higher proportion of fat and correspondingly lower amounts of water in her body. Alcohol is not fat soluble. A female and a male at the same body weight, both drinking the same amounts of alcohol, will have different blood alcohol levels. Hers will be higher due to less water in her body to dilute the alcohol.

The difference in weight and body fat will speed up the absorption rate in most women so that blood alcohol content will be:

Drinks per Hour	Blood Alcohol Content (BAC)
1	0.03
2	0.07
3	0.14
1 pint	0.45; she would be in a coma.

Breakdown and Removal of Alcohol

The removal of alcohol from the body begins as soon as the alcohol is absorbed by the bloodstream. Ten percent of the alcohol is excreted through the breath, sweat, and urine. The rest has to be changed chemically by metabolizing. The alcohol has to metabolize and change to acetaldehyde. Very rapidly the acetaldehyde breaks down to form acetic acid. It then leaves the liver and is dispersed throughout the body, where it is oxidized to carbon dioxide and water; 90 percent is metabolized and excreted by the liver.

The liver is the key organ in the breakdown process. The rate alcohol is metabolized by the liver may vary a little between individuals.

Effects on Health

Although moderate drinking causes no direct harm, continued heavy drinking can result in permanent damage to the:

Digestive system.
Circulatory system.
Central nervous system.
Brain.
Liver.
Kidneys.

Heavy drinking can also lead to malnutrition, ulcers, and gastritis.

BEHAVIOR CUES

· · · · ·

In order to identify at which level of intoxication an individual may be, the person's *behavioral cues* are used:

1. Inhibitions: talkative, relaxed, overfriendly, and mood swings. People with lowered inhibitions fit into the happy to excited stage of intoxication, depending on how extreme their actions are.

2. Judgment: erratic behavior, foul language, anger, and impulsive acts. People who fit this description are most likely in the excited stage and approaching the confused stage. Again, it depends on how extreme their actions are.

3. Reaction: loss of train of thought, eyes unfocused, speech slurred, and hands unsteady. People at this point have reached the confused stage.

4. Coordination: loss of balance, drowsiness, lack of dexterity and/or coordination. People in this state are in the fourth stage of intoxication, stupor.

CHAPTER

19

SPIRITS

DISTILLATION

· · · · ·

Distillation was one of the first processes used to separate one liquid from another. This method is simply the application of heat to a liquid, causing evaporation. Since different liquids evaporate at different temperatures, the mixture is heated only to a temperature where one liquid will evaporate and the balance will remain in liquid state. The process takes place in special containers designed to trap the liquid as it evaporates so that it can condense back to a liquid state.

The early use of the term *distillation*, about 800 B.C., did not necessarily refer to spirits. At the time, distillation was simply fermented liquid that, when allowed to evaporate, became stronger and more concentrated due to the loss of water. The term *distillatio*, as used by the Romans, defined a filtering process. Distillation is derived from the Latin term *distillare,* meaning to drip or trickle down.

The Romans used several different methods of filtration. One process, called *distillatio perfitrom,* involved passing wine through different kinds of materials to change the flavor. Another process of distillation was *distillatio per descensum.* The wine was placed in a perforated pot and allowed to drip into a lower pot containing additional flavoring elements.

In the first century A.D., the method of distillation changed to what we know it as today. The change was due to the type of container that trapped the condensation as the liquid was heated. This method of distillation began as an experiment, but soon spread throughout Asia Minor, Asia, and Europe. Sometime later, this method was refined by the development of an apparatus that simplified distillation.

Alembic was the name given to the apparatus developed by the Arabs. It was shaped like a hood with an extended tube. The alembic fits over a container of heated liquid, trapping the released vapors. The vapors condense and are led away from the heat via the tube, to cool into liquid form.

The distillation process was used by alchemists of the day, who sought a method to transmit base metal into gold. Interest in distillation was also shown by monasteries. They used the method to create medicines from herbs and roots.

With the use of distillation, the industries of the Eastern world were able to excel. Perfumes, colorings, and medicinal waters were derived from this method. *Kuhl,* the original term given to what we know today as eye makeup (kohl), later became *Al Kuhl* and referred to anything that produced a fine vapor during distillation. Al Kuhl or alcohol soon became the term used to describe vapors produced from the distillation of fermented beverages. It was inevitable that someone would stumble onto the distillation of liquid to produce spirits.

It is believed that in the 10th century, the first alcohol was distilled in Italy in spirit form. Until then, no written formula for alcoholic spirits existed. However, from this period on, there is a great deal of documentation on the production of alcoholic spirits.

In the following centuries, several nations referred to the product of distilled, fermented beverages in their own terms. The Arabs used the phrase *ruh al hamr* or spirit of wine, while the Greeks and Romans used *aqua vitae* or water of life. Other terms such as *eau de vie,* water of life, and *aqua ardens,* or firewater, were coined.

Alchemists, delighted in the discovery of alcoholic spirits, called them the elixir of life. Throughout medieval times, it was hoped this discovery would produce a medicine to heal the entire body. Using the spirit as the base, roots, herbs, flowers, and fruits were added to create a medicinal concoction as well as to hide the taste. During the 14th century, Black Death overtook Europe. The spirit elixir was used for the first time on a large scale as a medicine. It was also distributed as a purifier of water for those not ill.

Gradually, the use of distillation passed from doctor, alchemist, and monastery to private use. Wine makers and brewers created private enterprises using alcohol for other than medicinal purposes. Household distilleries emerged and the method of distillation improved. The still took on a new shape, which led to the design of the modern-day pot still. The still was no longer made of glass, as was the type used by the alchemist. It was transformed into a larger pot-shaped unit, predominantly made of copper. The lower half was called the boiler, the upper portion called the still head. The still head was shaped like an inverted funnel, its spout bent into a right angle that tapered off into a cooling coil.

The alcohol vapors produced by heating the fermented brew rose from the boiler to the still head. A pipe was connected to the head to lead the vapors away from the tube to be cooled. The pipe usually ran for some length, coiling through a tank of cold water beside the still, known as the condensation tank. By passing through the cold water, the vapors quickly condensed into spirit or liqueur.

Although the pot still helped to increase the amount of production, the distillation process itself was quite laborious. After each distillation, the still had to be cleaned and refilled. The distiller had to keep a constant check on the still head and pipe. If the pipe became clogged, an explosion was possible. At the same time, the temperature had to be increased to 173° F, which is the temperature that alcohol begins to boil and vaporize.

Despite the difficulties, production continued and, with household stills, started a new industry. The production of alcoholic beverages increased as the demand increased, especially for distilled spirits. This change moved distillers away from the production of sweet herbal concoctions toward new products such as whiskey, gin, vodka, rum, and brandy.

In Western Europe, particularly in Ireland and Scotland, the product of the fermentation of grain was being distilled as early as the 10th century. The production of this distilled spirit led to the discovery of whiskey. The spirit produced by the Hiberians (Irish) was known as *usguebaugh,* whereas the Caledonians (Scots) used the name *ulsegebaugh* or water of life. Eventually, both these terms were shortened to *viskel,* then whiskey.

The distilling of whiskey was quite common in Scotland, where it was distilled in almost every home. The still thus became a common household tool. Ireland was not far behind in the vast production of whiskey. Inevitably, the distillation process and the use of the still were brought to America.

Initially, all whiskeys in America were made in the style of the Scots and the Irish, using barley malt as the predominant grain. The American industry eventually started using corn rather than barley in distillation, as it was more plentiful. Whiskey made with corn was uniquely American. Corn whiskey became the popular spirit of this country and was given a new name, Bourbon.

Throughout the centuries the method of distillation has become much more refined, leading to much higher quality and more affordable products.

Definitions of Spirits and Malts

Alcohol	A volatile, colorless liquid obtained through the fermentation of a liquid containing sugar.
Alcoholic beverage	Any potable liquid containing from ½ to 75½ percent ethyl alcohol by volume.
Spirit	A potable alcoholic beverage obtained from the distillation of a liquid containing alcohol.
Proof (American method)	Was once called "gunpowder proof." To test the strength of the liquor, old-time distillers poured it on gunpowder and struck a match. If the liquor blazed up, it was too strong. Liquor at proper strength, mixed with the powder, would burn slowly with a blue flame.
	Mixing 50 percent water gave a slow, steady flame. That strength was considered perfect and was called "100 proof." Today, the same scale is applied to the alcoholic content of a liquor on the following basis: Pure, 100 percent alcohol is 200 proof—1 degree of proof is equal to ½ percent alcohol. Divide the proof by 2 and you get the percentage of alcohol by volume.

Proof is therefore a measure of alcohol strength. The proof number is always double the percentage of alcohol. The remaining percentage is distilled water, coloring, and flavoring. All alcoholic beverages fall into one of three basic categories (See Figure 19–1):

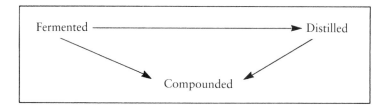

FIGURE 19–1
• • •
Alcoholic beverage categories

1. Fermented beverages made from products such as grains and fruits have alcoholic strengths ranging from 3.2 to 14 percent.
2. Distilled spirit beverages result from a pure distillation of fermented beverages.
3. Compound beverages are made by combining either a fermented beverage or a spirit with flavoring substances.

ALCOHOLIC BEVERAGES
• • • • •

Figure 19–2 summarizes the types and origins of alcoholic beverages.

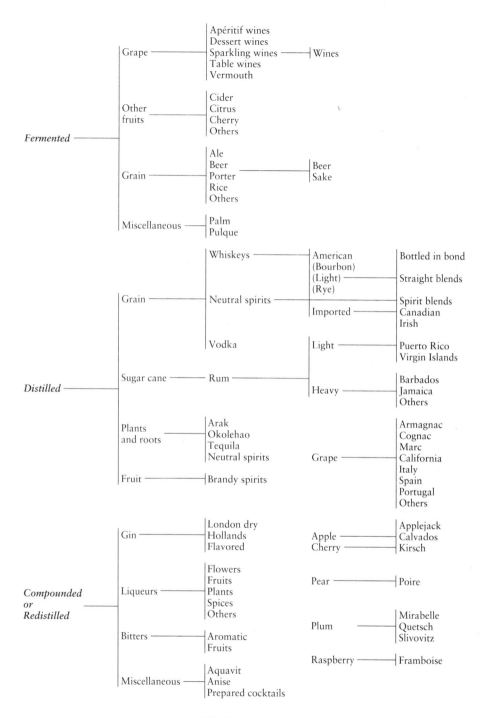

FIGURE 19–2

• • •

Alcoholic beverages

Production Process for Distilled Spirits

There are four necessary steps in the production of whiskey: mashing, fermenting, distilling and blending, and aging in oak barrels. For a flavored spirit, there is one more step called compounding (no aging is done).

Mashing

Mashing is the process of turning grains to sugar. Whiskey may be produced from any type of grain, but corn, rye, wheat, and barley are used most often.

The grains are first cleaned, then ground into meal. The meal is then cooked with water to release the starch. Dried barley malt is then added. The enzymes in the malt convert the grain starch to maltose or grain sugar. Wort is produced.

Fermenting

The mash is put into a fermenter (large tank). Yeast is added, which consumes the sugar and produces alcohol. This process takes from two to four days. The fermented mixture is called "distiller's beer."

Distilling

Separating alcohol from water by applying heat causes the alcohol to evaporate, the vapors are trapped and condensed. The distiller's beer is heated in an enclosed tank to boil the alcohol, but not the water. Remember, alcohol boils at 173° F, while water doesn't boil until 212° F. The steam from the boiled alcohol rises and is trapped. The vapors condense and become ethyl alcohol. U.S. law states that whiskey must be distilled at less than 190 proof (95 percent alcohol). It cannot be distilled at a higher proof because it would lose all the characteristics of the grain used and become a tasteless neutral spirit.

Most whiskeys are distilled from 140 to 160 proof and some as low as 125 proof. Some of the impurities, but not all, are removed through distillation; therefore, the colorless ethyl alcohol is still very harsh.

Compounding

Compounded beverages are made by combining either a fermented beverage or a spirit with flavoring substances. These beverages are derived from infusions, macerations, or percolations of products used. Distilling or redistillation is also a method of compounding. This process is used to flavor a fermented beverage or a natural spirit with flavoring substance. For example, gin is a distilled spirit with juniper berries.

Blending and Aging

After distillation, the ethyl alcohol is diluted with deionized (demineralized) water and then aged. Aging takes place in charred oak barrels. The oak gives whiskey its color, the char absorbs impurities, and time alone mellows the harshness. The end product is smooth and has a rich bouquet. The character of whiskey depends on the length of time it is aged. Heavy-bodied whiskeys are aged for a long time, eight or more years, whereas light-bodied whiskeys are aged for four years. If aged too long, whiskey can absorb undesirable wood flavors. It can only be aged in a barrel. Once bottled, it stays the same age until opened.

Whiskeys vary in alcoholic strength from 110 proof American bottled whiskey to 70 proof Canadian whiskeys. Most whiskeys sold in the United States are 80–86 proof, depending on the distiller and brand.

AMERICAN WHISKEY
• • • • •

1. Bourbon.
2. Corn.
3. Sour mash.
4. Tennessee.
5. Blended.
6. Straight.
7. Bottled in bond.
8. Rye.

These designations are rigidly defined by law and governed accordingly. See Figure 19–3 for a flowchart of whiskey distillery operations.

Bourbon

In order to be called Bourbon, this must contain at least 51 percent corn, be distilled at a proof not exceeding 160, and be aged in *new* charred, white oak barrels for at least two years. Examples: Jim Beam 80 proof, Early Times, and Old Grand Dad 86 proof.

Corn

Corn whiskey must be made from 80 percent corn mash and may be aged in used uncharred barrels. Example: Jim Beam Rye 86 proof.

Sour Mash

The difference between sour mash and other whiskeys is in the fermenting process. The yeast mash is soured with a lactic (milk sugar) culture (like sour dough bread) for a minimum of six hours. The fermented mash must contain at least 25 percent of the screened residue from the whiskey still and the fermenting time must be at least 72 hours. Examples: Beam's Black Label 90 proof and Chester Graves 90 proof.

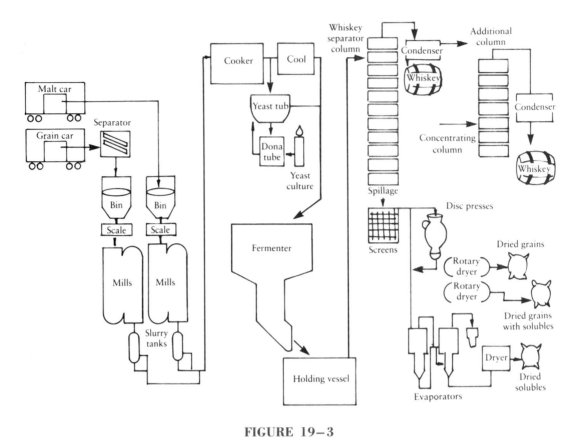

FIGURE 19-3

• • •

Flowchart of whiskey distillery operations

Tennessee

Tennessee whiskey is not Bourbon, although the two are very similar. The difference lies in the extra steps taken after distillation. Tennessee whiskey is seeped very slowly through vats packed with charcoal, called leaching. Following the leaching process, the whiskey is placed in charred, white oak barrels to be aged. Example: Jack Daniels Black Label 90 proof.

Blended Whiskeys

Blended whiskeys are balanced and light-bodied. A variety of straight whiskeys and grain neutral spirits that complement each other are blended together to develop a composite flavor characteristic that will always be uniform. Blends must contain at least 20 percent straight whiskey on a proof gallon basis and be bottled at not less than 80 proof. Seventy-five different straight whiskeys and grain neutral spirits go into premium blends. Examples: Seagram's 7 Crown 80 proof, Four Roses, and Corby's Reserve 80 proof.

Straight Whiskey

Straight whiskey is distilled at no more than 160 proof and aged at least two years in new charred oak barrels. Straight whiskey can be produced from corn, rye, barley or wheat grains, using 100 percent of the selected grain. Examples: Wild Turkey Bourbon 86.8 proof and Old Charter 10 years old.

Bottled in Bond

Bottled in bond is a straight whiskey, usually Bourbon or rye. The government requires that the whiskey be at least four years old, bottled at 100 proof, produced by only one distillery, and stored and bottled in a bonded warehouse under government supervision. Examples: Old Forester 100 proof, Beam's 100 proof 8 years old, and Old Grand Dad B/B 100 proof.

Rye

Rye must contain at least 51 percent rye grain, be distilled at no higher than 160 proof, and be aged in new charred oak barrels. Example: Jim Beam Rye 86 proof 7 years old.

IMPORTED WHISKEY
· · · · ·
Canadian Whiskey

Canadian whiskey is a whiskey blend and is light-bodied. It contains mostly Canadian corn, with a lesser amount of rye, wheat, and barley malt. For consumption in Canada, it is bottled at 70 proof. For export to the United States, it is bottled at 80–86.6 proof. It is usually six years old. If less than four years old, its age must be marked on the label. Examples: Seagram's VO 86.8 proof, Seagram's Crown Royal 80 proof, and Canadian Club 86.8 proof 6 years old.

Irish Whiskey

Irish whiskey contains no distilled spirit less than three years old. Irish whiskey is blended, deriving its individual personality from the native barley grain. It is made in pot stills and blended with pure, soft Irish water that has a very low mineral content. It is the only whiskey that is distilled three times. Only the choice center part of the distillate is retained each time, yielding spirits with a smooth, clean flavor. It is heavier and more full-bodied than Scotch and is usually 86 proof. Examples: John Jameson's 80 proof, Murphy's Irish 86 proof, and Dunphy's Irish 7 years old.

Scotch Whiskey

Production of Scotch malt whiskey begins with selection of the barley. After being cleaned, it is soaked in warm water for about 60 hours and then dried for 10 days or so, until it begins to sprout. The sprouted barley is then spread on screens over peat moss fires. The aroma of the smoke permeates the barley, which gives Scotch its unique smoky flavor. After several weeks of drying, the malt is cleaned and ground into meal. The meal is mashed and the yeast is added, then fermentation takes place. The resulting liquid is called mash beer.

The Scots use a different distilling process than that used in the United States. An old-fashioned pot still is used instead of a continuous still. Examples: Cutty Sark 12 years old and Cutty Sark 86 proof, Chivas Regal Salute 80 proof 21 years old and Chivas Regal 86 proof 12 years old, and Glenlivet 86 proof 12 years old. Most Scotch whiskeys are a blend of malts but some, like Glenlivet, are made from a single malt. See Figure 19–4 for a flowchart of the distillery and production process for Scotch.

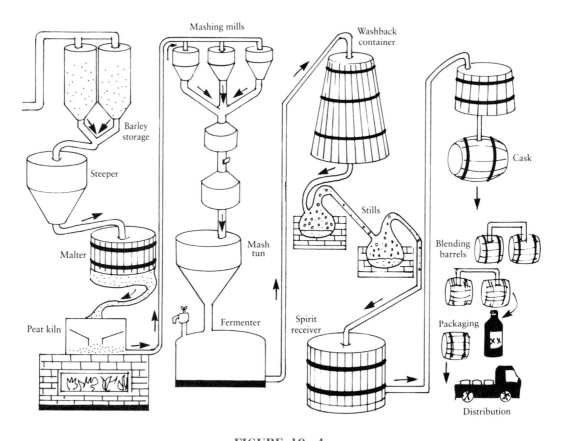

FIGURE 19–4
• • •

Distillation and production process for Scotch

288

GIN

· · · · ·

Gin is distilled from grain and receives its unique flavor and aroma from juniper berries and other botanicals. Gin can be made two ways, by being either distilled or compounded. Most brands sold in the United States are distilled. Compounded simply means a mixture of neutral spirits with juniper berries. Distilled gin is distilled completely.

The terms, *dry gin, extra dry gin, London dry gin,* or *English dry gin,* all mean the same thing—lacking in sweetness. Dry gins are delicate with the flavor of juniper and other botanicals toned down. They blend perfectly with other flavors and are ideal for mixing.

Two factors differentiate English and American gins. First, English gin is distilled at a lower proof than American. The second factor is the water, which influences the character of the fermented mash and the spirits distilled from that mash.

Genever gin is imported from Holland. It is highly flavored and rich in aromatic oils. It has a heavy taste and does not mix well with other ingredients. Dutch gins are full-bodied, with a substantial juniper character.

See Figure 19–5 for a flowchart of gin distillery operations.

VODKA

· · · · ·

The formula for vodka was brought to America in the 1930s via Paris. Vodka was first produced in Russia in the 14th century. It was distilled by the Smirnoff distilleries in Moscow, dating from 1818, until it passed out of the family's control with the 1917 revolution. Smirnoff was the first and only American-made vodka for many years.

Vodka is made from potatoes and various grains, mostly corn, with some wheat added. It may also be made from white beets, as in Turkey (izmaya), or from molasses, as in Germany (closter). Vodka, like whiskey, is an alcoholic distillate from a fermented mash. Whiskey, however, is distilled at a lower proof to retain flavor. Vodka is distilled at a higher proof and then processed still further to remove all flavors. Vodka, unlike whiskey, is not aged.

U.S. distillers filter their vodka through activated charcoal to further remove all distinctive character, aroma, or taste so that the end product is odorless, colorless, and tasteless. Flavored varieties of vodka are popular mostly in Poland and Russia, where infusions and mixtures with herbs, grasses, leaves, spices, and seeds are involved. Some are colored and, as vodka-based liqueurs, are sweetened and fruit flavored. They range from 70 proof and up.

The United States produces some fruit-flavored vodkas. These are orange and lemon, made with the rind of the fruit, and cherry, made from the pulp of the fruit and skins for color.

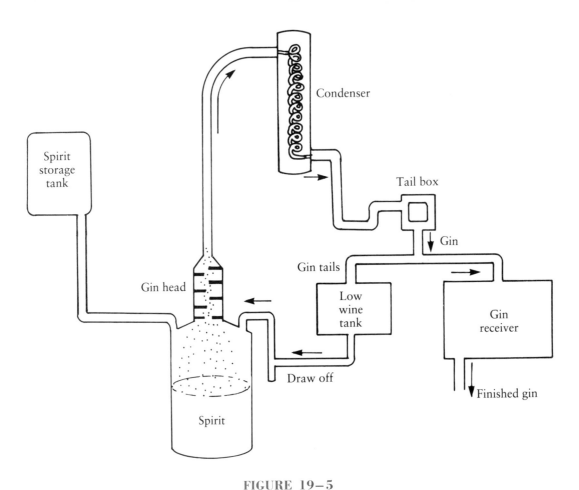

FIGURE 19–5

• • •

Flowchart of gin distillery operations

RUM

• • • • •

Rum is an alcoholic beverage distilled from the fermented juice of sugar cane, sugar cane syrup, sugar cane molasses, or other sugar cane by-products, distilled at less than 190 proof (whether or not such proof is further reduced before bottling, it must be less than 80 proof). The distillate must possess the taste, aroma, and characteristics generally attributed to rum.

Rum is produced wherever sugar cane grows, but most rums are produced in the Caribbean Islands.

There are four main classifications of rum:

Light bodied   Very dry, with a light molasses taste. It is produced in Puerto Rico and the Virgin Islands.

Medium bodied	Gold in color, slightly mellower, and has a more pronounced taste than light-bodied rums. It is produced in Haiti, Barbados, Trinidad, and Guyana.
Full bodied	Much darker and sweeter. Has a pungent bouquet and a heavy molasses taste. Dark rums differ because of a slower fermentation and special maturation processes. It is produced in Jamaica, Martinique, and Demerara.
Light-bodied (Batavia Arak)	Arak is a brandylike rum of great pungency and is used as any other rum. It is produced on the Island of Java, Indonesia. Its fermentation process is different from the other rums. The quality of Arak is obtained from the wild, uncultured yeast and specially cooked and dried Javanese rice that is placed in the fermenting tubs of molasses. The Arak is aged for three or four years in Java, then shipped to Holland, where it is aged for another four–six years, blended, and then bottled.

Rum was also produced in New England over 300 years ago. Molasses was imported from the West Indies. New England rum is now obsolete and was eliminated from the U.S. Standards of Identity in 1968. It was straight rum, distilled at less than 160 proof, with considerable body and pungency.

BRANDY

· · · · ·

The word *brandy* means distilled wine. Brandies are made by taking a wine base, from grapes or other fruits, and putting it through the distillation process. Although brandies are made in countries around the world, the best known are those of Cognac and Armagnac. Although all Cognacs and Armagnacs are brandies, not all brandies are Cognacs or Armagnacs. Only those brandies produced in the Cognac/Armagnac region of France are entitled to carry the word *Cognac* or *Armagnac* on the label.

Cognac and Armagnac

Before discussing these two very special products, Cognac and Armagnac, we should take a moment to understand some of the properties of their makeup. First of all, Cognac and Armagnac are spirits, and a spirit is defined as the essence of a substance extracted in liquid form, such as a strong, distilled alcoholic liquid. Second, we should understand that spirits may be produced from a wide variety of products, with each distillation varying in quality.

Another factor in understanding spirits is that they have no dependence on climate, locale, or cultural limits. They can be produced anywhere that a distiller decides to place the equipment. Of course, in the instance of Cognac and Armagnac, these are the world's elite spirits, and they are rated as elite because of the grapes from which they are distilled. In fact, these grapes are so outstanding and so widely recognized as grown in a very specific geographical setting that they wear their ancestry as one would proudly wear a coat of arms.

With this knowledge of their ancestral background, you can understand why Cognac and Armagnac make such pleasant products to study.

Cognac

Cognac is a brandy, but not all brandies are Cognac. Cognac is a brandy distilled from wine, made of grapes grown within the legal limits of the Charente and Charente-Maritime departments of France.

The city of Cognac, on the Charente River, is the heart of the district. The entire Cognac region was delimited in 1909; the seven subdivisions in 1936. The seven subdivisions in order of quality are:

1. Grande Champagne.
2. Petite Champagne.
3. Borderie.
4. Fins Bois.
5. Bon Bois.
6. Bois Ordinaires.
7. Bois à Terroir.

The Grande Champagne and Petite Champagne now account for about 30 percent of the total production of Cognac. These names bear no relation to the sparkling wines of Champagne. Champagne in French means open fields, a distinction made even clearer by the names of the five other districts, four of which refer to woodlands.

Cognac is distilled twice in pure copper pot stills soon after the wine has stopped fermenting. The wine is warmed in a tank and then boiled away by a steady coal fire. Two distillations are needed to get the fraction with exactly the right amount of alcohol. The first distillation produces a liquid of about 30 percent alcohol called *brouillis*. This is redistilled to make the raw Cognac, known as the *bonne chauffe,* which runs from the still white and clear at about 70 percent alcohol.

It takes 10 barrels of wine to make one barrel of Cognac. The new Cognac, which is colorless, is then aged in oak barrels. These barrels were traditionally made of Limousin oak, but the forest of Limousin can no longer supply all the needs of the Cognac shippers. Today, about half the barrels in the cellars containing Cognac are made of Trongais oak. It is the interaction between oak and brandy, as well as the continual oxidation that takes place through the porous wood, that gives Cognac its superb and distinctive flavor. It is the barrel aging (during which the brandy also picks up color and tannin from the oak) that refines a harsh distillate into a pleasurable beverage. Cognac, like all brandies, ages only as long as it remains in wood; it undergoes no further development once it is bottled. It is not the vintage that matters, as with wine, but the number of years spent in wood. Two years in a barrel is the legal minimum for any Cognac. Most good Cognacs have three to four years in wood.

The VS symbol means that the Cognac has been aged three or four years. The VSOP (Very Superior Old Pale) means that the Cognac has been aged five to seven years.

Cognac takes on color from the oak as it matures; normal commercial Cognac is diluted to 40 percent alcohol with distilled water and its sweetness and color are adjusted with sugar and caramel. The quality of the Cognac also depends on the soil. The soil at its best is as chalky as as in Champagne. From a top soil of 35 percent chalk to 25 percent to 15 percent is the progression from Grande Champagne to Petite Champagne to borderies. Beyond the borderies are the four bois with less and less chalk. The four bois are less delicate, with a distinct goût de terroir, or earthiness.

Cognac is made from the Ugni Blanc grape. White Ugni Blanc grapes produce wine having about 7–8 percent alcohol and about 10 percent acidity per liter. The best Cognacs have the most finesse, and then the Cognacs progress to a full-bodied and high-flavored spirit.

Fine Champagne is Cognac made from at least 50 percent Grande Champagne and 50 percent Petite Champagne grapes. A Cognac labeled Grande Champagne has been distilled entirely from wines made from grapes grown in the Grande Champagne district.

Some of the best Cognac houses include

Martell	Hine
Hennessy	Flapin
Remy Martin	Larsen
Courvoisier	Castillon
Otard-Dupuy	Delamain
Ricard Bisquit Dubouche	Denis-Mounie
Camus	Gaston de Lagrange
Salignac	Monnet
Prince de Polignac	

Armagnac

The world has only one other brandy that can be compared with Cognac, and it, too, comes from western France. Armagnac shares only its refinement and its very high standards with Cognac; the two brandies are poles apart in style and in the techniques used to make them.

Definition   Armagnac is an appellation controlée French grape brandy from Gascony. Its production, viticulture, distillation process, and aging are subject to detailed official inspection and strict controls.

Armagnac region   Armagnac is a remote country region located in the heart of southwest France, between Toulouse on the east, Bordeaux and Bayonne on the west, the Pyrenees on the south, and the Garonne Valley on the north. It is divided into three sections. Bas-Armagnac, Ténarèze, and Haut-Armagnac. This is the production area entitled to appellation d'origine status. Haut-Armagnac extends from flat plains in the northern part, through the eastern part, and into the hilly area of the southern part of the region. Ténarèze is located in the plain of the north-central area of the region. Bas-Armagnac is located in the plain of the north on the western side. Bas-Armagnac might be called the Grande Champagne of the region, except that it has sandy soil in place of chalk.

1. Bas-Armagnac is the most westerly growing area bordering on Les Landes. The land is sandy with a little clay in the soil. Prune flavor and aroma are the dominant characteristics of these renowned brandies. Eauze (pronounced Ay-oze) is the capital, as well as the center of the Armagnac market.

2. Ténarèze, centrally located, has a predominantly *argilo-calcaire* soil (a clay and limestone mixture) and produces Armagnacs with overtones of both prunes and violets that are considered on a par with those of Bas-Armagnac. Condom, the capital of this region, has an interesting Armagnac museum.

3. Haut-Armagnac is grown in the eastern region where the soil is mostly chalky with limestone outcroppings. Here, a large proportion of grapes is used for blending with the Armagnac of the other regions; some is used for such regional specialties as prunes (and other fruit) in Armagnac, as well as Armagnac-based liqueurs and apéritifs. The capital of Haut-Armagnac is Auch, the largest city in the area, with a population of about 25,000. In a park off the Place de la Libération is a statue honoring the most famous Gascon of them all, Armagnac's own D'Artagan, immortalized by Dumas père. His real name was Charles de Batz and he was born about 1615 in the old château of Castelmore, a short drive from Auch.

Types of grapes cultivated The three principal grape varieties used in making Armagnac are Folle Blanche, the St. Emilion, and the Colombard. Other traditional varieites include the Jurançon, Clairette, Blanquette, Mozac, and Plante de Grèce.

Other than the differences of soil, warmer climate, and the grapes, the big differences between Armagnac and Cognac come from the type of still; a continuous still is used for Armagnac, a type of double boiler in which the wine is distilled once at a much lower strength than for Cognac. Armagnac has a stronger flavor and scent than Cognac.

Comparisons of the flavors of Armagnac and Cognac always class Armagnac as rustic, as having a sharper aroma, and possessing a surprising smoothness. Armagnac is drier than Cognac. Sugar is not normally added, as it is to Cognac.

The main center of the industry are the little towns of Auch and Eauze, where a good deal of private buying occurs directly from farmers.

Production Processes

Vitification Only wines made from specified white grape varieties may be used to produce Armagnac, and they must be obtained through traditional wine-making methods without racking off so that the wines still contain their lees. No enological product may be added. The ideal base wine should be high in fixed acidity, low in alcohol.

Distillation In the past, the traveling still was a familiar sight trundling about the countryside, distilling the wine at individual vineyards and farms. Today, Armagnac is produced by the continuous method in a permanently installed copper still called the *alambic armagnacais*. (The pot still called alambic, a repasse, which is used to make Cognac via the double distillation method, is currently being used in a limited way by a few producers.)

When it first emerges from the still, Armagnac is called eau de feu (firewater) and is colorless with a powerful bouquet and flavor that mellows considerably after a few years in cask. Distillation is carried out in the winter and must be completed before April 30 of the year following the harvest.

Aging The alambic armagnacais' one-step technique gives Armagnac a greater proportion of aromatic and flavoring elements than Cognac. As soon as it comes out of the still, Armagnac is stored in hand-made casks of the region's tannic-rich Monlezun oak. At this point, the cellar master takes over—carefully and constantly checking the aging process. The Monlezun oak helps develop the remarkable complexity of flavor and the sparkling, rich amber color for which Armagnac is prized. When the dissolving of tannic matter and wood essences reaches its optimum rate, the brandy is transferred either to worked-out casks (i.e., no longer exuding tannin) or vats.

It is the cellar master's art of aging and blending that determines the essential quality of the firm's product, as well as its consistency. Once in a bottle, the brandy is stabilized and no longer ages.

Regulations and Label Language

On September 1 of the year following the harvest, Armagnac receives the designation Zero (Compte 0); the following September 1 it receives the designation One (Compte 1); and so on. The word *Armagnac* on the label categorizes all brandy from within the certified region. When Armagnacs come exclusively from either Bas-Armagnac, Ténarèze, or Haut-Armagnac, their place of origin may be indicated on the label. Most are a blend of two or three subregions.

Most Armagnacs shipped to the United States are classified VSOP (Very Superior Old Pale), VO (Very Old), or Réservé. Any of these classifications means the youngest brandy in the blend is at least Compte 4—about 4½ years old. In the United States, a three-star Armagnac indicates the youngest brandy in this blend is Compte 2, or 2½ years old. Extra, Napoleon, XO, Vieille Réservé, Hors d'Age, and similar label designations indicate the youngest brandy is at least Compte 5, or 5½ years old—although in these blends there will be greater amounts of older Armagnacs. In general, all Armagnacs contain much older brandies than regulations require.

How to Taste and Appreciate Brandy

Whatever its classified age, the following are recommendations on how brandy should be sipped and savored to appreciate their extraordinary aroma and flavor to the fullest.

Appreciation

Pour a little brandy into a clear, stemmed, glass brandy snifter. It should be about the size of an 8-ounce wine goblet, one that can be held comfortably in the palm of one's hand. The glass should not be more than one-third full. Hold the stem of the glass with thumb and forefinger. Examine brandy's sparkling amber color. Gently swirl the brandy around, allowing the aroma to develop. Lift the glass to your nose and let the bouquet envelop the nostrils, then inhale the heady scents with little sniffs. Try to recognize the overtones of prunes, of peaches, of hazelnuts, of violets, of what Gascons call the gout de terroir, the essence of the earth.

Tasting/Sipping

Next, taste the smooth, grape, deeply satisfying flavor in slow sips. Let it sit on the tongue before rolling it about in the mouth for a moment or two. Chew it to experience the subtleties of the "velvet flame," an initial brief moment of "dancing fire" on the tongue immediately followed by the sensation of velvety richness as the brandy is swallowed.

Savoring

When the glass has been emptied, cup it in the hand or warm it between the palms—and inhale deeply of the aromas it still exudes. This is an old brandy custom called fond du verre, the bottom of the glass. It is said that a glass that has held a fine brandy will still retain the bouquet the next day.

Suggested Uses

Brandy is becoming widely known all over the world for its versatility. Serve it in apéritifs, cocktails, punches, brandied coffee, and on the rocks, as well as an after-dinner digestif. In the Orient, brandy is actually sipped throughout the meal, complementing the distinctive flavors of eastern foods in the same way as a full-bodied beer or liquor. In cookery, brandy is the secret ingredient of well-known contemporary chefs in Europe and the United States who have taken a leaf from Gascony's notable chefs, La Ronde des Mousquetaires. In a remarkable way, brandy enriches and heightens the natural flavors in dishes, from hors d'oeuvre, to desserts, without being assertive.

OTHER SPIRITS
· · · · ·
Tequila

Tequila has its own special flavor that is almost tart. Tequila is obtained from the distillation of the fermented juice (sap) of the mescal plant, called pulque. The mescal plant is a species of the agava plant. It is a cactus plant that takes between 10 and 12 years to mature. At harvest time, its long leaves, or spikes, are cut off, leaving only the bulbous central core called the pina (pineapple). The pinas weigh between 80 and 175 pounds each. They are taken to the distillery where they are cooked in pressure cookers for several hours. Then they are cooled and shredded and the juice is pressed out. The juice, along with fibrous pulp, is mixed with sugar and the mash is fermented for about four days. In order to make tequila, the spirit must be redistilled to obtain the pure colorless liquor. It is then aged in oak barrels for approximately 35–56 days. Gold tequila is left for nine months or more in 50-gallon oak barrels that give it its color. Premium tequila is aged for over three years.

Mescal is made after fermentation; the pulque is distilled in pot stills to give low-grade alcohol.

Aquavit (Akvavit)

Aquavit is made from a fermented mash of either barley malt and grain or potatoes; it is flavored with caraway seeds. It is first distilled as a neutral spirit at 190 proof, reduced with water to 120 proof, and then redistilled with the flavorings. Caraway is the principal flavoring, but others, such as lemon and orange peel, cardamom, or anise, are used. It is similar in production to gin, except that the main flavor in aquavit is caraway rather than juniper berries. It is generally not aged and has an alcoholic strength of 86 to 90 proof. It is the beverage of Scandinavia. In Denmark, it is called Akvavit. It is usually taken with food with a beer chaser.

296

Bitters

Bitters consist of bitter and aromatic essences and flavors incorporated into an alcohol base. The flavors come from fruits, plants, seeds, flowers, leaves, bark, roots, and stems. Most bitters are proprietary brands. The formulas are a closely guarded secret handed down from generation to generation. These products are the result of infusion and distillation processes and their one common characteristic is bitterness.

Bitters are classified into two categories: for use as a beverage, or for use in a beverage. The best-known bitter is Angostura, which is made in Trinidad. It is used as a spice in cocktails. Bitters for use as a beverage, such as Campari from Italy, aid in digestion.

PROPRIETARY BRANDS
· · · · ·

Figure 19–6 shows some proprietary brand names of distilled spirits discussed in this chapter.

American Whiskey

Seagram's 7

Bourbon

  Jim Beam (blended)

  Old Grand Dad (straight, bonded)

  Early Times (straight)

  Wild Turkey (straight)

Tennessee

  Jack Daniels (sour mash)

Imported Whiskey

Canadian

  Canadian Club

  Seagram's VO

  Seagram's Crown Royal

Irish

  John Jameson

  Bushmill

Scotch whiskey

  Cutty Sark

  J&B

Imported Whiskey

  Dewars (White label)

  Johnnie Walker (Red label)

  Johnnie Walker (Black label) 12 years old

  Chivas Regal 12 years old

  Haig & Haig Pinch 12 years old

  Glenfiddich (straight malt) 10 years old

  Glenfiddich (straight malt) 12 years old

Gin

Beefeater

Boodles

Tanqueray

Bols Genever

Bombay

Bombay Sapphire

Vodka

Smirnoff

Fris

Absolut

FIGURE 19–6
· · ·
Some proprietary brand names for distilled spirits and aperitifs

Gin

Finlandia

Stolichnaya

Stolichnaya Cristall

Wyborowa (pronouned Vee-ba-rova)

Flavored Vodka

Absolut Citron

Absolut Peppar

Stolichnaya Pertsovstra

Stolichnaya Limonnaya

Rum

Virgin Island

  Barbancourt

  Lemon Hart

Jamaican

  Appleton—White

  Appleton—Gold

  Appleton—Dark

  Myers's—Platinum

  Myers's—Gold

  Myers's—Dark

Puerto Rico

  Bacardi—Silver

  Bacardi—Gold

  Bacardi—Amber

  Bacardi 151

  Bacardi—Black

  Captain Morgan—Spiced

Barbabos

  Gosling Barbabos

  Mount Gay Eclipse

Brandy (American)

Christian Brothers

*Cognac**

Courvoisier, VS, VSOP, XO

Courvoisier Napoléon

Hennessy, VS, VSOP, XO

Martell, VS, VSOP, Cordon Bleu

Remy Martin, VS, VSOP, XO

Remy Martin Louis XIII

*Armagnac**

Calvados

St. Vivant

Marquis de Coussade

Demontal

Tequila

Jose Cuervo—Silver

Jose Cuervo—Gold

Sauza

Two Fingers

Apéritifs

Quinnne apéritif (bittersweet)

Campari

Cynar (fortified wine, 16–24% alcohol)

Lillet

Dubonnet, red and white

Other Types

Dry white wine (12–14% alcohol)

Dry sherry (fortified, 1–20% alcohol)

Champagne (12–14% alcohol)

*Cognac/Armagnac Alph, grading:

VS (Very Superior)	2–6 years in wood.
VSOP (Very Superior Old Pale)	6–12 years in wood.
Napoleon	12 years in wood.
XO Xtra old	12–25 years in wood.
Medallion	12–25 years in wood.

FIGURE 19–6

• • •

concluded

LIQUEURS AND BEERS

LIQUEURS AND CORDIALS
· · · · ·

A liqueur or cordial is a spirit, usually brandy, whiskey, or grain alcohol, to which flavoring has been added. Various combinations of fruits, vegetables, herbs, and spices lend their flavors to the base spirit. To trace the popularity of liqueurs, it is necessary to reach back to their 14th-century origins, to elixirs brewed behind monastery walls and to the potions concocted by alchemists. While the students of alchemy searched for a fluid that could turn common metals into gold, the monks of several religious orders devoted themselves to producing liqueurs for medicinal purposes.

No discussion of the origins of contemporary liqueurs could proceed without mentioning two names that have bridged that span of centuries. Benedictine and Chartreuse exemplify the herbal blends that were developed by those ancient religious orders.

- Benedictine enjoys one of the most renowned reputations of all liqueurs. This famous French spirit, first made around 1510 by a member of the Benedictine order, is a complex mixture of herbs, plants, and spices incorporated into a Cognac base.
- The present recipe for Chartreuse dates back to 1764, when the Carthusian monks of France expanded the original recipe to include 130 ingredients. The intricate formulas for both the green and yellow variations of the liqueur remain in the hands of the Brothers to this day, entrusted to only five monks at a time.

Another of the first commercial liqueur distilleries—a company whose products continue to delight 20th-century palates—was started by Lucas Bols in Amsterdam in 1575. Other early distillers still in operation are Rocher Frères, founded in 1705, and the house of Marie Brizard, which began producing in 1755.

As the centuries progressed, liqueurs kept pace with changes in popular taste, as suggested by the 18th-century alterations in the formula for making Chartreuse. The 1700s ushered in a shift away from what were often somewhat harsh, medicinal concoctions toward beverages more suitable for pleasure drinking. As a result, there was greater experimentation with fruits and assorted sweetening agents. Recipes grew increasingly elaborate, with one old English formula for a "cordial water" calling for 67 ingredients, including gold and crushed pearls. The liqueur producers also indulged their sense of humor in naming new drinks. Translated into English, some of the more popular liqueurs were titled Illicit Love, Old Woman's Milk, The Longer the Better, and Up with Your Shirt.

Today, the steps involved in the manufacture of liqueurs employ the same basic techniques used hundreds of years ago. The individual processes of maceration, distillation, and percolation can each produce a liqueur by themselves, but are generally used in combination.

The simplest of these procedures, maceration, involves soaking the substances used for flavoring in base alcohol. After the desired length of time, ranging from a few days to several months, the alcohol assumes the qualities of the substance. Fruits are used with this method, as are such ingredients as coffee and vanilla beans.

Distillation requires the base spirits and flavor substance to be heated. The resulting vapor condenses in the still and forms a concentrated essence of the materials—usually plants, herbs, seeds, or dried fruit peels.

Percolation is very similar to the process of coffee making. The alcohol is placed in a lower chamber, with the solid materials in the upper compartment. The spirit is then dripped over the materials or is forced through them. Cocoa beans and vanilla pods are often percolated to release their flavor to the spirit.

The end products of these processes, whether blended or allowed to remain pure, are cut with neutral spirits and water to produce a liquid generally ranging from 50 to 80 proof (25 to 40 percent alcohol). Sugar or honey is sometimes added for sweetness. Since the liquid is clear or just faintly tinted at this point, color is frequently added.

Sharing the curative heritage of the herbal liqueurs are blends made from seeds such as caraway and anise, as well as from mint and coffee. As one of the oldest forms of liqueur, anisette has been enjoyed both for its aid to digestion and its pungent taste. Hippocrates was known to take the drink "anisum" from time to time. While aniseed is the primary ingredient in anisette recipes, other seeds and plants or citrus peels may also be used to subtly augment the flavor.

Absinthe, a liqueur based on the taste of anise, was popular in the late 19th and early 20th centuries. The characters in Ernest Hemingway's novels are frequently found sipping absinthe at charming outdoor cafés. The recipe for this strong, green liqueur came out of the 18th century, and relies on wormwood, an herb, as its principal ingredient. Around the turn of this century, wormwood was banned in most countries, as it was believed to cause madness and violent behavior, and today not much absinthe is produced anywhere in the world.

Several contemporary liqueurs retain the romantic tales surrounding their origins. One of the more colorful histories accompanies Drambuie, a Scotch whiskey–based liqueur. During the middle 1700s, the royal Scottish family of Stuart, the inventors of Drambuie, found themselves the victims of political turmoil and were deprived of their kingdom. In 1745, determined to reclaim the family birthright, Prince Charles Edward Stuart led an army of Highland clansmen in several successful battles against government troops. Although his forces pushed farther into England than any previous Scottish army, defeat finally caught up with "Bonnie Prince Charlie" at Culloden in 1746. The prince fled to the Island of Skye, off the Scottish coast, with a bounty of 30,000 British pounds on his head.

With fortune lost and army disbanded, the prince had to rely on the goodwill of the island's inhabitants. Among those who aided the fugitive Prince was John Mackinnon, forebear of the Mackinnon family, which today guards the secret of Drambuie. In his gratitude for the kindness showed him, Prince Charles Edward gave Mackinnon the family recipe for a unique liqueur made of aged Scotch whiskey, honey, and a secret essence of blended herbal oils, whose exact formula is known today by only one Mackinnon in each generation. The name Drambuie is taken from the Gaelic *an dram buidheach,* for the drink that satisfies.

The universal appeal of fruit is often enjoyed through a variety of liqueurs. Not long after the first shipments of exotic New World cargo appeared in Europe, the Dutch developed a liqueur that used bitter oranges from the West Indian island of Curaçao, and the product still carries the island name. Today, orange liqueurs are produced by many distilleries. One of the best-known and most successful is Cointreau, a product of France. The company has been owned by the family of Adolphe and Edouard Cointreau since 1849, and currently distributes its product in more than 200 countries. The base of Cointreau is a neutral spirit, which is processed with the peel of both the bitter oranges of the Caribbean and sweet oranges harvested in Mediterranean regions.

Grand Marnier stands as the rival to Cointreau among orange liqueurs. Dating from 1827, the firm of Marnier-Lapostelle presently devotes about 80 percent of its production to the elegant liqueur. Cognac is used exclusively as the foundation of Grand Marnier, with which only the peels of bitter oranges are used. Unlike the clear Cointreau, Grand Marnier has a deep golden color.

Cherries are one of the most popular and available fruits the world over and probably could not help but turn up in liquid form. The house of Peter Heering has been turning out a highly respected cherry liqueur since 1818. The Dutch firm uses an old recipe calling for the red cherries of South Denmark. Formally known as Cherry Heering, Peter Heering liqueur is consumed in many parts of the world.

Maraschino is a cherry liqueur with a markedly different character than Peter Heering liqueur. Special processing of the dark Marasca cherries of Yugoslavia, together with their pits, provides the cherry-almond flavor that distinguishes this liqueur. It was developed by Girolamo Luxardo in 1829 as a variation of a traditional, nonalcoholic beverage. The house of Luxardo has weathered considerable turmoil in its corner of Eastern Europe. After the original Yugoslavian distillery was destroyed in World War II, the present factory was built in Italy.

A bit closer to home, the famous American product, Southern Comfort, benefits from a fruit readily accessible on its own home soil. Originally from New Orleans, Southern Comfort subtly showcases the flavor of peaches, with undertones of oranges and herbs. All combine gracefully in a base of old Bourbon whiskey.

The versatility of liqueurs is a key to their continued success. Liqueurs are increasingly used as an ingredient in cocktails, offering almost limitless variety to the creative bartender. Gourmet cooking is another natural forum for liqueurs, particularly desserts. Since alcoholic content is dissipated with heating, only the concentrated flavor of the liqueur is imparted to the preparation.

Whether an ancient herbal blend or an exotic modern concoction, liqueurs add a special touch to the eating and drinking experience. It is only necessary to look at their distinguished history and promising future to realize that liqueurs are one of the world's most enduring pleasures.

Production Methods

Liqueurs are made by mixing or redistilling neutral spirits with fruits, flowers, herbs, seeds, roots, plants, or juices to which sweetening has been added. Liqueurs and cordials differ from all other spirits because they must contain at least 2½ percent sugar by weight. The sugar may be beet, maple, cane, honey, corn, or a combination of these. There are no hard rules. Liqueurs with a sugar content between 2½ and 10 percent may be labeled *dry* because they are not very sweet. Most liqueurs and cordials contain up to 35 percent of a sweetening agent.

There are two basic ways of extracting flavors when making liqueurs:

1. Cold method, generally using fruit flavors.
2. Hot method, using plant products, seeds, peels, and flowers.

Each method encompasses several processes, and each fruit or plant product is handled differently.

Infusion or Maceration

The cold method is used when the flavoring material is sensitive to heat. Cold extractions can take up to a year; attempts to make the process go faster by using heat would destroy the flavor.

1. If crushed fruits are steeped in water, it is called *infusion*.
2. If the fruit is steeped in alcohol, such as 120–130 proof brandy, it is called *maceration*.

The water or brandy eventually absorbs almost all of the aroma, flavor, and color of the fruit or berry. In some cases, when the stones (seeds) of the fruit are present, some of the oil from the stones is also extracted, which accounts for the slight bitter almond undertone sometimes found in such liqueurs as apricot, peach, and cherry.

When ready, the liquid is drawn off, allowed to rest for several days in a storage tank that will not impart any flavor (stainless steel), and then filtered. The mass of remaining fruit still contains both useful alcohol and some essential flavorings. In order to recover them, the mass is placed in a still and the last drop of flavor is extracted by distillation. The distillate may then be added to the original maceration in order to give it more character. The finished maceration is then sweetened to the desired richness by adding sugar and/or other sweetening material in syrup form. The finished product is sometimes aged before bottling.

Percolation

Another cold method, percolation or brewing is somewhat like making coffee. The flavoring agent, in the form of leaves or herbs, is placed in the upper part of the apparatus. Brandy or another spirit is in the lower part and is pumped up over the flavoring and allowed to percolate through it, extracting and carrying down the aroma and flavor. The process is repeated continuously for weeks or months until most of the flavor constituents have been obtained. It is then distilled to obtain whatever flavor remains, then mixed with the original percolate. It is then filtered, sweetened with simple syrup, and often bottled at once, although some plant liqueurs of this group are aged for a time.

Distillation

The hot extraction method is used mostly for seeds and flowers such as anise, caraway, orange peel, mint, roses, and violets. These materials can withstand some heat and benefit from a quicker extraction of flavor than the slower cold methods.

The distillation method is normally carried out in small to medium-sized copper pot stills. The normal procedure is to steep the flavoring agent—plant, seed, root, or herb—in alcohol for several hours, after which it is placed in the still with additional spirits and distilled. A vacuum is created so that distillation can take place at a lower temperature, preserving more of the floral aroma. The resultant distillate, always colorless, is sweetened with simple syrup and colored with natural vegetable coloring matter or approved food dyes.

Distinct Categories of Liqueurs

1. Fruit-flavored liqueurs are the most popular. The label will generally indicate which fruit was used to produce the liqueur; for example, the Midori label mentions melons, the Cocoribe label mentions coconuts, and the Peter Heering label indicates that the liqueur is cherry flavored.

2. Seed-based liqueurs do not use a single seed; they use a variety of ingredients with one seed flavor being predominate.
3. Herbs will not stand out, except for mint or aniseed. Herb categories use a combination of herbs and sometimes seeds and flowers (Chartreuse contains over 125 different ingredients).
4. Peels frequently give the flavor from the rind of the citrus fruit used; for example, the orange flavor of Curaçao comes from orange peels.
5. Crèmes is indicative of the creamy texture and sweet taste of the liqueur. Crèmes will take on the name of the dominant ingredient. They are usually sweeter than other cordials and are fruit flavored.

Fruit Brandies

The fermented mash of fruits other than grapes is the source of a wide variety of unique brandies. There are three categories:

1. Brandies made with apples and pears.
2. Brandies made with stone fruits such as cherries, plums, and apricots.
3. Brandies made from berries such as raspberries, strawberries, blackberries, and elderberries.

Fruit brandies are produced when the fully ripened fruit is gathered and thoroughly mixed or mashed with wooden paddles in a wooden tub where it is allowed to ferment—stones and all. After six weeks, when fermentation is complete, the entire contents is placed in a pot still and distilled twice. A small amount of oil from the stones is distilled again with the spirit. It is distilled to a fairly low proof, around 100 proof or less, so that the maximum fruit aroma and flavor are retained. Some of the most popular fruit brandies are Applejack and Calvados made from apples; apricot brandy made from apricots; Kirsch and Kirschwasser made from cherries; Prunelle and Slivovitz made from plums; Framboise made from raspberries; and Fraise made from strawberries.

How and When to Serve Liqueurs and Cordials

Liqueurs and cordials, being sweet and potent and containing certain beneficial, essential oils, are natural digestives. They are most popular as after-dinner drinks. During prohibition, however, liqueurs came into wide use as cocktail ingredients because their rich sweetness helped to cover up the harsh bite of the spirits bootleggers supplied. It was found that a dash or two gave a cocktail added smoothness, texture, and palatability.

In France, certain liqueurs were used in the form of highballs. Crème de Cassis was mixed with French vermouth and soda or with wine. A popular way of serving liqueurs is as frappés, made by filling a small stem glass with shaved ice and pouring liqueur into it.

Proprietary and Generic Brands

Proprietary liqueurs are ones that are produced under closely guarded secret formulas and marketed under registered trademark brands. Each one is produced by only one house. No other house may produce a product exactly like it. Generic brands are ones that are produced by many different companies all over the world. Since many producers use different flavoring formulas, there are variations in brands that use the same name. See Figure 20–1 for a list proprietary and generic brands of liqueurs and cordials.

Alize*	From France; blend of passion fruit and Cognac.
Amaretto	Aromatic apricot-almond liqueur; distinctive flavor and bouquet; made from almonds and apricots steeped in aquavit, a fusion of alcohol; today, one of the great-selling cordial flavors.
Amaretto di Saronno*	"The Italian liqueur of love."
Anisette	Sweet, mild, aromatic with pleasant anise flavor reminiscent of licorice; white and red; flavor blend of anise seeds, for which it is named, and aromatic herbs.
B&B Liqueur D.O.M.*	Delicate finesse of Benedictine D.O.M. with drier Cognac.
Benedictine D.O.M.*	Classic French herb liqueur.
Boggs Cranberry Liqueur*	Tart, tangy taste of juice of native-grown cranberries; red.
Campari*	Italian bittersweet spirits apéritif specialty; light ruby red; produced by infusion of aromatic and bitter herbs with orange peel.
Chambord Liqueur Royale de France*	From France; rich aroma and taste of framboises (small black raspberries) and other fruits and herbs combined with honey.
Chartreuse*	Classic herb liqueur with subtle flavor and aroma drawn from 130 wild mountain herbs distilled and blended in brandy. Two varieties: green (110 proof, brisk pungent, and reminiscent of exotic herbs) and yellow (80 proof; honey makes this the sweetest of the Chartreuse family).
Cherry Heering*	Danish cherry liqueur; flavor and aroma from the juice of fresh, ripe Danish cherries.
Cherry Marnier*	French cherry-flavored liqueur; rich cherry taste with a flavor hint of the cherry pit.
Cocoribe Liqueur*	Refreshing flavor of coconut and light Virgin Islands rum; white.
Cointreau*	Classic French specialty orange liqueur; white; fragrant, mellow bouquet, subtle hint of orange; produced by blending sweet and bitter Mediterranean and tropical orange peels.

*Proprietary brand.

FIGURE 20–1
• • •
Popular brands of liqueurs and cordials

Cream Liqueurs
  Baileys* (dominant brand)
  Carolans*
  Emmets*
  Leroux*
  Myers's*
  O'Darby*
  Crème de Grand Marnier*
  Mozart Chocolate*
	Dairy fresh cream blended with spirits and natural flavorings; Irish whiskey most widely used spirit; brandy, cordials, rum, and vodka also used. Flavor is rich, subtle, with mellow bite of spirit; shelf stable; some brands use nondairy creams.

Crème de Banana	Full flavor of fresh, ripe bananas; also called banana liqueur.
Crème de Cacao (brown)	Rich, creamy, deep chocolate flavor drawn from cocoa and vanilla beans, with hint of spices added.
Crème de Cacao (white)	Like brown Crème de Cacao, but not identical. With loss of color, chocolate flavor is less intense.
Crème de Cassis	Rich, fruity, with full flavor of black currants from Dijon, France.
Crème de Framboise	Raspberry-flavored liqueur.
Crème de Menthe (white)	Virtually identical to green Crème de Menthe. Because the green coloring has not been added, it can be used in more drink recipes.
Crème de Menthe (green)	Refreshing, tangy natural mint flavor, cool, clean, pleasant to taste; made as spirit flavored with several types of mint and peppermint.
Curaçao	Orange character, from the peel of bittersweet "green" oranges grown on the Dutch island of Curaçao in the West Indies. Clear amber; like Triple Sec but slightly sweeter and more subtle orange flavor; lower proof.
Drambuie*	Old Scotch whiskey delicately honeyed and spiced; produced in Scotland by subtle blending of Scotch with heather honey and gentle suggestion of herbs and spices.
Dutch Delight*	Imported from Holland; cream dessert liqueur flavored with chocolate and vanilla.
Frangelico*	Wild hazelnuts blended with berries and herbs.
Fruit-flavored Brandy	Flavor and aroma of selected ripe fruit identified by product name (blackberry, apricot, etc.); higher in proof and drier than companion liqueur (always 70 proof); always color of fruit.
Fruit Liqueurs	Flavor and aroma of fresh ripe fruit identified by product name (apricot, blackberry, etc.); lower proof and sweeter than companion fruit-flavored brandy; always color of fruit.

*Proprietary brand.

FIGURE 20–1

• • •

continued

Goldwasser	Flavor blend of herbs, seeds, and roots, and citrus fruit peels. Tiny flakes of gold leaf so light they cannot be felt on the tongue shimmer in this clear liquid; also called Gold Liqueur.
Grand Marnier*	From France; classic Cognac-based orange liqueur; flavor and bouquet from peels of wild bitter oranges.
Honey Blonde*	Honey-based imported liqueur from Denmark.
Irish Mist*	From Ireland; flavor blend of four whiskeys, honeys, heather, clover, and essence of a dozen herbs; amber.
Jagermeister*	From Germany; distinctive flavor blend of 56 roots, herbs, and fruits.
Kahlua*	Coffee liqueur from Mexico; rich flavor and aroma of choicest coffees; dark brown.
Kahlua Royale*	Mexican liqueur made from Kahlua, fine brandy, a hint of chocolate, and elegance of oranges.
Kokomo*	Highly mixable tangerine-pineapple–flavored liqueur.
Kummel	One of the oldest liqueurs; fairly dry, colorless, and usually 70 proof or over; essential flavor is caraway with a hint of cumin seed and anise.
La Grande Passion*	French blend of Armagnac with passion fruit.
Lemonier*	Lemon-peel liqueur; imported from France.
Licor 43*	Blend of vanilla and citrus flavors.
Liquore Galliano*	Golden Italian liqueur; distinctive flavor, rich, sweet, palatable; natural flavorings of seeds, herbs, and spices.
Liquore Strega*	From Italy; rich, fragrant, golden liqueur combining flavors of more than 70 herbs.
Lochan Ora*	Imported from Scotland; distinctive Scotch-based liqueur with subtle flavors drawn from ingredients from Curaçao and Ceylon.
Malibu*	From Canada; flavor blend of white rum and coconut.
Mandarine Napoléon*	From Belgium; a tangerine liqueur; flavor and bouquet of ripe Andalusian tangerines and Cognac.
Metaxa*	Brandylike Greek liqueur; grape base, slightly sweet, with a distinctive taste.
Midori*	Imported from Japan; light, refreshing taste of fresh honeydew melon; green.
Mohola*	From Japan; flavor of ripe mangos.
Monte Teca*	Tequila-based liqueur imported from Mexico; rich, golden taste.

*Proprietary brand.

FIGURE 20–1

• • •

continued

Opal Nera*	Imported from Italy. Color of black opal; anise and elderflower flavor with hint of lemon.
Ouzo*	Sweet, white Greek liqueur; licoricelike anise flavor; slightly drier and stronger proof than Anisette; when water or ice is added, Ouzo turns milky white.
Pear William	Delicate flavor of fresh Anjou pears from France's Loire Valley.
Pernod*	From France; blend of select anise seeds, special flavorings, and natural herbs on a spirit base.
Peter Heering*	Danish cherry-flavored liqueur produced since 1818 from the world-famous Danish cherries. Formerly known as Cherry Heering.
Petite Liqueur*	From France; Cognac and sparkling wine with a hint of coffee; amber.
Pimm's Cup*	Tall "sling" drinks imported from England. Pimm's Cup No. 1 is the Gin Sling.
Praline Liqueur*	Rich, mellow vanilla- and pecan-based flavor of the original New Orleans praline confection.
Ricard*	Anise and herb liqueur from France.
Rock and Rye	Whiskey-based liqueur that contains crystals of rock candy; flavored with fruits and sometimes contains pieces of fruit.
Sabra*	Flavors of Jaffa, Israel, orange and fine chocolate are combined in this Mediterranean liqueur.
Sambuca Romano*	Italian liqueur based on elderberry and anise flavor.

Schnapps
  Apple Barrel*
  Aspen Glacial
    (peppermint)*
  Cool Mint*
  Cristal (anise)*
  DeKuyper Peachtree
    (peach)*
  Dr. McGillicuddy
    (menthomint)*
  Rumple Minze
    (peppermint)*
  Silver schnapps (100
    proof peppermint)*
  Steel (85 proof
    peppermint)*
	Light, refreshing, easy to enjoy, unlike traditional liqueurs, which are made predominantly for after-dinner sipping and are too sweet and syrupy for straight drinking; enjoyed with many mixers, especially peach with orange juice.

Sloe Gin	Bouquet and tangy fruity flavor resembling wild cherries; red; made from the fresh fruit of the sloeberry.

*Proprietary brand.

FIGURE 20–1
● ● ●
continued

Southern Comfort*	High-proof American-made peach-flavored liqueur with a Bourbon whiskey base.
Tia Maria*	Jamaican coffee liqueur with the flavor of fresh coffee; dark brown.
Triple Sec	Crystal-clear orange flavor; like Curaçao but drier and higher in proof; flavor blend of peels of tangy, bittersweet "green" Curaçao and sweet oranges.
Truffles*	Liqueur du Chocolate; delicate combination of spirits and imported chocolate flavors.
Tuaca*	Golden Italian liqueur with hint of herbs and fruit peels on brandy base.
Vandermint*	Imported from Holland; Dutch chocolate with touch of mint.
Yukon Jack*	100 proof blend of Canadian whiskies.
Wild Turkey Liqueur*	Bourbon base; herbs, spices, and other natural flavorings; amber color.

*Proprietary brand.

FIGURE 20–1
• • •
concluded

BEER
• • • • •

Beer is a generic term for an alcoholic beverage made from the fermentation of grains and flavored with hops. The basic ingredients are malted barley, water, yeast, hops, and other cereals. Hops are added to give beer a special bitter flavor as well as to act as a natural preservative. Yeast is added to cause fermentation.

Production

Barley is soaked and sprouted. This is similar to making bean sprouts. The barley sprouts are then dried in a kiln. For darker beers, the barley sprouts are browned, giving flavor and color. After the barley is dried, it is mashed. This releases flavor and allows starches to be exposed. The starches will be converted naturally into sugar.

The dried ground barley sprouts are combined with hot water and cooked (brewing). Cooking brings out the flavor, and at this time, starches are covered into sugar. After being cooked, the mash is strained. The remaining liquid is called *wort*. Now the wort is boiled and hops are added. Once boiled (about 1 hour), the hops are filtered out and the wort is cooled. Once cooled, fermentation is ready to begin See Figure 20–2 for a flowchart of melting and brewing processes.

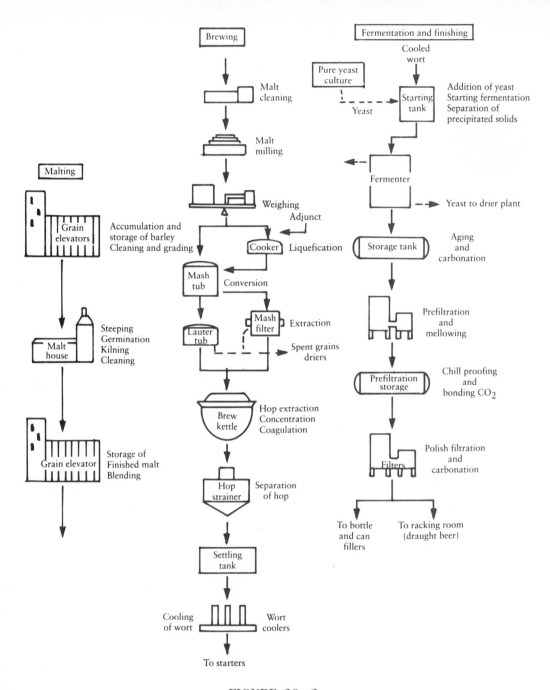

FIGURE 20-2

• • •

Flowchart of malting and brewing processes

Types of Fermentation

Bottom Fermentation

First fermentation   The first fermentation takes place at a cool temperature of 45–50° F for one to two weeks. Yeast added to the wort settles on the bottom of the tank; thus wort remains clear.

Second fermentation   The second fermentation lasts one to nine months in cold surroudnigns. Temperatures vary, usually 32–40° F. This is called the lagering stage or storing period. At this time, beer develops its balanced flavor.

To get a second fermentation, the beer is *krausened*. This process is the addition of partially fermented wort; this has sugar present and causes more fermentation. Beers made this way are lager, pilsner, and malt liquor.

Top Fermentation

First fermentation   The first fermentation takes place at a higher temperature than bottom-fermented beer, 59–68° F. The higher temperature gives more fermentation over a shorter period of time, about one week. Like bottom fermentation, there is a second fermentation.

Second fermentation   The second fermentation involves the addition of sugar to the fermenting beer. The beer is *primed* with sugar and sealed in kegs. The added sugar increases fermentation and allows for higher alcohol content. If beer is too sweet, hops are added to increase bitterness.

Traditional English ales are sent to pubs while the second fermentation is still progressing. When the keg goes out, it must be aged at least 48 hours before consumed and after being tapped. It must be consumed within two days. This beer is unpasteurized and tends to go sour, so it must be consumed quickly. Beers made this way are ale, porter, stout, sake, and bock.

Pasteurization

To kill remaining yeast cells, beer is heated to 140–145° F for approximately 20 minutes, then cooled. Another method is flash pasteurization: heating beer to 180–185° F for one minute. Pasteurization affects the taste of beer.

Types of Beer

Bottom Fermented

1. Lager: Bright light beer with high carbonation. Most American beers fall into this category.

2. Pilsner: Term found on many light beers; usually clear; good carbonation; process originally from Pilsen, Czechoslovakia. The city uses natural soft water (few minerals) to make Pilsner. The process is almost identical to lager.

3. Malt liqueur: A malt beverage brewed like beer but has higher alcohol content. (Examples: Colt 45 and Schlitz malt liquor.)

Top Fermented

4. Ale: A beer originally without hops, usually served fresh (unpasteurized). Slightly bitter with full body. (Examples: Molson Golden, and Ballantine.)

5. Porter: Dark malt base; rich in flavor; some use roasted barley unmalted.

6. Stout: Very dark, heavy rich beer; uses heavily roasted barley. (Example: Guinness Stout.)

7. Sake: Japanese rice beer, often confused with wine because it is still (no carbonation). Sake is high in alcohol, 14–16 percent, and should be served at 90–100° F.

8. Bock: A brew made in water to be consumed in the spring. Originally used sediments from other beers to achieve special full flavor. Now the term denotes season of production.

Beers and Ales as Food Products

Beers and ales are complex food products. They contain:

Water	85.0–90 percent by weight.
Alcohol	3.2–8 percent by weight (Sake 16 percent).
Carbohydrates (sugars)	3.0–6 percent by weight.
Protein	0.3–0.5 percent by weight.
Calories	10.0–17 per ounce.

The alcohol content of U.S. beer varies from 3.2 to 4 percent by weight, while malt liquor varies from 3.2 to 8 percent by weight. Ales average 4.5 percent and fuller ales, such as stout, average 6 percent by weight. The average U.S. beer has 12½ calories per ounce; bock beer, malt liquor, special ales, stout, and porter have a higher caloric value. There are also low-carbohydrate beers that have one-half to two-thirds the calories of regular beer.

Packaging

The three forms of packaging are kegs or barrels, bottles, and cans. The beer, under pressure, passes through closed pipe lines into the containers. Beer cannot be kept or stored in direct contact with wood, as it will take on the unpleasant woody flavor. Metal kegs of aluminum or stainless steel are used almost exclusively. These kegs are built to withstand pressure of about 300 pounds per square inch (PSI).

Beer so packaged is not pasteurized but is kept under refrigeration. Beer that is bottled or canned is pasteurized, making it sterile and killing any yeast that might still be active. If this is not done, additional carbon dioxide gas could form and the bottle or can could explode.

Pasteurization takes place at 140 to 145° F, where it is kept for 20 minutes. It is then cooled rapidly. The peak quality of pasteurized package beer is not indefinite; for cans it is four months, while for bottles it is six months. The principal difference between draft beer and bottled beer is that pasteurization diminishes the fresh flavor.

The following are beer container equivalencies.

Keg or barrel (31 gal.)	= 13.8 cases of 12-oz. cans or bottles
½ keg (15½ gal.)	= 330 6-oz. glasses
Pony (¼ keg—7¾ gal.)	= 164 6-oz. glasses
Tap (1 gal.)	= 21 6-oz. glasses

Dispensing Draft Beer

The three cardinal points of beer service are cleanliness, temperature, and pressure. Beer is one of the most delicate and perishable food products and is highly susceptible to extraneous odors, bacteria in the air, and strong light. It should be stored in a spotless, well-ventilated room with a constant temperature of 40° F.

Temperature

The ideal temperature is 40° F for beer and 50° F for ale. Do not chill below 40° F; the nearer the beer is to 45° F, the better the taste. Imported beers should be served at 48–50° F and ales or Irish stout at 55° F. Beer that is too cold is flat and cloudy. If it is too warm, the gas breaks away from the liquid and too much gas is lost. When that happens, it is called wild beer. Maintain a constant and uniform temperature.

Pressure

Pressure must be watched and controlled to maintain an even flow of beer from the tap. Since some of the natural pressure of the carbon dioxide gas is bound to be lost between the time the barrel is opened and the last glass of beer drawn, additional pressure must be supplied. One of two methods is used: air or carbon dioxide. Carbon dioxide ensures a more even supply of gas from the first to the last glass and eliminates the possibility of foul air being drawn into the system, as may happen when air pressure is used.

Handling Packaged Beer

Bottled beer should be stored in a dark, cool place. It should not be exposed to the direct rays of the sun, as beer is extremely sensitive to light and will, after a short period of time, take on a strange odor and flavor commonly called skunky. It may also become cloudy. Beer in cans is not affected by light, but should be kept in a cool place. At home, it should be stored in the lowest, coolest part of the refrigerator and not on the door shelf as the constant jostling and the drafts of warm air from the kitchen could hasten the beer's deterioration.

Service

When serving bottled or canned beer, allow the glass to remain on a flat surface. Pour the beer so that the stream flows straight into the center of the glass. Do not tilt the glass and pour down its side as it will not release enough carbon dioxide. Pour the beer in a natural manner and not too fast, which may cause overfoaming.

Never wash beer glasses in soapy water. The soap leaves a fatty film on the glass that will break the bubbles of the gas, thus destroying the desired collar of foam. Use a nonsoapy detergent, but make sure that the glass is rinsed well before it is used.

G·L·O·S·S·A·R·Y

Accompaniments: Items that accompany a course, food item mandated by the chef.

à la carte: Foods prepared to order. Each dish priced separately.

à la Russe: The Russian way.

al fresco: Outside dining; i.e., on sidewalk, patio, lawn, or poolside.

Appetizer: A food or drink that stimulates the appetite, usually the first course served in a dinner.

Banquet: A dining function in which all guests are served at one time, and all factors are predetermined; that is, menu, number of guests, price, and so on.

Banquette: A type of seating arrangement in which guests are seated facing the dining room with their backs against a wall or partition.

Blazer: An oval, rectangular, or round pan mostly used for tableside cooking.

Breathe: To breathe a wine means to allow air to come into contact with it to improve the taste.

Buffet: A display of ready-to-eat foods presented on a table or sideboard where guests select their food items. Guests may serve themselves or be aided by a serviceperson.

Carte du jour: Menu of the day.

Casserole dish: An ovenproof dish used in the baking and service of various food items.

Check register: A managerial tool used to record the check numbers issued to specific servers. Used as a control to prevent employee theft.

Chef de rang: Table captain.

Chef de service: Dining room manager.

Commis de rang: Front waiter.

Commis de suite: Food runner (back waiter).

Condiments: Seasonings or additional ingredients for a food or beverage; may be requested by the guests; for example, salt, pepper, Worcestershire sauce.

Cover: A single place setting on a guest's table.

Cruet: Small glass bottle for holding liquid condiments such as vinegar and oil.

Crumbing: The act of removing food particles from a guest's table with the use of a plate and a folded napkin or crumber.

Débarrassage: The act of clearing a guest's table of plates, flatware, and so on.

Débarrasseur: Busperson.

Decanting: The process of separating the wine from its sediment after several years of bottle aging. Done by pouring the wine into a separate container, leaving the sediment in the bottle.

Demi-tasse: Half cups in which espresso is traditionally served.

Deuce: Table for two.

Entrée: The main food item ordered by a guest.

Family-style service: Enough portions for a table of patrons served on one platter or in one bowl from which patrons may help themselves. Usually means sizable portions of food.

Finger cup: A small cup filled with warm water and a slice of lemon. Used by the guest to cleanse the fingers when eating foods that require use of the fingers; for example, barbequed ribs.

Flatware: Collectively, all forks, spoons, and serving utensils used in the dining room.

Flight: Row, as in a flight of glasses in a table setting.

Forecasting: Predicting future needs and activities that will influence the operation of a restaurant.

Front of the house: Those areas of a restaurant where the server meets the guest, such as dining room, lobbies, guest rooms, meeting rooms, and so forth.

Guéridon: Wheeled cart from which food is served in the dining room.

Highlighting: The practice where a particular item is emphasized so as to leave a lasting impression on the guest.

Intermezzo: A pause or intermission between two courses. Sherbet or sorbet can be served to cleanse the palate.

Linen: Term used for all cloth handled in the dining room, usually pertaining to that which will be placed on dining tables.

Logbook: A book used for recording the past performance of a restaurant; for example, number of guests served on past occasions.

Maître d': Master of. A contraction of maître d'service or maître d'hôtel. In the United States, indicates a dining room manager, in France, a food and beverage manager.

Must: In wine making, liquid that is produced after the grapes have been pressed.

Order: Foods selected by patron and recorded by server, who relays list to kitchen by voice, in writing, or by computer.

Prix fixé menu: A menu offering several courses for one set price; the price, or prix, has been set or fixed.

Réchaud: Heating unit designed to be used on a guéridon for tableside cookery.

Reservation: An arrangement established between a guest and a restaurant for dining at a specific date and time.

Rests: Equipment that keeps the cutting end of a knife off the tablecloth.

Service plate: A plate used to replace a show plate and used as an underliner for all courses preceding the entrée. *Note:* If a course is served on a plate of the same size as the service plate, the service plate should be temporarily removed.

Service set: A large fork and spoon held in specific ways and used to transfer food items from one service container to another.

Service station (side stand): A small work area or supply closet in the dining room. Usually containing items used frequently during service.

Service towel: A clean, pressed linen napkin used by a serviceperson during service for serving hot plates and wiping small spills during service.

Serviette: A plate covered with a neatly folded napkin or just a napkin used to carry items such as flatware to a guest's table.

Show plate: A decorative plate used to make the tabletop more attractive.

Side work: Defined duties for each servicemember to perform prior to opening the dining room.

Silencer: A pad or cloth, rubber or felt, placed between the table and the tablecloth to reduce noise.

Sommelier: Wine steward.

Station: One or more dining tables that a serviceperson or brigade has the responsibility of serving.

Suzette pan: A circular pan, the most frequently used pan for tableside cooking. Named after an opera singer who was being entertained by the Prince of Wales in A.D. 1900, who served the first flaming dessert.

Table d'hôte: From table of the host. In modern context, a menu in which the price of a complete meal changes according to the entrée selected.

Tea hottle: A pear-shaped bottle used for brewing tea.

Tips: To ensure prompt service; a percentage of the bill left for service. Tips may be kept by the worker to whom they are given, may be pooled so all workers share an equal portion, or may be divided into shares given to other employees such as the débarrasseur.

Turn sheet: A management tool used to distribute parties evenly throughout the dining room. Used in restaurants that operate on a first-come, first-served basis.

Underliner: Any plate placed under a service item containing food or beverage.

Verbal selling: Servers discussing the menu with the guests.

Waste plate: A plate placed before guests for the discarding of bones or shells.

WEIGHTS AND MEASURES

Teaspoons

1/8 teaspoon = a few grains
1 teaspoon = 60 drops
1 teaspoon = 5 milliliters
1 teaspoon = 1/3 tablespoon
3 teaspoons = 1 tablespoon

Tablespoons

1 tablespoon = 3 teaspoons
1 tablespoon = 1/2 fluid ounce
2 tablespoons = 1 fluid ounce
4 tablespoons = 1/4 cup
4 tablespoons = 2 ounces
5 1/3 tablespoons = 1/3 cup
8 tablespoons = 1/2 cup
10 2/3 tablespoons = 2/3 cup
12 tablespoons = 6 ounces
16 tablespoons = 1 cup
16 tablespoons = 8 fluid ounces

Dry volume measure

2 cups = 1 pint
2 pints = 1 quart
4 quarts = 1 gallon
2 gallons = 8 quarts
8 quarts = 1 peck
4 pecks = 1 bushel

Liquid measurements

1 pint or 2 cups liquid measure = 1 pound
2 pints or 1 quart of liquid measure = 2 pounds
1 tablespoon = 1/2 liquid ounce or 15 grams
1 cup = 16 tablespoons or 8 liquid ounces or 227 grams
2 cups = 1 pint or 16 ounces or 1 liquid pound or 454 grams
4 cups = 2 pints or 1 quart or 32 liquid ounces or 907 grams
1 quart = 64 tablespoons
1 liter = 66 2/3 tablespoons

Cups

1/8 cup = 1 ounce
1/8 cup = 2 tablespoons
1/4 cup = 2 ounces
1/4 cup = 4 tablespoons
1/3 cup = 5 1/3 tablespoons
3/8 cup = 6 tablespoons
1/2 cup = 4 ounces
1/2 cup = 8 tablespoons
1/2 cup = 1 tea cup
1/2 cup = 1/4 American pint
1/2 cup = 1 gill
5/8 cup = 10 tablespoons
2/3 cup = 10 2/3 tablespoons

3/4 cup = 6 ounces
3/4 cup = 12 tablespoons
1 cup = 8 ounces
1 cup = 16 tablespoons
1 cup = 1/2 American pint
1 cup = 2 gills
2 cup = 1 pint
2 cups = 1 pound
4 cups = 1 quart
16 cups = 1 gallon

METRIC AND OTHER MEASUREMENTS

New Metric Sizes	U.S. Fluid Ounces
1.75 liters	59.2 ounces
1.0 liters	33.8 ounces
750.0 milliliters	25.4 ounces
500.0 milliliters	16.9 ounces
200.0 milliliters	6.8 ounces
50.0 milliliters	1.7 ounces

Case packing requirements for 200 ml distilled spirits bottles may be changed from 60 bottles (as indicated) to 48 bottles per case under proposed rulemaking notice published by BATF.

Distilled spirits

New Metric Sizes	U.S. Fluid Ounces
3.0 liters	101.0 ounces
1.5 liters	50.7 ounces
1.0 liter	33.8 ounces
750.0 milliliters	25.4 ounces
375.0 milliliters	12.7 ounces
187.0 milliliters	6.3 ounces
100.0 milliliters	3.4 ounces

Closest Present Container— U.S. Fluid Ounces	Mandatory Number of Bottles per Case
Jeroboam—102.4 ounces	4
Magnum— 51.2	6
Quart— 32.0 ounces	12
Fifth— 25.6 ounces	12
Tenth— 12.8 ounces	24
Split— 6.4 ounces	48
Miniature— 2.0 ounces	60

*Includes still wines, champagnes, and sparkling wines.

*Wines (all types)**

Metric	U.S. Equivalent
10 milliliters = 1 centiliter	0.338 ounce
500 milliliters = 50 centiliters =1/2 liter	16.97 ounces = 0.52835 quart
1000 milliliters = 100 centiliters = 1 liter	33.8 ounces = 1.0567 quart
U.S.	Metric Equivalent
1 ounce	2.9575 centiliter
16 ounces = 1 pint	0.4732 liter
32 ounces = 2 pints = 1 quart	0.9463 liter
64 ounces = 4 pints = 2 quarts = 1/2 gallon	1.8926 liters
128 ounces = 8 pints = 4 quarts = 1 gallon	3.7853 liters

Table of measurements

1 dash	= 1/6 tsp. or 1/32 oz.
1 tsp.	= 1/8 oz. to 1/6 oz.
1 tbsp.	= 3 tsp. or 3/8 oz. to 1/2 oz.
1 pony	= 1 oz.
1 jigger	= 1 1/2 oz.
1 wine glass	= 4 oz.
1 tenth	= 4/5 pint or 12.8 oz. or 1/10 gal.
1 fifth	= 25.6 oz. or 1/5 gal.

American	French (Gay Lussac)	British (Sykes)
70 proof (35% alcohol)	35 proof (35% alcohol)	38.8 under proof (or 61.2 proof) (35% alcohol)
80 proof (40% alcohol)	40 proof (40% alcohol)	30.0 under proof (or 70.0 proof) (40% alcohol)
86 proof (43% alcohol)	43 proof (43% alcohol)	24.8 under proof (or 75.2 proof) (43% alcohol)
100 proof (50% alcohol)	50 proof (50% alcohol)	12.5 under proof (or 87.5 proof) (50% alcohol)
150 proof (75% alcohol)	75 proof (75% alcohol)	31.3 over proof (or 131.3 proof) (75% alcohol)

Other measurements

A·P·P·E·N·D·I·X

C

DINING ROOM EQUIPMENT IDENTIFICATION

Dinner knife

Dessert knife

Fish knife

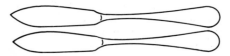

Butter/cheese set

Butter spreader

Butter knife

Steak knife

Dinner fork

Dessert/Salad fork

Fish fork

Snail fork

Cocktail fork

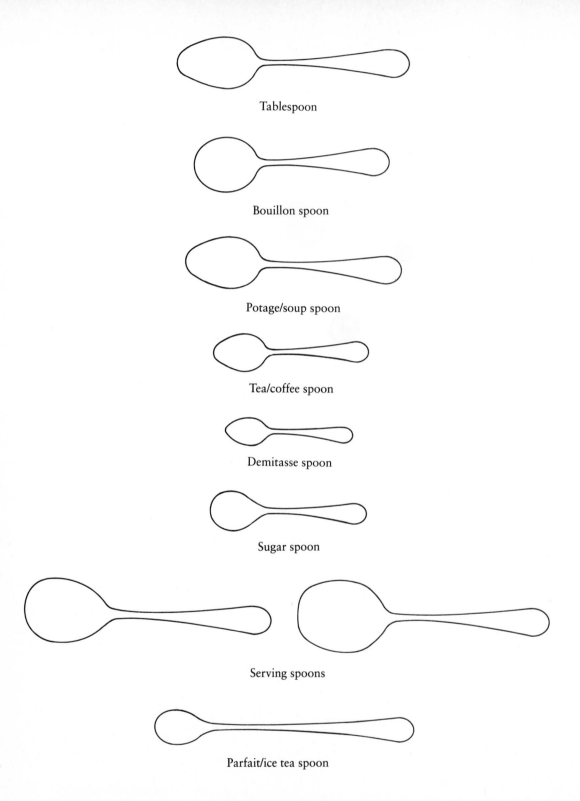

Tablespoon

Bouillon spoon

Potage/soup spoon

Tea/coffee spoon

Demitasse spoon

Sugar spoon

Serving spoons

Parfait/ice tea spoon

Sugar tongs

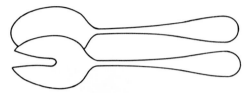

Salad servers

Pie/pastry server

Cake knife

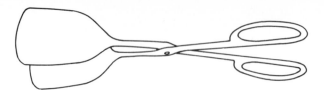

Pastry tongs

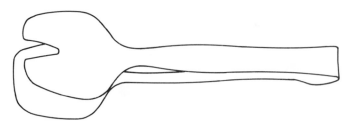

Pastry tongs

Snail dish

Snail tongs

Lobster fork

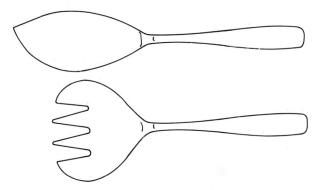

Fish serving set

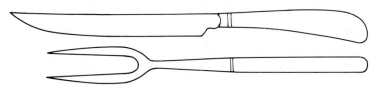

Carving set

Water pitcher

Teapot, 8 oz. / coffeepot, 32oz.

Water pitcher with ice guard

Creamer pitcher

Sugar basin with lid   Sugar basin

Sauce boat

Sauce ladle

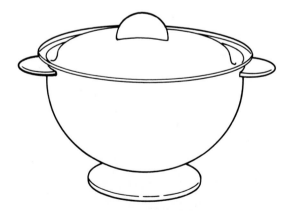

Soup tureen with lid

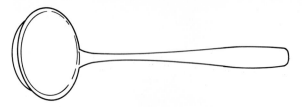

Soup ladle

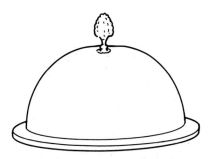

Plate cover (stackable)

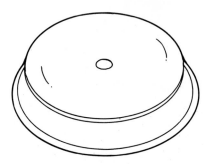

Cloche (plate cover)

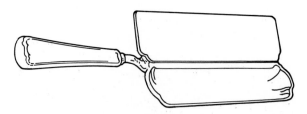

Table crumber/scraper

Wine service basket

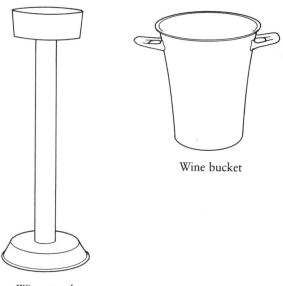

Wine bucket

Wine stand

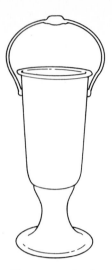

Champagne bucket

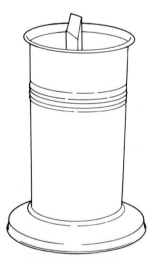

Cake server holder

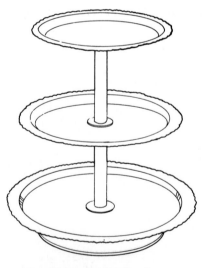

Pastry display stand
(three tier)

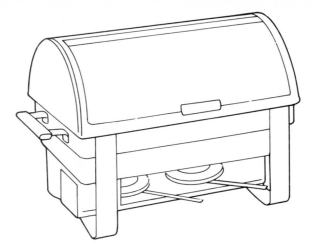

Chafing dish with foldback lid (closed)

Chafing dish with foldback lid (open)

Cover display holder chafing dish

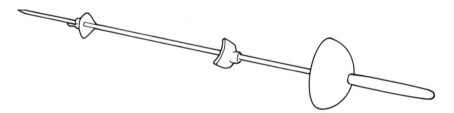

Flaming sword

A·P·P·E·N·D·I·X

D

GLASSWARE

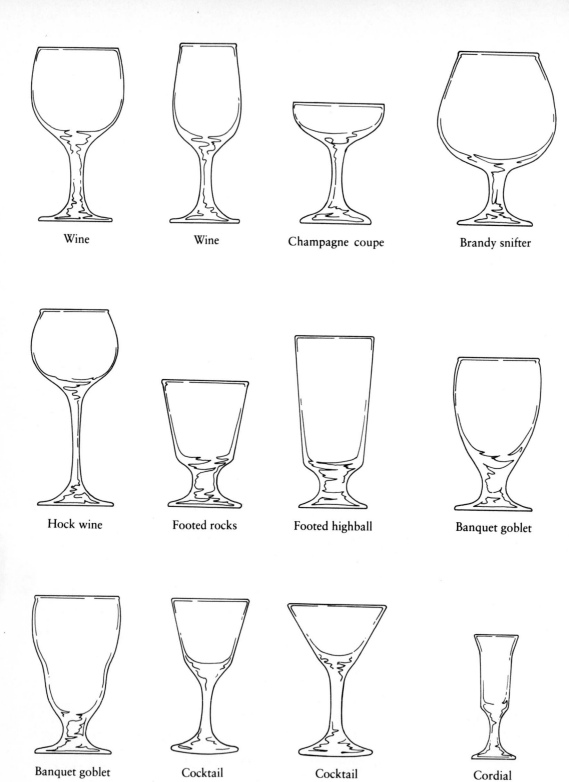

Wine

Wine

Champagne coupe

Brandy snifter

Hock wine

Footed rocks

Footed highball

Banquet goblet

Banquet goblet

Cocktail

Cocktail

Cordial

Sherry

Pony

Whiskey sour

Rocks

Old-fashioned

Highball

Tall highball

Champagne tulip

Pilsner

Lined shot

Mug

Pilsner

Mixing glass

Lid

Tea hottle

American Diabetes Association and the American Dietetic Association. *Exchange Lists for Meal Planning*. Alexandria, Va.: American Diabetes Association, Diabetes Information Service Center, 1986.

American Spice Trade Association. *Food Service Seasoning Guide*. New York: Food Service Department, American Spice Trade Association, 1969.

Boxer, Arabella; Jocasta Innes; Charlotte Parry-Crooke; and Lewis Esson. *The Encyclopedia of Herbs and Flavorings*. New York: Cresent Books, 1984.

Brody, Jane. *Jane Brody's Nutrition Book*. New York: W. W. Norton, 1981.

Cichy, Ronald F. *Sanitation Management*. East Lansing, Mich. Educational Institute of the American Hotel and Motel Association, 1984.

The Culinary Institute of America. *The New Professional Chef*. 5th ed. Edited by Linda Glick Conway. New York: Van Nostrand Reinhold, 1991.

Dalsass, Diana. *Miss Mary's Down-Home Cooking*. New York: New American Library, 1984.

Dittmer, Paul R., and Gerald G. Griffin. *Principles of Food, Beverage and Labor Cost Control for Hotels and Restaurants*. 3rd ed. New York: Van Nostrand Reinhold, 1984.

Dowell, Philip, and Adrian Bailey. *Cook's Ingredients*. London: Dorling Kindersley, 1980.

Dykstra, John J. *Infection Control for Lodging and Food Service Establishment*. New York: John Wiley & Sons, 1990.

Escoffier, A. *The Escoffier Cook Book*. New York: Crown Publishers, 1969.

Eugen, Paul. *Classical Cooking the Modern Way*. New York: Van Nostrand Reinhold, CBI, 1979.

Farrell, Kenneth T. *Spices, Condiments, and Seasonings*. Westport, Conn.: AVI Publishing, 1985.

Food and Drug Administration, Division of Federal State Relations, State Training and Information Branch, "Hazard Analysis and Critical Control Points," Draft, May 1991.

Fuller, John; John B. Knight; and Charles A. Salter. *The Professional Chef's Guide to Kitchen Management*. New York: Van Nostrand Reinhold, 1985.

Gisslen, Wayne. *Professional Cooking*. 2nd ed. New York: John Wiley & Sons, 1989.

Gunst, Kathy. *Condiments*. New York: G. P. Putnam's Sons, 1984.

Haines, Robert G. *Math Principles for Food Service Occupations*. 2nd ed. Albany, N.Y.: Delmar Publishers, 1988.

Hamilton, Eva May; Eleanor Whitnew; and Frances Sizer. *Nutrition Concepts and Controversies*. 5th ed. St. Paul, Minn.: West Publishing, 1991.

Heath, Henry B. *Source Book of Flavors*. Westport, Conn. AVI Publishing, 1981.

Herbst, Sharon Tyler. *Food Lover's Companion*. New York: Barron's Educational Series, 1990.

Kotshevar, Lendal H. *Standards, Principles and Techniques in Quantity Food Production*. 3rd ed. Boston: CBI, 1966.

McDowell, Milton C., and Holly W. Crawford. *Math Workbook for Foodservice Lodging*. 3rd ed. New York: Van Nostrand Reinhold, 1988.

McVety, Paul J., and Bradley J. Ware. *Fundamentals of Menu Planning*. New York: Van Nostrand Reinhold, 1989.

Montagné, Prosper. *Larousse Gastronomique*. Edited by Charlotte Turgeon. New York: Crown Publishers, 1977.

National Restaurant Association. *Current Issues Report,* Nutrition Awareness and the Foodservice Industry. Washington, D.C.: National Restaurant Association, 1990.

Pauli, Eugene. *Classical Cooking the Modern Way*. Edited by Marjorie S. Arkwright, R.D. New York: Van Nostrand Reinhold, 1979.

Peddersen, Raymond B. *Foodservice and Hotel Purchasing*. Boston: CBI, 1981.

Peterson, James. *Sauces: Classical and Contemporary Sauce Making*. New York: Van Nostrand Reinhold, 1991.

Ray, Mary Frey, and Beda A. Dondi. *Professional Cooking and Baking*. Encino, Calif.: Bennett & McKnight, 1981.

Saulnier, L. *Le Repertoire de la Cuisine*. Distributed in the United States by Christian Classics, Westminster, Md.

Stobart, Tom. *Herbs, Spices and Flavorings*. Woodstock, N.Y.: Overlook Press, 1982.

U.S. Department of Health and Human Services. *Dietary Guidelines for Americans*. Washington, D.C.: USDA Home and Garden Bulletin No. 232, U.S. Department of Health and Human Services, 1990.

The Surgeon General's Report on Nutrition and Health. Public Health Service Publication No. 88-50211. Washington, D.C.: Public Health Service, U.S. Department of Health and Human Services, 1988.

Wason, Betty. *Cooks, Gluttons and Gourmets, a History of Cookery*. Garden City, N.Y.: Doubleday, 1962.

I · N · D · E · X